SANDSTONE GOTHIC

Andrew Riemer was born in Budapest and came to Australia in 1947 with his parents. He studied at the Universities of Sydney and London and was a member of the Department of English at the University of Sydney for a number of years. Andrew Riemer is currently a writer, a literary and cultural journalist and the chief book reviewer of the *Sydney Morning Herald*. His previous books are: *Inside Outside* (1992), *The Habsburg Café* (1993), *The Ironic Eye* (1994), *America with Subtitles* (1995) and *The Demidenko Debate* (1996).

SANDSTONE GOTHIC

ANDREW RIEMER

ALLEN & UNWIN

Copyright © Trieed Pty Ltd, 1998

All rights reserved. No part of this book may be reproduced or transmitted in any form or by any means, electronic or mechanical, including photocopying, recording or by any information storage and retrieval system, without prior permission in writing from the publisher.

First published in 1998
Allen & Unwin
9 Atchison Street, St Leonards 2065 Australia
Phone: (61 2) 9901 4088
Fax: (61 2) 9906 2218
E-mail: frontdesk@allen-unwin.com.au
Web: http://www.allen-unwin.com.au

National Library of Australia
Cataloguing-in-Publication entry:

Riemer, A.P. (Andrew P.).
  Sandstone gothic.

  ISBN 1 86448 626 0.

  1. Riemer, A.P. (Andrew P.). 2. College teachers—Australia—Biography.
  I. Title.

378.94092

Set in 11/13pt Times by DOCUPRO, Sydney
Printed and bound by Australian Print Group, Maryborough, Victoria
10 9 8 7 6 5 4 3 2 1

'It's amazing how many people teach these days,' I said. 'Everyone I know is either a teacher or a student. What do you think it means?'

White Noise, Don DeLillo

PART I

A Sentimental Education

1

Sometimes it seems to me that the forty years, a lifetime, I spent in the shadow of the magnificent neo-Gothic folly Edmund Blacket fashioned for the University of Sydney were no more than a long infatuation with the world that building mimicked in honey-coloured sandstone. When disenchantment came, it was slow, gradual and intermittent. As it grew, and as that backward-looking community changed, I came to realise that my decision to embark on an academic career—unlikely though it had seemed at the time—was prompted by far more than mere professional ambition. It had as much to do with the long and perplexing process of self-fashioning that began when my parents and I arrived in Sydney in February 1947.

In those days just after the end of the Second World War, the imperative was to assimilate into a society which, officially at least, entertained no doubt about its nature or aspirations. We had strayed into a late-colonial world that drew reassurance from its origins in a distant place. To become an Australian, you were obliged to become British, even though there were few visible signs of Britishness in the strangely perplexing city we explored in the first weeks after our arrival. With the passage of time, we began to understand, however, the extent to which Australian life was suffused with memories and fantasies of Britain, particularly of England, the centre of a powerful mythology.

Signs of that were everywhere. Portraits of the royal family adorned the walls of banks and post offices, of the classrooms of the broken-down school I attended. Everyone stood to attention when they played 'God Save the King' at the cinema—which we soon learnt to call 'the pictures'. The streets of the suburb where we lived were named after English towns and counties. Many of our neighbours spoke of going 'home' one day, even though none of them had ever seen that home. Longing for England gave substance to what seemed an otherwise formless, unsatisfactory existence.

Such predispositions were encouraged by the unrecognised propaganda of the time. At school we were taught to sing 'Rule Britannia' and 'Land of Hope and Glory'. We learnt about the glorious victories of Agincourt and Trafalgar. We were urged to respect the splendours of

English civilisation. Shakespeare, we were assured, was the greatest poet the world had ever known. Watt and Stephenson had enriched humanity by harnessing the power of steam for manufacture and transport. Churchill had stood up single-handed against the Nazis while other nations wavered or allowed themselves to be overrun. Though we lived in a distant part of the globe, our lives were enriched by the unbreakable ties that bound us to the greatest civilisation of modern times.

When George VI died we shuffled into the school assembly hall while someone played Chopin's Funeral March on an out-of-tune upright piano. The headmaster, standing beneath the King's black-draped portrait, delivered the commemorative oration. He spoke about the passing of a great man, whose courage had been an inspiration to all during the darkest days of the war, a man unshaken in his faith in God's mercy, an example to others, both as a loving father and as a loving king. Then we sang 'Abide with Me', the late King's favourite hymn, and—for the first time—'God Save the Queen'.

My parents and I stayed up late into the night to listen to the broadcast of the King's funeral. The solemn voices, describing the cortege as it made its way to the thud of muffled drums in the background, rose and fell in the whining, crackling static. Some time later, we listened to the coronation and thrilled to the cries of *'Vivat! Vivat Regina!'* as the young Queen was invested with crown, orb and sceptre. Everyone seemed to rejoice that the Second Elizabethan Age had dawned. We went to The Embassy Cinema in Castlereagh Street to watch the colour film of the coronation, and also to marvel at Hillary's conquest of Everest: the most fitting gift, the soundtrack announced, to mark the inauguration of a glorious reign. When the Queen arrived on her royal tour, the first time a reigning monarch had set foot on Australian soil, my mother and I stood in the blazing summer sun, waiting to catch a glimpse of her as the cavalcade of shiny black cars flowed past. And when the first of that line of sleek limousines emerged from the waves of heat rising from the asphalt, we were thrilled to see for an instant a white-gloved hand and a slender young woman. The crowd cheered and waved Union Jacks, and my mother and I, having made the long trip to town in a crowded train and almost fainting from the midsummer heat, cheered along with them.

So it was inevitable, in a way, that I should carry that process of learning to worship all things English to its logical extreme in spending the greater part of my life teaching English Literature in the University of Sydney. When I achieved what had seemed at first an unlikely goal, I fancied that I had completed the risky adventure of reinventing myself. The trouble was, however, that the world had changed by then.

The ideals that sustained Australian life in the heady postwar years of optimism had begun to fade. The sentimental combination of nostalgia and yearning for progress, which formed the spirit of that earlier, perhaps more innocent time, was no longer deemed valid. Fewer and fewer people saw a bright, limitless future for the land of milk and honey, which would rise to ever greater heights of prosperity and civilisation by remaining firmly rooted in its British traditions. Instead, Australians became fascinated by—perhaps obsessed with—the darker side of their world.

Eventually they grew fond of telling stories of brutality, dispossession and exploitation. In place of social harmony we found conflict and enmity. The very bases of the myths on which my own efforts at transformation had been built came at length to seem suspect and shameful. Australia's British antecedents were no longer a source of pride or promise, but evidence of servitude and oppression. In such a climate, the ideals and aspirations reflected by the virtuoso essay in parody Blacket had fashioned for the university seemed risible. The building continued to stand as a charming anachronism, a fit setting for television commercials and corporate functions. But the university that had been nestling around it for the best part of a century and a half by the time I decided to call it a day in 1994 had changed beyond recognition.

To those, like myself, who had been enraptured by a sentimental education into the ways of a late-colonial society, the university now seemed chaotic, lacking all respect for the past, for traditions, for knowledge and even perhaps for truth. To others, of course, those of us who held such views seemed only remnants of a discredited *ancien régime*. In my last years at the university, it seemed as if nothing of any particular value had replaced those lost illusions. It was small consolation to know that the illusions had to be lost, that they could not survive into a more robust world, one offering fewer certainties. Nevertheless, on the day when I gave my last class to a group of bored and resentful undergraduates, I was aware that when I first walked up the university's long drive as a student in 1954 I was making my way towards a finer world than the one I was about to leave forty years later with undisguised relief.

2

For people of my generation, going to university was exceptional. I spent the last years of school at a well-regarded boys' high school which had produced several celebrated figures, whose achievements were wearyingly invoked at every opportunity. Yet of the hundred or so boys who took their Leaving Certificate at the end of 1953 only a handful of us went on to study at university. The majority, many far more gifted and studious than I had been, did the sensible thing. They went to work in banks, with insurance companies, or chose to become trainee teachers, surveyors or accountants, or clerks in the public service. To go to university was considered a luxury, despite the recently introduced Commonwealth Scholarship scheme which remitted fees to anyone matriculating with a mark of more than sixty per cent.

That I was one of the small number to attend university was due almost entirely to my parents' (and my own) determination to validate the decision they took after the war to leave Europe and look for a new and better life in Australia. In their world, going to university was circumscribed by all manner of political, social and religious prohibitions—and not merely the notorious *numerus clausus* in such countries as Hungary, which severely limited the number of university places available to Jews and other undesirables.

Nevertheless, the particular difficulties of migration, of living in an unfamiliar and largely perplexing environment, produced a significant dilemma once the unexpected miracle took place and I learnt that I had done well enough to be awarded a Commonwealth Scholarship. The problem was choosing the appropriate faculty. In a way, I had been well prepared for that contingency: as soon as the possibility of my being able to attend university arose, my parents and I determined that the only sensible thing would be for me to become a medical student. Accordingly, on a rain-sodden day in February 1954 I made my way to the enrolment office to register as an undergraduate in the Faculty of Medicine.

It was astonishing folly. Nothing in my decent though unremarkable career at school suggested that I was cut out for the medical life. My best subjects were English, History and French. Deciding to study medicine was a consequence of the inevitable mixture of caution and ambition common among newcomers trying to survive in an unfamiliar world. From the perspective of the time, when we had spent only seven years in Australia, becoming a doctor seemed a safe and prudent ambition: that I had no skill or liking for the scientific life was somehow irrelevant. The Faculty of Medicine, however, was not prepared to overlook that shortcoming. I failed miserably at the end of my first attempt. I found some consolation in the fact that two out of every three candidates did not survive the brutal weeding out that took place each year. On the other hand, I had failed so abysmally that I was denied the opportunity of taking posts the following January. That should have been warning enough, but I persisted, failing the year again. The second time around, I qualified for posts at least, but it did me little good because in January 1956 I failed for the third time in two years, so setting something of a record in the annals of unsuccessful medical students.

So I had wasted two years, except that later on I imagined that those years had not been wasted, but had pointed me in the direction my life should take. In 1956 I enrolled in the Faculty of Arts. My parents were indulgent and long-suffering. The prospect of financing me through the degree caused them great hardship—money was short, and even in those days there was very little you could do with an Arts degree apart from teaching in schools. Nevertheless, they agreed to see me through, much to the outrage of their friends who thought that my parents were out of their minds. I should be made to find a job, they advised, instead of wasting even more money. I, for my part, had no ready justification to offer, except to say what no one (not even my parents) were inclined to take seriously: that I would study English with the aim of becoming an academic.

Why English? At the time, the question did not detain me for an instant. Studying English Literature seemed the most natural and indeed inevitable thing. In later years I realised how that decision too had been prompted by the overarching imperative of those years: to find an identity and a way of life that would reconcile me to what continued to seem in many ways a life in exile. I cannot explain otherwise why, without a moment's hesitation, I sketched out so relentlessly the rest of my life in the course of those bitter days early in 1956 when I smarted with anger and shame at having failed Medicine I yet again.

English was not the natural or inevitable choice. I had achieved the same modest success in French and History during my last years at school. I had a facility with words which in later years helped me cut corners and smooth over the joins in all sorts of ways. But I had displayed no particular literary bent. Certainly, I liked reading, and spent far too much time buried in books borrowed from the City of Sydney Public Library deep in the bowels of the crumbling Queen Victoria Building. For all that, though, I had precious little of a literary background, especially in English, and came to my studies in what I now realise was a state of remarkable innocence. The decision to concentrate on English studies was prompted only by the desire to move in to the centre of the kind of Australian life which, I felt, I could tolerate. To put it simply, I was attracted by style, rather than substance. In my two years as a medical student I had glimpsed from a distance enough of that style to recognise English studies as my ideal goal.

In truth, there was a certain style—subtle, imperceptible to the outsider, but nevertheless substantial—in the Department of English in those days. Several members of the small department occupied splendid rooms at the very heart of Blacket's great building. That gave them considerable éclat in a rigidly hierarchical institution which observed with meticulous care ceremonies of rank and status impossible to maintain in the world at large. Their handsome, high-ceilinged, dark-panelled rooms conferred on them an extraterritoriality that I also came to relish in time.

The instruction I received from the fortunate inhabitants of those wonderful rooms was, by contemporary standards, formal and impersonal in the extreme. Teaching was conducted entirely by means of lectures. Small-group, face-to-face teaching, which was to become an irresistible fad by the seventies, and was to contribute in the main to the financial difficulties the humanities experienced once the palmy days of prosperity were replaced by the austere atmosphere of the eighties, was unheard of. There were, it is true, one or two classes each term that were described as optional tutorials; but they were nothing more than lectures where the lecturers did not wear black gowns. It was not until I reached the honours year in 1959 that we, the undergraduates, were required to make any contribution to classes.

Otherwise lectures conformed to an inflexible, seemingly tradition-hallowed pattern. After the first year, then as now an indigestible smorgasbord ostensibly intended to provide an introduction to the subject, we studied writers, not individual texts—except in the case of Shakespeare, who had special privileges conferred on him by having several of his plays nominated each year. Apart from Shakespeare, the courses were organised more or less chronologically in terms of centuries or the reigns of English monarchs: principally Elizabeth, James and Victoria. Within these confines the more significant authors were discussed according to a seemingly invariable pattern. Depending on their importance, writers were allocated two, three, on rare occasions four lectures each. In the course of those lectures we would be treated to a brief biographical sketch, an account of the principal works together with information about sources, collaborations and the like. The lectures would usually conclude with a survey of the state of scholarly and critical opinion.

Of course, the people who taught us—some of whom were to

become my colleagues and friends in later years—displayed all manner of individual characteristics, which led to inevitable likes and dislikes among students. Most unjustly ridiculed perhaps was Thelma G. Herring, a remarkable scholar of Renaissance drama who became one of Patrick White's earliest and best critics, and also his friend. She was a woman of extraordinary intellectual and personal integrity, a feminist before feminism had made any impact on academic life, who was nevertheless delighted when she heard that a famous American scholar had complimented her for writing like a man. Her lectures were models of their kind: comprehensive, erudite, well-balanced. Yet she was the most insufferable of teachers, with an absolute disdain for the tyranny of the clock, usually running well beyond her allocated time, droning on in an infuriating sing-song that rose heavenward, as did her head, at the end of each carefully constructed sentence. Her lectures were endurance vile; we suffered (or at least those of us who had not given up attending them) those seemingly inchoate, monotonous rambles with bad grace. Only on looking at the perfunctory notes the more diligent among us managed to take did we realise the extent of the learning and good sense that informed her teaching.

G. A. Wilkes, on the other hand, could do no wrong, especially where the women in his classes were concerned. When I was an undergraduate Wilkes was the heir apparent to the prestigious Challis Chair of English Literature—occupied at the time by Wesley Milgate, a retiring, genial man, the most elegantly witty of my teachers, for whom the carefully concealed beastliness of academic life soon proved irksome. Wilkes's lectures conformed to the departmental model. They were delivered in a manner as dry as Thelma Herring's, yet enlivened by his presence and personality. He read slowly, deliberately from pages of ruled paper covered in a small, spidery hand. From time to time he would lift his head with its mass of golden hair to look out at the audience as he repeated the salient phrase—a habit he retained throughout his long and distinguished career. Several of my women friends would never contemplate missing one of his lectures, no matter what other blandishments were on offer, and despite the fact that Wilkes taught the more weighty and intractable writers—Milton and George Eliot for instance.

R. T. Dunlop—I must describe these people in the way they were known to us—was the best-liked member of the small department among students, especially those in the first year, where he had the bulk of the teaching in a dreadful, draughty barn, the Wallace Theatre, built a few years earlier to accommodate the large bulge in enrolments after the end of the war. Dunlop charmed us with his urbanity and sophistication. Yet the way he taught or what he taught was little different from his colleagues' practices.

That was equally true of Harold Oliver, the only member of the department for whom I developed a pronounced dislike—which he entirely reciprocated, as I found out much later. Oliver, to whom nasty rumours clung like a swarm of blowflies, was vain and self-impressed, constantly harping on his great achievement in the international scholarly world, not at all averse to pushing shamelessly his own scholarly barrows in courses and examinations papers. Even he, however, was transformed when he stood behind the lectern, in the way that some priests are said to be transformed into inspiring preachers once they mount the pulpit. Much as I disliked him, I remember with respect the subdued brilliance and comprehensiveness of his lectures on E. M. Forster, who was considered a contemporary writer in those days.

In that way, Oliver was also an exponent of that characteristic Sydney style, which came to exert such a pronounced influence on me during my years as an undergraduate. Admittedly, the decorative or cosmetic elements of that style made much greater impact than its substance. I found, indeed, that the idea of studying English was far more alluring than its reality. It was not until the last year and a half of the four-year honours course that I made any significant engagement with the subject; until then I found much of it boring, pointless and meretricious. Before that, the glamour of those splendid rooms around the clock tower was more alluring than the day-to-day grind of undergraduate life.

I found, disappointingly, that there were not many opportunities to enter that magic domain. Indeed, during my first two years they were restricted to the ceremony of handing in essays. That took place in a high chamber beneath the clock tower called the Muniment Room. In those days it was the centre of the English Department's life—the common room, what passed for an office and where (unbeknown to us) fierce disputes and battles sometimes raged. In my student days it was presided over by the most daunting member of the department: Miss Roberts, the secretary, a tyrannical stickler for what she regarded as the proprieties of academic life.

Nevertheless, something of that atmosphere also pervaded the draughty lecture halls where we listened—enthralled or resentful—to conducted tours of the glories of English literature. It was implicit in the very formality with which our teachers approached their task, always beginning their classes with the magic formula, 'Ladies and Gentlemen . . .'. The severe black gowns they wore (supplemented in Thelma Herring's case in winter with a close-fitting hat to ward off the cold) were like priestly robes, indicating that on entering the lecture hall they had left their ordinary selves and the everyday world far behind.

It was by no means that they aped English manners and modes of speech. For instance, the McCaughey Professor of Early English Literature and Language, A. G. Mitchell, an expert on Australian speech, could not have been mistaken for anything but an Australian— or a Sydneysider indeed, according to his Melbourne detractors. Yet they indicated in all kinds of subtle ways that they belonged to the great republic of English studies, for which the accidents of place and climate were nothing but inconsequential trifles. Their teaching remained innocent of the fact that they were professing their discipline on a hill above the roar of traffic along Parramatta Road. Their mien made no allowance for that: they would have given the same lectures, you felt, in identical ways, wherever English literature formed the focus of cultural life. To have acknowledged the isolation of their students from the physical origins of that culture would have seemed insulting, for it would have indicated that we were in some ways inferior—marginalised in the jargon of today's cultural discourse.

In time, such habits and casts of mind, which were to absorb me at first emotionally, later intellectually, came to seem indefensibly vain and irresponsible. Judged by the standards of contemporary academic and cultural life, those learned figures in their austere black gowns seemed to dwell in a nostalgic cloud-cuckoo-land, with an almost monastic contempt for the ordinary. And it is also true that the more vain or less cautious made it clear that for them the most valuable and absorbing life lay elsewhere—in those Oxford colleges and libraries where they seemed to have encountered the most significant experiences of their lives.

Preserving the great traditions of scholarship in Sydney was, in quite palpable ways in some instances, a form of exile. I, for my part, conscious of my own life of exile (though I was never quite sure from what), picked up more readily perhaps than many of my contemporaries the small, unrecognised hints conveying that longing and desire. I began to suspect that for several of my teachers life in Sydney was a curious state of suspension: six years of anticipation, waiting for the moment once every seven years (except for the interruption of wars and other misfortunes) when they could board a great liner and sail through the Heads towards Oxford, the land of heart's desire. As I became more confident that my absurd ambition of becoming an academic might indeed be fulfilled, I too began concentrating on the possibility of escape, so that at length university life became indistinguishable for me from what had once seemed an impossible miracle: travelling to England.

The practices and ideals of the English Department—in many ways of much of the university in those years—seem bankrupt from the perspective of the present, less romantic, less optimistic age. And it is true that in the course of the forty years I spent there the edifice did crumble, revealing the unsure foundations on which it had been so hastily raised. Yet the first, and for me the most traumatic, challenge to those assumptions and certainties came from an unexpected quarter. At the time of my return to Sydney in 1963, the department embarked on one of the many self-inflicted martyrdoms that characterise academic life.

In the course of the sixties, the old Sydney department, of which I was to be the last product, became the object of strenuous criticism for its antiquated and inappropriate ways. The complaint was not so much that it failed to acknowledge the accidents of time and place, that its members were teaching their discipline to increasingly ill-prepared and culturally deracinated students, but that they had failed to keep pace with developments in the subject in Britain, and also in America to a lesser extent. The grounds for those complaints were provided by the department's close links with the ideals and practices of Oxford. I was educated in an almost unsullied historicist atmosphere. The department's courses—especially for undergraduates in the four-year honours stream—were meant to provide a systematic survey of English literature, with some acknowledgment of the contribution of Americans, though not in my day of any Australian writer. The bias was, therefore, predominantly antiquarian, despite the gestures towards more recent writing—principally Joyce, Yeats, Eliot, Virginia Woolf and E. M. Forster. In some ways these practices were perhaps as anti-intellectual as its detractors claimed they were. Almost no emphasis was placed on literary theory, on aesthetics, let alone on the political implications of literature and literary study. Nor were there strenuous attempts to form taste or to encourage discrimination—the department's greatest failing, according to a group of influential academics who arrived, mostly from Melbourne, in 1963. In short, the department appeared guilty of amateurishness and dilettantism, preferring gentlemanly scholarship to intellectual rigour and adventurousness. Its easygoing survey of what would now be called the canon of English literature seemed to ignore the knottiest of literary and intellectual problems.

It is undeniable that such charges carry some weight, at least from the perspective of the more demanding and much more neurotic vision of English studies that came to dominate the department for a few years in the sixties. To attempt to justify those older, perhaps naive ways in the contemporary intellectual climate is probably pointless. Nevertheless, even though I have come to recognise the fragility of a way of life and of ideals that appealed to me so strongly in my years as an undergraduate, I am convinced that the inevitable loss of the vision informing them has impoverished academic and cultural life. Fundamentally, the department (and indeed the university itself) was unashamedly elitist. Since only a tiny proportion of school-leavers went on to university (at a time when most people left school after their third year of secondary education), academics could persist in the conviction that they were catering for the brightest and most dedicated. That attitude manifested itself in all sorts of ways, not the least in the apparent indifference to students, for which university people were to be so strenuously criticised in later years. There was indeed an icy, magisterial disdain in much of their dealings with us. And yet few of us resented it, because it was recognised by many— certainly by me—as a sign of respect. It was a wonderful liberation to be left to your own devices, without the watchful eye of those in charge. It seemed to mark more surely than any other ceremony our entry into the adult world, our being responsible for ourselves. That independence came at a price, it is true. As long as we fulfilled the department's minimal requirements by handing in a few pieces of written work, no questions were asked about our diligence or application. Of course, the examinations in November revealed all: those who failed to meet rigorous standards could expect little mercy. Yet none of us would have imagined that the responsibility was anyone's but ours. Most understood that our teachers equipped us with the means of meeting the standards required of us. To have taken steps to supervise our progress in the way of contemporary academics would have seemed a breach of good manners—or intolerable intrusion.

Nothing that has happened since those days has lessened my sense that such attitudes and practices represented a fundamentally civilised vision of university life. There was a certain courtesy in our teachers' remoteness and also something admirable in the impression they gave that they saw their prime responsibility as being lodged in their discipline rather than in us. Although contemporary attitudes find such inclinations shockingly irresponsible, I revelled in them. For the first time in my life I found true independence, an opportunity through the long academic year to discover the spaces of my own life free of all but the most minimal interference. I felt fully alive.

3

The relaxed rhythms of an Arts degree allowed me to discover another beguiling aspect of university life, one perhaps just as nostalgic and sentimental as the rituals played out in the great Quadrangle, yet exhilarating for all that. What I remember most vividly about those years, indeed, is not the instruction I received in English literature, but the activities and diversions you could indulge in, as long as you were prepared (as most of us were) to submit to a month or so of furious cramming in October. Everyone accepted that one of the rare privileges we enjoyed was the liberty to waste time, because in doing so many of us discovered ourselves.

For me the opportunities for leisure afforded by my new life as an Arts student seemed the most wonderful of blessings. I had worked very hard while studying Medicine, especially in the first, optimistic year. In that year I had almost no free time. Each day, except Friday afternoon, was occupied by lectures and laboratory classes. By lunchtime on Fridays, when theoretically I had the afternoon to myself, I was usually so exhausted that all I could think of was to get home as quickly as I could. In that draconian climate I had little opportunity to make friends. In most of the lectures and practical classes we had to occupy seats or spaces at benches allocated according to a strictly alphabetical system. Most of the people I met, therefore, were those whose names began with P, Q, R and S. It proved a limited and not entirely enthralling circle of acquaintances. As far as I remember I did not even once go to a party during my first year.

The distress and humiliation of failure at the end of that year forced me into two quite contradictory resolutions: to work even harder, and to find some way of keeping boredom and resentment at bay. As things turned out, I was more successful in achieving the latter. The true beginning of my new life occurred in the winter of 1955, halfway through my second attempt to pass the first year of the course in Medicine. One day, even more despairing than usual, I made my way to a ramshackle wooden hut at the end of a dank alley which housed the office of *Honi Soit*, the student newspaper. With my heart in my mouth, I knocked on the door and asked, in the faintest of voices as I remember, whether there were anything for me to do.

At that time the paper was a frivolous affair, not too interested in causes or in saving the world. It reflected the particular flavour of the 1950s, an irresponsible time, hedonistic in the postwar prosperity from which so many sections of society benefited. In the five years of my association with *Honi Soit* most of the people who helped to put it together were principally intent on having a good time. While our self-indulgence lacked the ideological basis of the hedonism of the sixties and the eighties, it was in essence no different from the atmosphere of those more spectacularly irresponsible decades. There were exceptions, of course, those who saw beyond mere high spirits: a young woman called Eva Hauser, for one. In later years, as Eva Cox, she was to mould opinion and influence social policy in significant ways. Back then, when she fetched up one day in the offices of the paper to offer her services, she seemed somehow out of kilter with the temper of the time. Most of us were too intent on fun to attend to what she was trying to say. Others, such as Peter Wilenski, were obviously more concerned with student politics—the Students' Representative Council, the Union, the university branches of the two major political parties. Wilenski in particular seemed to regard his association with the paper as merely an aspect of larger political ambitions. Several active and highly motivated student politicians avoided it entirely, for it obviously carried insufficient clout to make it worth their while associating with it.

It was at *Honi Soit* that I came to know several people whose lives have taken them far beyond the confines of that little, self-important world. Among them only Robert Hughes struck me as exceptional at the time; others—Clive James for instance—had not yet revealed their brilliance. With Hughes, though, there could be no doubt that he was out of the ordinary. There were in my circle of acquaintances several people from established, often cultivated backgrounds: offspring of solid rural families or members of the great legal clans. None, however, radiated the patrician air that struck you as soon as you came within Hughes's orbit. Memory tells me that he was wearing a beret when he first breezed into the *Honi Soit* office offering to draw cartoons. It was intended, I am sure, to suggest something debonair, insouciant. Even then, some people suspected that his flamboyance was that of a poseur, though I think that in those years he was fully dedicated to his several incarnations—first as the existentialist artist; next as the champion skier; the intellectual; the bon viveur.

A large part of his confidence and energy was generated by the sense he gave that he was very well-connected, although seemingly in reduced circumstances. He was the youngest of four children. At the time I knew him his brothers were already making names for themselves in the law. His father had been dead for some time. Those circumstances accounted in large manner, it seems to me, for the edge of insecurity to his wonderful theatricality, as someone obliged to make his mark among his elders who might well have regarded him as a trifle wet behind the ears. In the years that I knew him he lived with his mother in a large—the word 'stately' came inevitably to mind—house in a good street in the Eastern Suburbs. Or perhaps it was only a part of the building. In any event, I remember high, cool, somewhat cobwebby rooms.

In those years Robert was disconcerting; you could not be sure where his obvious talents might lead him. His great ambition seemed to have been to become a painter. Indeed, on the last time I saw him before he left Australia he seemed finally to be headed in that direction. I was having dinner with friends at Vadim's at the Cross, which used to be celebrated and notorious at a time of stringent licensing laws for serving spirits (in coffee cups) at all hours. Hughes was being entertained in an elegant restaurant across the street by Major Rubin, a well-known collector and patron of the arts. He saw us sitting just inside the plate-glass window of Vadim's, and ran across, bubbling with excitement, with that slight stutter that always seized him at such times, to tell us of his great good luck. Rubin would be buying some of his paintings, so setting him on the road to fame. We must celebrate, he said, ordering cognac, but rushed back to his host before it arrived.

For *Honi Soit* he drew a series of amusing little sketches, dinkuses as they were called, to break up columns of type or to fill awkward spaces. Many of them showed devils with pitchforks doing unpleasant things to squirming, writhing figures. They were inspired, Hughes insisted, by his experience of Riverview, the Jesuit college at Lane Cove, where there was much emphasis on sin and retribution. He had not had a good time there, he used to add. Those little sketches and the few larger drawings he made for the paper revealed a bold line and a mordant wit with more than an edge of cruelty. The one or two paintings he showed me seemed much less striking.

He had other ambitions too—and part of his charm was that you could never tell whether he was in earnest or had made it all up on the spur of the moment. He might become a professional skier, he announced one day. His family had connections with the first of the clubs to be established at Thredbo, at the time no more than a couple of huts and a rickety, wheezing chairlift. We did not know, however, how much of his tales of derring-do on the snowfields was to be believed.

In those years the university's ski club owned a prefabricated hut, a remnant of the Snowy Mountain construction works, high above Guthega dam. It was an uncomfortable, isolated place which offered cheap accommodation. To get there, you could often rely on the services of the district postman, who made a bit of extra money by driving people in his rattling van to the handful of huts above the dam. When the snow was heavy, however, the road was blocked beyond the power station at Munyang, some six or seven kilometres and several hundred metres below the huts. Then you had to walk on skis up the cruel incline, carrying clothes and provisions for a week, arriving exhausted, frozen, suicidal. One year Hughes failed to turn up. We didn't give it much thought: the weather had turned foul, and we guessed that he had decided to give it away. As it grew dark, I remember, a blizzard set in: huge sheets of snow streaming horizontally in the fierce wind. By morning the storm had passed, we woke to a clear sunny sky above the sparkling snow-covered hills. As we were cooking breakfast, we heard stamping and shuffling on the porch. It was Hughes, pink-faced, smiling, obviously pleased with himself. He'd been caught in the blizzard. He remembered what Antarctic explorers did: he buried himself up to the neck in snow to keep warm. I don't think any of us believed him, but we were too polite (or perhaps intimidated) to say so.

I realised a long time ago that we underestimated him in those days. To some of us he seemed just another of the many who made all sorts of extravagant claims about their abilities, their connections and their prospects. Hughes had more style, that insouciance which remains such an attractive aspect of his personality. But he seemed to have been cut from a similar cloth. He was, of course, very young, unformed—just as we all were. But our reluctance to pay much heed to him had another, fundamental cause, one intimately connected with those notions of identity and belonging that were preoccupying me in an idiosyncratic way during those years. It was beyond our imaginative, even perhaps moral, capacities to consider that one of us might conquer that great, and in so many ways mythological world we thought of as 'abroad'. Our communal or national sense of inferiority seemed to debar us from hoping for such unthinkable achievements. That was hardly a rational attitude, but it was widespread nevertheless, a matter I think of unstated but devoutly held beliefs.

Such self-denigration was a result of the particular quandary of our generation, a quandary, moreover, that was even then fast disappearing, though only the more perspicacious—Hughes among them—recognised it. We were living in a world still experiencing some of the after-effects of war. Travel was difficult and expensive. And Europe was a dangerous, menacing place. Much of it still lay in ruins in the first half of the 1950s. Britain suffered from appalling economic hardships, which prompted thousands to seek a better life in Australia. The political climate grew increasingly alarming: those were the years—the Berlin blockade, the Suez crisis and the revolution in Hungary during the mid-fifties—when the great powers seemed bent on an inevitable path to nuclear collision. Australia's long isolation during the war years exacerbated our communal suspicion and timidity.

Significantly, whenever we listened to (and sniggered at) the ambitions of people like Hughes, the world we imagined that they wanted to conquer was England, or perhaps France. Few of us gave America even a passing thought: it found little place in our dreams and longings. We did not recognise how rapidly the world was changing, how England was already becoming essentially foreign to us, or how much certain aspects of American intellectual and cultural life would come to guide our halting progress towards self-knowledge and self-sufficiency. I understand now that most of my Australian-born contemporaries were just as beguiled by fantasies of Europe as I was in those years. They dreamt that they too might find fulfilment and satisfaction there one day. I have also realised that the discontent and nostalgia we newcomers brought with us increased for a time that sense of dependency. I am reminded that Hughes's splendid North American career was achieved only by way of his time in England, for he, too, was initially beguiled by fantasies of Europe not substantially different from mine.

4

Only one of the people I knew at university departed from such conventional ways of thinking, and looked beyond England to America—where she was to forge a remarkable public and academic career. At the time, I did not know Jill Ker (Jill Ker Conway as she is now) at all well. We did, however, have some friends in common; I would talk to her occasionally at parties and dances. The parties where I met her were usually held on the North Shore, those well-heeled conservative suburbs of Sydney which then had a far more individual and distinct style. Nevertheless, even at the time, many people looked with mild amusement or outright hostility on what they saw as a stuffy, conformist and bourgeois world. Being the product of generations of bourgeois conditioning—especially on my father's side of the family—I relished that world, and felt grateful too that I had found acceptance there.

A Sentimental Education

Jill Ker seemed to fit perfectly into that environment. Many years later, she wrote frankly in *The Road from Coorain* about the sense of intolerable constriction she suffered during those years. In Australia, she came to feel, being a woman imposed all kinds of barriers in her way: intellectually, professionally and emotionally. What I remember of her during those years betrays none of that. Jill, the daughter of a rural family, seemed to belong naturally to that conventional upper-middle-class environment, the social rituals of which she played out with consummate ease.

She was, however, different. Alone among those young women, she was academically ambitious, gifted and highly successful. I came to know her during her last years as an honours student in History. Hers was generally acknowledged to be an outstanding year. There was a friendly rivalry between her and Milton Osborne, the other gifted student in her group. That did not seem to affect their friendship: Milton and Jill moved in the same circles, shared many friends, liked doing similar things. Socially, Jill's poise and confidence were her most remarkable attributes. Some mean-spirited people thought of her as no more than a stuck-up bluestocking: humourless, self-impressed, intellectually snobbish. None of them, I think, ever watched as she kicked up her heels at a party. But it is true that even in those unguarded moments she did not lose her composure. Most of us were convinced that a great future lay ahead for her—we were right as it turned out, though not quite in the way we had imagined.

Yet, as some knew—and as she was to confess in later years—there was a great shadow over her life. She never let on about her troubled relationship with her tormented mother, a woman of fierce pride and possessiveness who awed many of Jill's friends—fortunately perhaps, I never met Mrs Ker. We knew a few sketchy details about the hardships of Jill's childhood on the Western Plains, and we also knew that her father had died some time well before we met her, though the circumstances of his drowning, with the hint of possible suicide, were never mentioned. The death of a brother in a car accident became common knowledge, but again it seemed to most of us that Jill had managed to deal with it with her customary poise.

She even managed to hide a good measure of her disappointment and anger when she received the setback that became instrumental to her decision to leave Australia. She graduated with first-class honours and the University Medal in History—a distinction she shared in that year with Milton Osborne. The achievement was notable in itself, but all the more remarkable because in those years the Department of History was niggardly in awarding such distinguished degrees. John

Ward, the Professor of History, later to become one of the university's less distinguished Vice-Chancellors, was said to have insisted that first-class honours degrees must be reserved for those whose work would be recognised as outstanding contributions to the discipline. In other words, as rumour had it at least, no concession was made to the inevitable differences in skill, sophistication and technique between the work of a final year undergraduate and that of a fully trained professional historian. Accordingly, first-class degrees (let alone university medals) in History were exceptional. Only the introduction of travelling scholarships for postgraduate studies by the Commonwealth Government, a year or two after Jill's time, made the History Department change its ways and join the race to obtain as many of those coveted prizes for its students as it could.

By the time Jill's and Milton's extraordinary results set everyone by the ears, Jill had obviously decided against aiming for an academic career in Australia, or in Britain. In *The Road from Coorain* and more thoroughly in *True North*, an account of her life in Canada before she moved to the United States to take up the presidency of Smith College, Jill wrote of her disillusionment with the practices and ideals of the Sydney History Department. They were, she remembers, far too dry, far too unimaginative, scornful of the intellect, chained to the study of historical 'fact', unable to break free of the tyranny of documents and data into a more speculative world.

In her memoirs she sees such uninspiring modes of teaching as the result of the Sydney History Department's—indeed Australia's— worship of British ways and institutions, the dusty memories of Oxford 'scholarship' and the discouragement of intellectual curiosity that seemed to have marked many of the people who taught us. The recognition came to her, she writes, that she had to break out of that mould, that the fundamentally colonial cast of Australian intellectual life (or what passed for it) was an outmoded and nostalgic impediment both to her own development and that of society at large. The intellectual challenge and inspiration she discovered in North America showed her how to escape the prison-house of nostalgia and thoughtless worship of British models.

It is evident from her books that her particular predicament as a woman contributed strongly to the sense that she must leave behind the world which was symbolised for me, so alluringly, by the turrets and crenellations of Blacket's essay in nostalgic pastiche. The greatest blow, she remembers, came not so much from the university, but from her inability to win a cadetship in the diplomatic service. I recall seeing her a few days after she had received word that her application had failed. Milton Osborne had been accepted. She had no quarrel with that, but it riled her that another of their contemporaries, far less accomplished than either, had also been offered a place. She was convinced, I remember her saying on the one occasion when she lifted her mask a little, that she had been passed over because she was a woman. Some have disputed that claim, citing the possibility that she may have been considered temperamentally unsuitable. If that was so, the selectors were doubly in error, for in the decade she spent at Smith College she managed to take that already notable institution to greater and greater achievements by means of the expert combination of diplomacy and ruthlessness people in such positions always need.

Being scorned by the diplomatic service was the final insult, the catalyst that confirmed her decision that she must seek a life for herself not merely outside Australia, but also away from that self-satisfied, decaying society in England that the Australia of the day worshipped so unthinkingly. Jill's choice was unerringly accurate for her. I saw her shortly before she sailed for America in 1960, at a party given by her friend Nina Morris. Jill arrived late, I remember. Her eyes were shining with excitement: she was about to set out on the great adventure of her life. I also remember that she was even more lively than usual. She was beginning to change, but on that night she was still one of us.

I saw her again nine years later. Nina and I had recently married: we were spending my sabbatical year in London. Jill and her husband, the Canadian historian John Conway, were passing through. We called on them in a chintzy, genteel hotel in Knightsbridge, behind Harrods. Jill had been transformed. It was much more than the slight North American twang she had acquired. Her presence, the way she dressed and carried herself all spoke of that transformation. She was even more assured and confident than she had been in Sydney. Here was someone obviously used to exercising influence, and on a large scale too. In that sense she had become worldly in ways she could not have achieved in Sydney.

I, by contrast, thought that I had not changed much since I last saw her—except for losing my hair. And in most ways I had not. I was no longer a student at the University of Sydney but a member of the Department of English. My intellectual and cultural horizons had not, however, changed substantially. Whenever an opportunity to travel arose I thought automatically of England and Europe. America never entered my calculations. Indeed, my first visit to America—after, that is, the three febrile months my parents and I spent there on our way to Australia in 1946 and 1947—only took place after I had left the university.

5

The friendships that began through my association with *Honi Soit* emerged in large part as I was beginning to discover that I had certain talents—while the talents themselves were nurtured, I am sure, by the confidence friendships are able to confer.

At the time I could see no affinity between my determination to make a life for myself in the university (despite my less than diligent application to my studies) and those trivial talents that I discovered with *Honi Soit* and, a little later, the annual revue performed in the raftered barn of the long-since demolished Union Hall. Studying English Literature seemed a serious, responsible business—it was to be a long time before postmodern playfulness announced its presence in academic culture. My talents, by contrast, were for parody, pastiche and satire of a generally obvious sort. *Honi Soit* provided many opportunities to indulge those inclinations—and also for language games of a type entirely different from Wittgenstein's. I discovered a facility for parodying the pompous, polysyllabic style of the *Bulletin*, or the sensationalist machine-gun sentences of the *Sun* and the *Daily Mirror*. I also slipped into the paper literary parodies of the kind undergraduates then were fond of writing: Joyce, of course, and Proust too, because I had actually read forty or fifty pages (but no more than that) of *Remembrance of Things Past*. It was the annual revue, however, that gave me the greatest scope to indulge in the arts of mimicry. The high point of my career as a scriptwriter came in 1957 with *Brass Monkeys*, long remembered for its obscurity, pretentiousness and for the Wagnerian demands it made on its unfortunate audiences.

My contributions to the revue were, as far as I can recall, two sketches. One concerned the man who read the time on the telephone: 'At the third stroke, the time will be ten forty-three and twenty seconds . . .' I called him George, seated him at a desk with a gong and brought his gun-toting girlfriend on stage to berate him—between announcements of the exact time—for infidelity. Predictably, at the climax of the sketch she gunned him down, pushing him off his chair to make the next perfectly timed announcement into the microphone.

The most substantial—and as far as the audience was concerned the most infuriating—piece I wrote for that revue was, hindsight tells me, the most sinister in import in many ways. It was a parody of Chekhov, with overtones of Dostoyevsky, called, predictably enough, 'The Idiots'. I bitterly regret that I did not keep a copy of it, not because I think it had any particular merit, but because it would have given me a mirror in which I could see my younger self. The sketch was, I now realise, a disturbing portent of things to come. It revealed a particular cultural and even psychological dilemma, intimately connected with questions of identity, of belonging and—at the farthest remove—with the dangers inherent in being a 'virtuoso' in a language not fundamentally your own. 'The Idiots' chimed in, it seems to me, with the provisional, hypothetical and essentially parodistic way in which I was beginning to experience some success with my formal academic studies in English.

At the time, 'The Idiots' seemed nothing more than fun, an opportunity to display my new-found sophistication. The sketch consisted of a group of people—five, I think—engaged in what I took to be a typically Russian conversation. They talked about their longing for spring. They remembered the past, especially the great frost when the Neva froze solid and the Tsarina commanded an organ to be wheeled onto the ice so she could listen to (or was it play?) Bach in the sparkling winter air. There was talk, too, of people lying on the shelf beside the stove through the bitter winter night, to be found frozen dead in the morning beside the cooling stove. Writing and polishing 'The Idiots' and the sketch about George coincided with the months when, for the first time, I became absorbed by my studies in English—or at least as far as much more important activities allowed. As I have suggested, I could see nothing but coincidence in that at the time: it was only much later that I recognised the symptoms of a particular quandary which I was never entirely able to solve—only to mask or disguise.

It had been one thing to announce to the world that I was really cut out for the literary life. In practice, as soon as I began attending lectures in English Literature I discovered the extent of the gulf between my fantasies and the reality of English studies. Much of the work seemed trivial. I particularly remember the tedium of trying to read overlong, indigestible nineteenth-century novels: *Vanity Fair*, *Bleak House* and George Meredith's *The Egoist*—the last of which, I must confess, I have never managed to read to the end. I found their ponderous sentimentality or almost childish jocularity intolerable. This was not what I thought literature should be about.

Matters did not improve much in my second year. I had managed to pass the first-year examinations without, however, gaining a credit, the qualification required for entering the honours stream. The department was very indulgent in these matters, and allowed me to enrol in the honours course as a probationary candidate. By the end of the year I had perfected my skills in parody and mimicry sufficiently to walk away with a high distinction, so allowing me to continue as a candidate in the honours school. But I knew in my heart of hearts that my success had been due largely to sleight of hand. The second-year syllabus seemed just as dreary as what had gone before. It had a pronounced bias towards literature from the eighteenth and early nineteenth centuries—with additional texts, most threateningly Anglo Saxon, as the honours component. Eighteenth-century fiction—principally Fielding, Smollett and the Gothic romances—proved as unattractive as the heavy Victorian fare of the first year. Significantly, the only work to make any impression on me from that period was the tongue-in-cheek playfulness of *Tristram Shandy*.

Nor was I much happier with the Romantics who dominated the second half of the year. It was then that I developed my dislike of Wordsworth and Shelley—the one ponderous, it seemed to me, the other almost farcical in his ecstasies. Not even Keats managed to speak to me, except, I remember, for 'La Belle Dame Sans Merci'. Coleridge was, however, another matter—there was something significant in the fact that I was able to appreciate the sophisticated archaisms in 'The Rime of the Ancient Mariner' in ways that I could not come to terms with the subtle delicacy and restrained passion of Keats's verse. The abyss of that part of the course, however, was Scott—I soon abandoned any attempt to read *Old Mortality* or *The Heart of Midlothian* or any of those wordy historical romances that seemed to me entirely stillborn. For many years I pretended that these dislikes were the products of sophisticated literary judgments. They were, of course, nothing of the sort; rather they reflected the quandaries of the linguistic quagmire in which I found myself, and the idiosyncratic, indeed eccentric, literary experience I brought to my studies.

As a consequence of having missed out on a normal childhood, I had not been introduced to the life of the imagination in ways that children living in happier circumstances usually experience. Even in the early years of my life in Budapest I was soon catapulted from the world of childhood stories—*Struwwelpeter* and the brothers Grimm—into the harsh realities of war. Before starting school in Australia in March of 1947, when I was eleven years old, I had attended no more than a week or two of preschool. During the war, my mother had taught me to read, and I somehow picked up the ability to count, as most children are able to do. In the hectic

A Sentimental Education

eighteen months between the end of the war and our setting out on the long journey to Sydney I read very little. Paradoxically therefore, I was both naive and sophisticated, as I was to remain during our early years in Australia.

My true engagement with literature at university did not happen until the syllabus came to focus on the dramatists of the sixteenth and early seventeenth centuries—Shakespeare's predecessors, contemporaries and heirs. I remember precisely how my fascination with those plays began. Until then we had studied several of Shakespeare's plays, but Shakespeare was somehow beyond me: he was too grand, too awesome, and too much cultural capital had been invested in him for me to approach him with anything but timid respect. His contemporaries, I was to find, carried no such cultural baggage.

John Webster, the most gifted and exciting of Shakespeare's imitators, was nominated, together with a clutch of his contemporaries, on the syllabus for the second year of my course. In those days before the cheap paperback, books were very hard to come by. The holdings of the university library, in that other mock-Gothic fantasia, the Fisher Library, nowadays the MacLaurin Hall, were inadequate even for the needs of the small student population of the time. But I was lucky with Webster: I managed to borrow the volumes of Lucas's *editio maior* containing the two best and best-known plays, *The Duchess of Malfi* and *The White Devil*. Webster's plays opened many doors for me. Renaissance drama became an obsession, an all-consuming passion—and it was to lead eventually to Shakespeare himself. After Webster's grand melodramas, I discovered the dark passions and intrigues of Chapman's plays centred on the historical figure of Bussy d'Ambois, where monks versed in necromancy raise hellish spirits from the deep. I stumbled on the whirling revenges and counter-revenges of *The Revenger's Tragedy* and its bizarre, cut-out abstractions who seemed, paradoxically, more alive than the well-rounded characters of Dickens and Thackeray whom I found pallid by comparison. I read voraciously and indiscriminately. In the dusty stacks of the library I found volume after volume of old collections of plays which appeared not to have been opened for decades. I discovered the charm of those scholarly 'conservative' editions which preserved the chaotic spelling of Shakespeare's age. And I also stumbled on shelves of thin volumes bound in grey boards with sand-coloured linen spines, the publications of the Malone Society. These were not merely conservative reprints of obscure, often anonymous plays, retaining the orthographic eccentricities of the sixteenth century, but facsimiles, reproducing the typefaces and design of old books—catchwords at the foot of each page, compositors' signatures and, in some instances, near-illegible, and for that reason all the more enthralling, black-letter type.

Among those forgotten books, much more than from the formal teaching I received in Renaissance literature, I found my vocation. During the course of my third year in the English Department I determined that I would make the drama of Shakespeare's age my field of speciality. At the time, I thought that the decision was prompted by the recognition that those long-forgotten plays offered a rich field for scholarly research. That was undoubtedly so, but my fascination with early drama proceeded from the same source as the other aspect of the syllabus for that year which had a profound impact on me—though I was not to pursue that interest until I became a book reviewer and literary journalist in the years just prior to my leaving the university in 1994.

That field was contemporary fiction. Of course, what the Department of English understood by contemporary fiction in 1958 was, to say the least, conservative and unadventurous. Its basis was firmly lodged in the ideals of Bloomsbury. Joyce was, naturally, a towering presence. So were Virginia Woolf and E. M. Forster. One or two Americans also found a place, Hemingway principally. Lawrence, by contrast, was, if not overlooked, certainly somewhat looked down on—though his time was to come, with a vengeance, in the early sixties, when the department's life seemed to revolve around him. 'Contemporary fiction' in the late fifties also stretched back in time with considerable generosity. So we studied Conrad and Arnold Bennett too. Far less emphasis was placed on younger British novelists, though Evelyn Waugh was acknowledged.

As was the case with my discovery of Renaissance drama, I found far greater interest and excitement in reading books not included on the syllabus. Indeed, the lectures I attended proved, with only one or two exceptions, not particularly enthralling. But reading was—indiscriminately, voraciously, without the least concern for aesthetic or literary principles, more a voyage of exploration than systematic study. I read a great deal of ephemera, most of which has been forgotten, most of which I have forgotten too. I read mainly English and American fiction—Australian writers remained, as far as I was concerned, dreary chroniclers of the bush, a subject in which I had no interest. Someone gave me a copy of *The Tree of Man* for my twenty-first birthday. I read the first page about Stan Parker cutting a clearing in the bush and decided that I had read enough. Another twenty-first birthday present proved, however, far more enticing. It was also a new novel, Thomas Mann's *Confessions of Felix Krull, Confidence Man*. Something, I was not entirely sure what, fascinated me about Mann's jesting, ironic tale of a hotel valet who starts a life of impersonation in a small Rhineland town of vineyards, twisting lanes and bourgeois propriety. Perhaps it was that I was encountering images of that dream-Europe (not the Europe I had known) for which I had never entirely stopped yearning. Or perhaps I recognised in the novel something of my own character as a literary or academic confidence man.

Throughout the years of my academic life I did not attach any particular significance to these areas of literature that engaged my interests—whereas my academic engagement with Dickens and Wordsworth, Milton and Keats, Austen and Tennyson was merely cerebral and professional, in the way that a construction engineer might be fascinated with the materials he uses without feeling the least emotional attachment to steel and concrete. Only latterly, as I have been trying to make sense of this, have I come to suspect the deep, perhaps disturbing explanation for that phenomenon.

The great outburst of creative energy on the London stage that began in Shakespeare's youth came out of nothing. A new world was fashioned from words, gestures, old stories and emotions. But it had no background, there was little resonance to it. In that sense those comedies and tragedies, stories of impassioned love and overweening ambition Elizabethan playwrights churned out with such relish and nonchalance, were also innocent, creations, as it were, *ex nihilo*. Much of the fiction I read, I now realise, revealed something similar. The books I enjoyed most belonged, in one way or another, to the great endeavour of modernism—debased and trivialised in some instances but significantly present, nonetheless. There also was evidence of a conscious break with a discredited past, of a deliberate attempt to fashion the world of the imagination anew with fresh, at times outrageous means. I too was refashioning the world, remaking myself in a new image, coming to the traditions of literature and culture with a curious mixture of confidence and naivete. For me there was no past, or rather only a past remote from the slow, instinctive acquisition of the language in which the imaginative traditions of English literature were nurtured. With those hoary plays and modern books the peculiarity of my cultural background seemed of far less moment—I could wash my inadequacies, even ignorance, away.

6

The Department of English saw these matters in a rather different light. Those were not the days of options, generous choices for students to exercise. It offered its future graduates the means of gaining competence in a body of knowledge, not the opportunity to indulge in unformed and immature likes and dislikes. In order to earn my degree, therefore, I had to buckle under and come to terms with writing for which I had little liking or sympathy—the great staples of eighteenth- and nineteenth-century literature which constitute a complex, multi-faceted tradition deeply immersed in the cultural experience encoded in the English language. Even at the time, despite my boredom and bouts of resentment, I could see the virtue and good sense in that, for I realised that I was seeking professional and academic qualifications, not self-fulfilment. But none of that made it any easier to satisfy my teachers that I did indeed possess such competence.

My gifts as a mimic and ventriloquist came to my rescue. I learnt how to conduct an argument in an essay or examination, and also how to use the vocabulary and discourse of the critical fashions of the time. In that I was no different from most undergraduates, then or now. Nor are such essentially imitative practices necessarily to be frowned on, it seems to me, despite the preoccupation with originality and personal response that became a fad in the sixties, and continues to influence academic attitudes in various theory-clad guises. I, like most youngish university students, was far too immature to reveal any worthwhile originality, and had too little experience of life to make my personal responses valuable. I acquired professional skills in honing and perfecting my technique in dealing with the topics and propositions (often harbouring concealed trip-wires) that our essays and examinations invited us to discuss by employing sanctioned and traditional modes of critical and scholarly writing.

No doubt I was somewhat more successful than many, perhaps most of my fellow students. But I recognised the tricks and illusions that allowed me to write authoritatively about writers and books in which I had only limited interest. I have wondered since those days whether some of my contemporaries were less successful students because they were more respectful in their approach to the subject. Did they, I ask myself sometimes, have scruples of the kind I could not possess because of my essential indifference? I did not hesitate for a moment, for instance, to write with some panache I think, about the symbolic complexity of, say, Conrad's *Lord Jim*, even though I found that suety meditation on personal honour almost intolerably pretentious. But as I approached the task of making something of the topic in much the same way that I would go about solving a crossword puzzle, I discovered great fascination in the intellectual exercise, if it may be called that. *Lord Jim*, that verbose, pompous novel, became interesting not for itself but because I could do something interesting with it. I was discovering, in short, that my interest lay in literature as an academic and intellectual pursuit, not as something essential and meaningful to my emotional or even perhaps spiritual life.

I have no doubt that the practices and ideals of the English Department of the day did not discourage such inclinations. The model of scholarship the department followed, based, on the whole, on the precepts of Oxford, were diametrically opposed to the fashion for encouraging personal engagement with literature, which was to rule briefly in the sixties, derived from the ideals of the Cambridge English school, and particularly from the missionary zeal of F. R. Leavis. I think that most of the people who taught me would have regarded the nurturing of taste, even perhaps of opinion, as something of an impropriety, an invasion of individual preferences and sensibilities. Their job, as they saw it I think, was not to inculcate aesthetic, let alone ethical discriminations, but to disclose the complex traditions of English literary history. But precisely because they were not primarily interested in the value or pertinence for our time of the discipline they professed, that tradition they disclosed was not frozen into dogma. Rather their practices allowed, indeed encouraged, individual tastes, preferences, even quirks and eccentricities, as long as these were recognised as individual, personal predilections, and not confused with the essential objectivity of English studies.

It was for that reason, I am sure, that my eccentricities were tolerated and in some ways encouraged in an intellectual climate which seems to me to have been more civilised than the hectoring of various kinds that came to dominate the study of literature in later decades. But my brittle, parodic mimicry had intrinsic limitations. I am certain that if I had not discovered the heady world of Renaissance drama my success as a student would have stopped short at a certain well-defined point. Those hoary, at times crude but always wonderfully inventive and energetic plays did make my pulse race, did engage feelings in ways I had not experienced before. And with that, I am equally certain, came academic work of a higher calibre, even perhaps of value.

I received much encouragement in that new-found interest from Wesley Milgate, the Challis Professor of English Literature. That was the first substantial contact I had with a member of the department.

Milgate agreed to supervise my honours thesis, in which I chose to examine a largely neglected form of Renaissance drama known as domestic tragedy. In terms of the sixteenth century's attitudes, 'domestic tragedy' was a contradiction in terms, for the grave matters of life and death with which tragedy deals were supposed to be the preserve of the high-born, those capable of great passion, great ambition and great evil. The affairs of ordinary people were considered, by contrast, the domain of comedy, where nothing grave usually happens, where everything ends to the satisfaction of all.

Towards the end of my third year I made an appointment with Milgate to put the thesis proposal to him. Why was I interested in domestic tragedies, he asked. I explained to the best of my abilities that I was fascinated by the attempt to convert matters and ways of life which were usually considered trivial and the source of laughter into the material of tragedy. And besides, I added (with a little greater courage and confidence, I remember), no one had looked at those old plays for many, many years. I am sure that this clinched the matter: I was proposing to do something that had not been done before, at least in Sydney within living memory. I see it as highly significant that Milgate did not ask the next question, a question that would have followed inevitably a few years later, after his early retirement and the arrival of the Melbourne Leavisites: were these creaky old plays good enough? That question did not arise, for the fact that I had found them interesting was, I think, sufficient justification according to the broad and generous ideals of those days.

Milgate proved a tactful supervisor. By the standards of later decades—when often steamy relationships developed between candidates and their supervisors, spilling at times well beyond the academic into the personal, even the sexual—he may appear to have been irresponsible in letting me go my way as much as he did. I tend to think, though, that it was more a matter of trust rather than that mistrustful, on occasions destructive interference that was to go in the guise of care and responsibility in later years. I saw him two or three times during my honours year. Our relationship was strictly academic, the personal was never allowed to intrude. A few weeks before the submission date I showed him the draft: he corrected my spelling and grammar, pointed out a few inconsistencies, and made one or two more substantial suggestions. But that was that. I did as he had suggested and submitted the work to the magisterial Miss Roberts.

I have little recollection of the examination papers for my degree, except that the clever game playing, which I practised as assiduously as before, had an edge of real excitement and even commitment to it in the papers I wrote on Renaissance literature. There I felt that I had found my true calling. Waiting for the results was agonising. I gave in to self-doubt: my parents' friends had been right all along, I decided. Aiming for an academic career had been egregious folly: I had set my sights far too high, the consequences were bound to be disastrous. Days, weeks went by. I bumped into a few members of the department but none of them indicated anything by word or gesture. They were feeling sorry for me, I decided. Then, a day or two before the official publications of the results, I had word in a roundabout fashion from the head of one of the residential colleges that I had done very well. I was disinclined to believe her; I was also disinclined to believe the line of small black type in the *Sydney Morning Herald*, according to which I had graduated with first-class honours in English Literature.

7

So it seemed after all that I was on my way to the academic life I had spoken about so flippantly and with such little hope four years earlier. Shortly after the results were published Milgate got in touch, asking me to see him. On my way to the appointment I ran into a couple of people from the department. I fancied I noticed a change in they way they spoke to me. Was I already one of them? Milgate was friendly in a reserved fashion. I should apply for a scholarship to Oxford, he advised, to do more work on Renaissance drama. To fill in the time until the beginning of the English academic year in October, he offered me a teaching fellowship for two terms. I would be required to take the bulk of the first year tutorials the department was proposing to conduct in 1960.

I began teaching in March. The department gave me a desk in a former laboratory just behind the main building. You reached it by way of the Vice-Chancellor's Quadrangle, a small, handsome space separating the main Quadrangle from Science Road. In spring it is usually filled with azalea blooms around a Florentine bronze statue of Mercury—with a suggestively upraised finger on which wags used to put doughnuts for birds to peck at. I shared that dark (and in winter perishingly cold) room with the other teaching fellows, three women, all members of the Early English Literature and Language side of the department. When one of us was teaching, the others vacated the room, but since the other three gave most of their classes elsewhere, and spent the rest of the time at home or in the library, I had the room to myself to all intents and purposes. It was not one of the handsome panelled rooms beneath the clock tower, but it was heaven, nevertheless.

My teaching duties required me to take six or seven classes a week on a five-week cycle. That meant that I had to hold a class on the same topic thirty or thirty-five times. Some of my friends thought that this would be enough to drive anyone insane. Certainly, by the end of five weeks it was hard to sound fresh or invigorating on *Bleak House* or *Much Ado About Nothing*. I also discovered that although these tutorials were meant to encourage discussion, they soon collapsed into monologues held in front of assiduously note-taking students. The only exception I recall was a lively group—whom I saw no more than four times—where an intense student called Bruce Beresford would often take over the discussion. He seemed enthralled—obsessed might be a better word—by Mahler, a somewhat recherché composer in those days. Otherwise I soon found that coaxing students into talking was much harder than getting water out of stone.

I also discovered that I liked teaching and seemed to have a gift for it. I enjoyed the challenge of how to subject often vague, provisional, at times contradictory novels, plays or poems to the kind of scholarly scrutiny we practised in those days. By the standards of later decades our methods seem antiquated, as well as antiquarian. We were intent on recovering as far as possible what a work might have conveyed to its contemporaries. So, for instance, when the turn of *The Merchant of Venice* came, I naturally mentioned the fear and suspicion of Jews in Elizabethan England, particularly after the trial and execution for treason of Dr Lopez, the queen's doctor. I do not remember experiencing any qualms or any need to remind my students of the infernal history of European anti-Semitism in the twentieth century, which my parents and I had narrowly escaped. Such personal or even communal concerns seemed irrelevant to the academic study of *The Merchant of Venice*.

That intellectual climate made teaching easier for me in many ways. The selection of texts on the first-year syllabus contained a number of works which, privately, I found tedious and tendentious. I had to teach Fielding's *Joseph Andrews*, to my mind almost intolerably jocular and pointless in its seemingly endless series of one-liners and prat-falls. Three or four years later, the new climate in the department would have forced me to acknowledge what I thought about that tediously over-written novel. During my academic apprenticeship, however, such preferences, eccentricities or quirks could be ignored—indeed, they had to be ignored. *Joseph Andrews* is a key text in the development of English fiction; anyone making an even half-hearted attempt to study or teach English literature in an academic context must come to terms with it, must understand why it exercised such influence over later writers, and why many people continue to hold it in high esteem. It would have seemed absolutely improper to use a class on the novel as an occasion to persuade students why its reputation was unwarranted, or indeed the result of social and cultural conditioning by a powerful and self-serving elite. The attitudes of later decades saw our failure to engage with such practices as irresponsibility. Nevertheless, despite the many earthquakes and volcanic eruptions I have encountered in academic life, I continue to regard the scholarly fashion we followed in those days, and the ideals it represented, as more civilised than the hothouse atmosphere that has shrouded the humanities, and particularly the study of literature, for many years.

The experience of those months, the need to prepare classes, to learn routines of work, the numbing boredom of many of the tasks—for instance, marking two hundred essays on the one topic—did much to contain and convert the romantic fantasies of academic life as I had observed it from the outside during my student years. Teaching in a university, I came to understand, was a profession, not a calling or a religious vocation. It demanded the degree of dedication any profession should demand, and a particular commitment as well. You had to be convinced that what you were doing was worthwhile, honourable and of some benefit to society. The dangers of professional arrogance and self-absorption had always to be acknowledged. In some ways being an academic was more encompassing than other professional ways of life: the monastic ideal still echoed faintly in the universities of the time, and not merely because the physical model for our university had been tinged by the monastic and ecclesiastical. Nevertheless, it was essential to resist the temptation to withdraw into that world of rituals and ceremonies, a world that could so easily ignore the unsatisfactory reality beyond those protective confines. That indeed was one of the reasons why I proved something of a disappointment when I decided to take up the travelling scholarship I won in 1960 not in Oxford but in the more plebeian and much less renowned University of London.

The justification (or excuse) I found was a result of the first of many instances of ineptitude I experienced throughout my academic career at the hands of the university's administration. I had missed out on receiving one of the newly established travelling scholarships offered by the Commonwealth—another of the occupants of the laboratory off the Vice-Chancellor's Quadrangle managed to bag one. Naturally, I sank into deep gloom. Milgate and Wilkes both cheered me up—that left the way open, they reminded me, for one of the university's own, and only a little less lucrative scholarships: I should apply for one as soon as the advertisements appeared.

Weeks, even months went by and there was no sign of an advertisement. Finally I screwed up enough courage to mention it to Milgate, who promised to look into it. He sent me a note the next day: the person in charge of those advertisements (an idiot, the tone of the letter implied) had forgotten to announce the competition. Applications were now open, he added. I put in the relevant papers and within two or three weeks received word that I had won the Hannah Fullerton Travelling Scholarship for two years. I should write without delay to Oxford, Milgate said, because time was running out. As it happened, time had run out. I received a letter telling me that all places for the 1960–61 academic year had been filled, but that they would treat an application for the following year favourably.

I was piqued, but also relieved. Some instinct told me that it would be unwise to do my postgraduate work in Oxford. My reluctance was largely the product of self-doubt. It was one thing, I thought, to practise my arts of mimicry surrounded by the mimicry of Blacket's sandstone extravaganza. How would I fare in the place that had furnished the model and the inspiration for such dreams? Would I be found out for what I feared I might be: an imitation? Suddenly, those images of dreaming spires that had sustained so many of my fantasies only a year or two earlier seemed menacing. And besides, I realised, my ambition to become an academic had been provoked in part by the urge to find some way of living in Europe again. And for me, Europe meant not a provincial city dedicated to the higher reaches of the mind (and, admittedly, the production of cars) but a metropolis of the kind I imagined London to be. I realised (with a perspicacity which still surprises me) that I could never devote myself fully or unconditionally to the academic life. I needed a world where I could assume other personalities, other incarnations, somewhere to be anonymous or at least one of the crowd. The more I thought about it, the more the University of London—where I was told a place could be found for the academic year beginning in October of 1960—seemed to answer my needs.

Milgate was obviously disappointed when I put it to him that I should apply formally for a place in London. He pointed out to me the close links between Oxford and several members of the Sydney department, and that an Oxford DPhil was a far more valuable asset than a London PhD. He offered to continue my teaching fellowship to give me an income until the place in Oxford became available. What he said made good sense and in many ways it was alluring, too, for I had not entirely lost the effects of my nostalgic and sentimental education. Besides, I respected Milgate and liked him very much; it upset me that he was not in favour of my studying in London—and I also feared that it might make him somewhat less well inclined towards me. Nevertheless I knew that going to Oxford would court disaster.

I played my trump card. I was in my twenty-fifth year. I could not afford to wait any longer to start gaining the necessary qualifications for my academic career. Reluctantly, but without the least ill will or resentment, Milgate undertook to make inquiries about a place for me at University College, London. A few weeks later I received a letter advising me that I had been accepted as a postgraduate student, to be supervised by the Reader in English, Mr Arthur Brown. Milgate said that he had heard something about him, no more than that. I left Sydney at the end of August, wondering, when it was too late of course, whether I had made the right decision. I could not have known at the time that had I not insisted on taking up my scholarship in that year, I would never have been able to find a position in the university and so spend thirty years more in the shadow of Blacket's imitation of those Oxford colleges which—as things turned out—I have only visited briefly, mostly as a tourist and sightseer.

8

When I set out from Sydney for the great adventure, I did not imagine that another nostalgic imitation would provide the focus of my life for close on three years. The British Museum Reading Room in London, nestled within the great storehouse of the spoils of an empire, was modelled on the Pantheon in Rome, the best preserved monument of the city's imperial past. There is a particularly English arrogance in calling that huge space, topped by a shallow dome, a reading room. It smacks of undue modesty; but it is a modesty so absurd that its opposite was obviously intended. From the moment I set foot inside, I was aware that here was greatness, a repository of untold riches— particularly of the mind. The 'room' exudes a sense of power, too, the kind of power you sense among Rome's crumbling remnants of its imperial past, and in particular in the soft golden glow inside the Pantheon, where all the gods had found their proper station. And the library's gods were on display in the Reading Room, on tier after tier of shelves reaching to the base of the great dome. These were, in a sense, as much spoils of empire as the great Assyrian lions, Attic marbles and Egyptian stelae cluttering the museum's galleries on either side of the Reading Room.

To gain admission was in itself, as I found, a ceremony of induction. On my first day, armed with a letter from the University of London certifying that I was a bona fide candidate for a doctorate, I was directed to a pair of huge wing doors, higher than any doors I had ever seen or indeed doors need to be. Beyond them I came upon a tall counter in elaborately carved wood. An official behind the counter, and from a considerable height, looked at me through small, steel-framed National Health glasses. To achieve that impression of superiority, he must have been sitting on a platform a foot or two above the floor. Slowly, deliberately he inspected the letter of introduction, apparently considering each phrase, each flourish of the signature. Next he pushed a large, leather-bound ledger to the front of the counter, where a somewhat lower shelf allowed just enough space to prop up the volume. Dutifully, I wrote my name and address, and signed in the appropriate place. The official inscribed—there is no other word for it—something beside my name, with a steel nib. He did the same on a small, buff-coloured rectangle of cardboard. Without a word he handed it to me: it bore my name and a number in curving copperplate. It was my reader's ticket, a passport to mysteries.

The British Museum became, in later years, a riot of bag-searches, hidden television cameras, metal detectors and light-beam warning systems. Now that the library has finally moved to a new building a mile or so away, this high-tech wizardry will, no doubt, be even more astonishing. In 1960, a time of innocence, all that lay in the future. The Reading Room was reached through a pair of glass doors, in front of which a uniformed underling inspected readers' tickets in the most cursory way imaginable. Once through the doors you found yourself in a short, narrow corridor painted in institutional cream—lavatories to the right, a bank of coin phones to the left; in the middle a wooden bench. Another pair of glass doors led to the great rotunda.

My first impression was overwhelming. What I remember most vividly was the sound of the room—not silence, not noise, but something indefinable, haunting and a little menacing too, as befits a holy place. There were strange sounds: odd sighs as books were carefully closed, the soft clang of something coming into contact with wood or metal, the swish of a door, footsteps, indistinct, murmured conversations, a sharp noise here and there as someone dropped something, the rattle of castors—sounds of a world where silence was supposed to reign. And yet these sounds were dispersed, floating among their own echoes as they rose to the great dome, falling to the ground again, mingled, otherworldly almost, transformed in their resonant voyages around the library. Enveloping them were the curious sounds of spectres, of the unseen but not inaudible workings of the great machine.

I remember standing in the doorway for a moment or two, astonished by that audible silence, which seemed to share some of the watery quality of the light as it seeped through the openings in the cupola. It was a dark autumn day; most of the lamps above the desks were already alight. Only then did I begin to take in the physical appearance of that extraordinary place.

The centre of the Reading Room was occupied by an enclosure surmounted by a metal grille. Behind it sat four or five librarians, each in front of a small aperture in the grille, to receive request slips for books, to offer advice and to discourage the troublesome and the contentious. It was they who dealt with your anguish when your request slip was returned with one of the disasters listed on the back—lost, at the binders, on permanent loan elsewhere, damaged by water, destroyed by enemy action—ticked with a bold, confident flourish.

Concentric rings of shelves, with irregularly placed gaps, as in a maze, surrounded the central desk. These contained the catalogues of the library. On my last visit I discovered that the library had succumbed to the computer terminal, but the catalogues were still there, and the learned still pored over them with the intense dedication I remembered from a quarter of a century earlier. Using the catalogues required both muscle and perseverance. They were outsize, arm-breaking volumes of thick, stiff paper with details of the library's holdings pasted to the pages on strips of paper. The bibliographical description of each book, whether conveyed in fading copperplate or typewritten, seemed, in my first weeks, to defy reason. There were none of the familiar Dewey numbers I had grown used to at Sydney University. Instead, each book was assigned a series of seemingly random and meaningless numbers, interspersed with letters, both capital and lower case, as well as the odd dash or slash. One slip in transcribing elaborate catalogue entries could provoke disaster—instead of the book on Aristotle you had requested, a dust-coated attendant would deposit on your desk a late-nineteenth-century tide chart for Skegness. What is more, because the details of the catalogue were progressively pasted onto those thick sheets bound (twenty or thirty at a time) into the volumes of the catalogue, there was little sense of accumulation, of the stream of editions of *Hamlet,* for instance, from the first seventeenth-century printing to the latest scholarly text. Everything was a jumble—amateurish I thought, remembering what I had read of the English cult of the dilettante.

Beyond the outermost circle of catalogue shelves, the desks of the British Museum Reading Room shot out like the spokes of a great wheel. These were testimony to the Victorians' love of opulent practicality. Readers sat in rows, separated from the person on the opposite side of the desk by a partition covered, like everything else, in pale blue leather, which contained the most beguiling array of contraptions to make the labours of the mind a little less arduous. There were pen-stands, concealed ink-wells guaranteed to avoid spillage, little flaps and shelves which could be lowered to have books and other necessities placed on them; a curious lathe trestle to support folios and other large volumes, a place for you to rest your spectacles, even a receptacle for a magnifying glass should one be needed. On my first day in the Reading Room I had to stop myself playing with these marvels.

Many of the permanent readers were, like myself, postgraduate students—from Canada and the United States, India and Pakistan, a few Australians, New Zealanders and South Africans, although only a tiny handful, I remember, from the former African colonies. In summer planeloads of American scholars would arrive to work on their latest projects, as did some French and German researchers, as well as the rare visitor let out from behind the Iron Curtain, people forever looking nervously over their shoulders. The bulk of the population was made up, however, of the professionals: mature men and women who made a living—although often a very poor one—by accepting research commissions from commercial institutions or from wealthy individuals determined to discover an illustrious lineage or to find proof of their theory that the earth was flat or that Elizabeth I was a man. These researchers worked with extraordinary dedication on projects that must often have made their hearts sink. They were there as soon as the library opened, in their worn jumpers and cardigans, wearing shoes ground down by the daily trek from the tube station to Great Russell Street; and they were always the last to leave in the evening as the warning bells sounded.

There were the writers and translators too: Ann Keep, who worked on a series of handsome books on the art of the world; the novelist and biographer Vincent Brome. And then there were the eccentrics: the woman who sang; the Fagin-like creature in a caftan who wandered between the rows of desks with his ear-trumpet firmly in place; the elderly gentleman in the egg-spotted suit who seemed to spend most of his time engaged in acrimonious disputes with the librarians behind the metal grille. These and other more transient curiosities provided a kind of sideshow in the great rotunda. They were mostly tolerated—at least until they caused such nuisance that one of the librarians would gently take them by the elbow to shepherd them through the glass doors. But they were usually back the next day.

I spent two or three weeks among the toilers and eccentrics of the main Reading Room. Then, because of the nature of the work I was doing for my thesis, I moved to an annex, a large rectangular hall called the North Library, a holy of holies (with green leather desks and chairs) where some of the library's most treasured possessions, the so-called case books, matter printed before the year 1700, were to be inspected. I spent the next two and a half years among the scholars and sages of the North Library, gathering material for a thesis I had not thought until then I would write.

9

That blow came a day or two after I enrolled at the University of London and managed to find my supervisor's room in University College, in a warren of alleyways behind the long, dreary stretch of Gower Street. The college had been badly bombed during the war. The handsome building in Gower Street survived, but everything behind it had been levelled. The college had to make do with makeshift accommodation in warehouses, storage blocks and whatever room people could find in the nearby streets.

I had no preconceptions about what the place might look like. I knew that the University of London itself was something of a parvenu—at least in the eyes of Oxbridge grandees—which had come into being through the amalgamation of several older foundations and one or two newcomers. Before leaving Sydney I received in the mail a small booklet about University College, with a brief history attached. It had been founded in 1828 at the instigation of Jeremy Bentham to provide an education for those who did not meet the stringent qualifications for entry imposed by Oxford and Cambridge: principally Catholics, but also Jews and dissenters. The booklet was silent, however, on the most bizarre aspect of the ceremonial marble-floored entrance hall in the part of the building which escaped bomb damage: Bentham's embalmed body, in clothes appropriate to a radical gentleman of the early nineteenth century, standing upright in a glass case and surveying with cold eyes the life of the institution he had helped found. It said nothing either about the jumble of soot-stained buildings where I finally managed to find the Department of English.

It was housed on the upper floor of an unadorned brick structure of indeterminate age. The first thing I noticed as I reached the top of the stairs were four white doors bearing the legends WOMEN, MEN, GENTLEMEN STAFF, LADIES STAFF. A little further along the corridor I found a door marked MR A. BROWN. I knocked and heard a muffled voice reply. There too I did not know what to expect. I had a few vague notions of what an Oxford academic might look like, garnered mostly from old Ealing comedies and *Brideshead Revisited*, but in the days when I dreamt of walking among dreaming spires, it was the *mise en scène* rather than the actors peopling it that formed the substance of my dreams. I had no preconceptions about what I might find on the other side of that door.

What I found was a tweedy, ginger-haired and ruddy-faced middle-aged man sitting in a shabby leather armchair. I noticed a large red handkerchief flopping out of his breast pocket. He sported a splendid moustache, like those worn by Battle of Britain aces in wartime movies—and, indeed, I was to learn that Brown had been in the RAF, though not shooting Jerry down over the Thames. The other vivid impression I retain of that first meeting is of the mess, books and papers lying everywhere, charts leaning up against tottery piles of books on the floor, cardboard boxes crammed full of little slips, cards, memoranda. Years later, after Brown died suddenly in Melbourne of the hypertension that had already given him the flushed cheeks I saw on that first meeting, the executor of his will asked me to look through his scholarly papers. It was the same mess, the same chaos. By then I had learnt, however, that the true scholar's life is conducted in the midst of chaos, adrift among the galaxies of facts and theories, the monuments and chimeras of the past where nothing may be inessential or discarded. By that time I had come to mistrust people of tidy habits and minds, suspicions that were confirmed when I looked at the desks of ideologues of various kinds who—in the 1960s and again in the 1990s—came close to tearing apart the Sydney English Department.

I remember that Brown half rose from his battered armchair as I walked into the room. We shook hands. Brown supported himself with one hand on the faded leather of the chair; I leant down with an inevitably respectful mien. That instant has stayed with me because even then I realised that it somehow crystallised the streams of uncertainty that were flowing past me—an unfamiliar society, its ways and rituals known only from a distance, second-hand; being apprehensive about how I would shape up, whether I would negotiate the hurdles I saw lying in wait for me everywhere; inability to decide whether Brown's curious half-rising from his chair was meant to indicate informality or arrogance; the thousand hesitations, in short, of one unsure of himself.

I have only the haziest recollection of how the interview went after that. There was, I think, desultory talk of my sea voyage, a comment about how I was the second Australian recently to sign up with Brown. We discussed the courses I had taken in Sydney, and as we talked I became aware of a curious detachment, even indifference in Brown. He seemed almost bored by our interview. Then he pulled the handkerchief from his breast pocket, fished in his trouser pockets until he found a small, tarnished silver box. I realised what was coming: I had read about it in books. He shook some dark brown powder onto the back of his clenched fist, raising it to one nostril then the other, sniffing loudly. I was impressed: I had never seen anyone take snuff before.

That seemed to be the signal for the business part of the meeting to begin. I bristled when Brown asked me whether I felt confident enough about my command of English. But the moment passed. He told me that initially I would have to enter the master's programme, and then, in six months or so, I might transfer to a doctorate if I were up to scratch. As it happened, I was saved from more than three or four weeks of such apprenticeship when Brown—whose real trade was bibliography and textual scholarship—discovered that those somewhat arcane aspects of English studies had been exhaustively covered in the Sydney honours course of my time. In the meantime, he went on to say at that first meeting, we had better determine an area of research, for whichever degree I would eventually take. I reminded him that I had specified a topic in my application. 'Remind me,' he said as he told me that my documents were in departmental files—shorthand, I realised later, for the sad fact that he had no idea where he had put them.

The topic I had chosen was, at the time, a practically unknown mid-seventeenth-century dramatist called Richard Brome. He was to remain neglected until the emergence of cultural studies made a few—very few—people take notice of him. I became interested in Brome's plays at the suggestion of Milgate. One day in the summer before I took up the temporary position to tide me over until I set off for England, I got a message that he would like to talk to me. I hurried up the grand staircase of the main building. Milgate's door was ajar, and he waved me in.

He had a book, he said, that I might find interesting. It was a small, thin volume covered in shiny tan leather, with the faintest remnant of a device embossed in gold. It was old, I realised; but only when I opened it did I realise how old it was. It was a collection of plays by Richard Brome printed in the middle of the seventeenth century. I knew about such books, we had studied them in the course on bibliography and editorial procedure. I knew about folios and quartos, octavos and duodecimos, about the rules of imposition, about signatures for gatherings, about the practices of the printing shops of the time, about catchwords and those techniques of casting off copy that could cause endless difficulties and errors. I knew about pirated texts and false ascriptions on title pages; I knew about conventions of abbreviation and how errors and mistakes could come about because certain letters that no-one would confuse today—such as p and x—looked almost indistinguishable in most sixteenth- and seventeenth-century hands. I knew all that and much else besides, but I had never seen, let alone handled, an example of what had come off the presses in those centuries. And now here it was with its strange lineny paper, where you could see the watermark on some pages even without holding them up to the light; its bold, slightly old-fashioned but wonderfully clear and elegant typeface, catchwords dutifully in place at the foot of each page, signature markings to guide the binder boldly visible just where the practice of the time had demanded. I thanked Milgate and promised to take care of the precious object. He remarked that Brome was interesting—strong commendation from one who had cultivated, as did many of his colleagues, the Oxford style of understatement. I spent the next few days reading the five or six plays in the collection: they were, indeed, interesting.

Richard Brome was such a minor playwright that he had found no place at all in Thelma Herring's grand tour of the plays of Shakespeare's age. I remembered a reference to him in connection with the great Ben Jonson, something about his having been Jonson's servant, and a joke in *Bartholomew Fair* about Brome, 'my man', sweeping the stage. The plays turned out to be comedies of London life—merchants and their wives, apprentices, artisans, con-men, the occasional country bumpkin, the kind of stuff, in short, that you could find in dozens of plays of the time. The plots were much the same too: good honest folk usually prevailed over exploiters and charlatans; true love almost always found its reward. But there was something else that seemed enthralling. Even more strongly than in similar plays I had read, Brome's none-too-subtle characterisation and language declared his liking for the merchants, tradesmen and their families who people his plays. There was no

A Sentimental Education

condescension and no sentimentality either. He looked at everyday life in ways that made his plays fresh and honest in comparison with the grand passions and over-coloured emotions of the usual staple of Renaissance drama. There was one play set in and around a place called the 'Sparagus Garden, where barren women went to eat asparagus spears—guaranteed, it seemed, to ensure fertility. Another had a nicely alluring title: *The Antipodes.* It was one of those upside-down-world tales where lawyers pay their clients, schoolboys flog their masters, wives are faithful and goldsmiths honest. None of this was 'great' literature or drama. But it was unusual, lively and besides—Milgate assured me when I returned the book to him—no one had looked at Brome carefully. It seemed ideal for a doctoral dissertation in an intellectual and academic climate where research topics were supposed to be original. That requirement proved to be my undoing.

Brown seemed neither impressed nor unimpressed when I reminded him that I had been accepted as a doctoral candidate to write a thesis on Brome. He took some more snuff—I didn't dare ask, I remember, whether I might smoke. 'Yes,' he said, 'yes'—without enthusiasm. He thought it would do. He'd think about it for a day or two; and we would confirm the arrangements later. Then, before bringing the interview to a close, he launched into a complicated anecdote about the stationer who had printed and sold the volume of Brome's plays Milgate had lent me. I couldn't see much point to it but listened attentively, of course.

A few days later I went back to see him at the time we had agreed to find that he was not alone. A large, loose-limbed man—in his early thirties I guessed—was sitting in the leather armchair, his legs sticking out at odd angles, his arms flopping over the sides. He seemed American, and when he began to speak, after Brown made a cursory introduction, I was surprised, even shocked perhaps, to discover that he spoke with an accent which reminded me of hit-men in American movies. His name was Sam Schoenbaum—at the time it meant nothing to me.

In later years Schoenbaum became the doyen of Shakespeare studies on both sides of the Atlantic. His word was law: he could make and unmake careers and reputations with one stroke of the pen. In 1960, when I met him, he was merely one of an army of American academics exploiting their princely salaries and entitlements to spend as much time in England as in their own universities. He seemed pleasant enough. What was I working on? Richard Brome, I told him. He paused for a moment, and then said—with words which have burnt into my memory—'Oh, I don't think you can; it wouldn't be original work'.

I was astonished, almost literally as if someone had given me a swift blow to the head. Brown, I noticed, was impassive, as detached as on our previous meeting. Schoenbaum went on to mention a name—I can't now remember it, and I think I never heard it again—who was about to publish something 'big' on Brome. Had I ever considered James Shirley? I knew about Shirley. He was important enough—though still decidedly 'minor'—to have two or three lectures to himself in Thelma's tediously comprehensive survey. I could remember nothing of interest about him except that he had written a lyric I rather liked:

> The glories of our blood and state
> Are shadows, not substantial things . . .

and that most of the heroines in his plays, in common with the heroines of many another playwright of the time, were called Leonora.

As if on cue Brown said, 'Now that is interesting', and I recognised that word again. Schoenbaum muttered some encouragement. I said—lying, and I knew they knew I was lying—that I'd go back to Shirley to see what I thought of his plays as candidates for research. I left Brown's room in a daze, knowing however that I would indeed be writing a thesis on Shirley, whom I hadn't read, apart from perhaps two plays—and those, memory told me, were dreary enough. But I had been cornered, and had to accept it.

The 'big' study of Brome—indeed any study devoted to him—did not appear. I could never understand why Schoenbaum had chosen to put such an effective spoke in the wheel of my plans. Was he keeping the topic for one of his students in America? Or was it that unfocussed, purposeless malice that I was to meet time and time again among academics of all persuasions? A sequel some years later to that disturbing meeting gave me cause, at least, to suspect the worst in retrospect. By then, though, I had seen enough of the academic world from the inside not to be surprised.

It happened about ten years after Schoenbaum steered me so effortlessly away from Richard Brome to James Shirley. I saw him often in the two years or so it took me to write my confident but meretricious study of that pedestrian playwright. He seemed friendly enough, and even offered me work for a couple of weeks preparing a bibliography for his revision of a nineteenth-century history of English Renaissance drama—he was a great reviser of other people's work. We lost sight of each other until 1969 when Nina and I spent a sabbatical year in London. By then Schoenbaum was well on the way to the top of the scholarly pole. He was just coming to the end of a contract with his university that allowed him to spend most of his time in London; he had bought a small flat near Bloomsbury where he settled with his wife, whose accent also turned out to be unadulterated Brooklyn. He had aged a great deal in that time; he seemed even more loose-limbed, clumsy, shambling than before. If you looked closely, there was something not quite right with his face—a mild stroke, gossip whispered. I felt sorry for him.

Then I ran up against some decidedly odd behaviour. On our way to London that year, Nina and I bought a second-hand car in Switzerland. We planned to return to the Continent in the summer, and the Schoenbaums got wind of it. At the time Sam was anxious because he was afraid that his contract might not be renewed. Money was short, he said, so he wasn't sure how they would get to Paris to stay with friends who'd invited them for the summer. Could we give them a lift?

We set out one June morning. I filled up the tank at Dover because in those days petrol prices in France were even more murderous than in Britain. On the ferry Schoenbaum forked out their share of the passenger supplement for the crossing. When we were back in the car at Calais he announced that his gammy leg was playing up. For the next three or four hours, he demanded frequent stops so that he could dangle his leg out of the open door. Just before we reached Paris, we needed more petrol for the small tank. No offer of a contribution. We dropped them off—relieved to see the last of them—somewhere near Luxembourg Gardens.

A month later we were all back in London. Sam was in high spirits: his contract had been renewed, it was even more magnificent than before. He was probably feeling expansively generous: would I contribute something to a volume of essays on Shakespeare he was putting together? I jumped at the opportunity, flattered, thrilled, exhilarated. I had been interested for some time in the possible influence of Hermeticism and Neo-Platonism on Shakespeare's last plays, particularly *The Winter's Tale*. I suggested a piece along those lines. He thought it would be splendid; and then said that it was splendid when I gave him an eight-thousand word manuscript six weeks later. He was sure it would grace his volume. I hurried back to our Kensington flat, on tenterhooks until Nina arrived home from work, to tell her the good news. We made a night of it at a neighbourhood French restaurant.

Two or three days later Schoenbaum came up to me in the North Library. He was sorry but he couldn't use my piece. It was not up to scratch.

I was shattered, devastated—only clichés are able to describe my distress and fury. I could make no sense of what had happened. I stayed away from the British Museum for a time—I couldn't bear to walk through those glass doors, past tne great wheel of desks towards the passage leading to the North Library. Irrationally, perhaps, the strongest emotion I experienced was shame. Eventually, of course, I had to take up work again. I made sure to avoid coming close to Schoenbaum, whom I saw almost every day. Before long we did bump into each other at the catalogues. He was bright and cheery. I turned away without a word—not a wise thing to do, perhaps, but irresistible. At the same time I began to think a great deal about that day in Arthur Brown's room when Schoenbaum deflected me so effortlessly from Brome. Old suspicions began to well up, though I realised all along that such was the coward's way.

In the mid-seventies the great scholar of Renaissance civilisation and culture, Frances A. Yates, wrote a book on Shakespeare's last plays. In the chapter on *The Winter's Tale* I was dismayed to find arguments similar, perhaps identical to the essay I had written in 1969. Was this coincidence or had Schoenbaum told her about the argument of my essay without identifying the source? The bitterest pill came a few years later when I published my own study of those plays. With gritted teeth, I was obliged to acknowledge Yates's 'pioneer' work in establishing the links between Shakespeare's late plays and Hermetic doctrine. In 1981 I saw Schoenbaum at a Shakespeare conference in Stratford. He weaved through the crowd spilling onto the lawn at the opening reception on a warm summer evening. He had read my book, he said, all smiles. Splendid. Splendid.

10

In 1960, after that strange meeting in Brown's room, no idea came to me as an alternative to the less-than-alluring prospect of spending two years with Shirley. Dutifully, I read my way through his collected works, which had been edited by a well-meaning and no doubt terminally bored clergyman in the first half of the nineteenth century. As I finished one volume and embarked on the next, my spirits sank lower and lower. I was sustained through those dreadful weeks only by the great adventure of London itself.

In the first week or two I spent as much time as I could being a tourist and a sightseer. I went to the Abbey, visited St Paul's, looked

A Sentimental Education

at the great curve of the Thames, stood outside Buckingham Palace to watch the changing of the guard, walked along Piccadilly and the Strand, found Peter Pan in Kensington Gardens and listened to Big Ben chiming the hour. Very soon, however, a different and much more exhilarating experience evolved: I began to live in London, learning its patterns and rhythms. I became expert at using the Underground and cracked the codes of the bus routes. I discovered which were the best times to visit the automatic laundrette. I found out how to make my limited funds stretch as far as cheap seats at the theatre and concerts. I discovered the newspapers, especially the Sundays—wonderful, bulky cornucopias you could lug to Hyde Park or Kensington Gardens on a sunny day—and there were, I was surprised to find, quite a few sunny days during the long autumn of my first year in London. At length, despite many difficulties, alarms and occasional bouts of depression (prompted on the whole by the dreary James Shirley), I realised that I had found a congenial and exhilarating environment. Those were wonderful years, and not merely in retrospect.

The unfolding of that infatuation with London began in Molyneux Street, a short stretch of modest, unadorned early-nineteenth-century terraces on the western extremity of the West End, just around the corner from the noise and chaos of the Edgware Road. In 1960 Molyneux Street was a quiet backwater, still a working-class or at best lower-middle-class street of pensioners, charladies, storemen, bus drivers. The little neighbourhood seemed entirely cut off from the world around it: on one side the brilliantly messy life of Paddington with its barrow-traders, teddy boys and pimps, and shabby-genteel Bayswater, where gaunt elderly ladies in darned frocks and moth-eaten furs could be seen hurrying to the tube station, on their way to the theatre or the opera. On the other side, the posher parts of Marylebone—the great patrician streets and squares; Harley Street with its titled surgeons and heart specialists; Bryanston Square, where discrete *mezuzahs* were fixed under the lintels of ample black double doors; Montagu Square, the preserve of the gentry and lesser aristocracy.

Molyneux Street knew nothing of those worlds. Minutes, even hours perhaps, could go by without a car driving past; carts were far more common, though still infrequent. A large lorry regularly made its way down the street, stopping at round metal plates covering the coal-holes for the mostly welfare-assisted residents. Apart from a small pub and a tiny grocery, the street was quiet, frozen in a time which had already passed elsewhere in the great city. It did not last, of course. At the end of my years in London, when I was living in a flat half a mile or so away, I went to take a last, sentimental look at Molyneux Street. It had already begun to change. There were flowerboxes in many windows. A few stylish cars were parked at the kerb. Doors had been painted in glossy, fashionable colours. The little pub, where two years earlier no-one under sixty seemed welcome, had been transformed into an Italian restaurant. The people going in and out of those shiny front doors looked as if they were called Cynthia and Simon.

In October 1960, when I stood, surrounded by my trunks and suitcases, on the pavement in front of a chipped door in Molyneux Street, the Cynthias and Simons had not yet arrived. Instead I was greeted by a little wizened man in a cloth cap who was called Mr Gotts. He and his daughter occupied the only flat, on the first floor of the small three-storey terrace—apart from the basement flat, that is, which the landlady, Miss Craig, an out-of-work actress, shared with her friend Brenda and a very large, very classy dog. The rest of the house was taken up with bed-sits, larger or smaller rooms, each with a basin, a gas ring and heater, and a voracious meter constantly demanding to be fed with sixpences and shillings. During the bitter weeks of January and February, when sixpences and shilling pieces were as rare in London as Spanish doubloons, everyone would sit wrapped in blankets waiting for the magic moment when you would get a few of those fabulous coins in the change and so find a little, brief warmth.

I had come to Molyneux Street because of my friend Jim Carlton, later to become a Federal politician, who had left Sydney two or three years earlier to take up a position with an engineering company. He had worked for a while in Bristol, and then moved to the firm's headquarters on the edge of London. When he heard that I was on my way to spend a couple of years in London, he wrote asking whether I'd like him to get me a room in the place where he was living. I accepted without hesitation, glad to have one problem solved, and even more pleased to have a friend nearby.

Jim had the best room in the place. It was on the ground floor overlooking the street, with a high ceiling and, as such accommodation went, space enough to move. My room was on the top floor, under the low-pitched roof. It was small and narrow, and just fitted a small bed, a table with two chairs, a decrepit armchair, a wardrobe and a cupboard built around the sink, gas ring and heater. The place smelt damp and musty, I realised after I managed to get the sticking door open. There was also a strange, heady smell lingering in corners. I couldn't imagine what it could be, but it was unpleasant and sinister in some indefinable way.

Late that night, as I tossed and turned, sleepless in an unfamiliar world, I heard heavy footsteps on the groaning, creaky stairs. Then sounds of fumbling and metal jangling against metal. I could hear the scrape of a key against a lock, followed by the squeaky protest of a resistant door, then the shuddering thud as it was forced shut. Silence. In a few moments I was aware of that smell again, sweet, sickly but pungent, creeping through the crack under the door. In the four months or so I spent in Molyneux Street I never saw my neighbour. But on almost every night I was woken by the scrape and thud of the door, and I would lie like a latter-day Proust, waiting for that smell to seep into my room. There was, I remember, a period of a few weeks when no scraping was heard, when nothing came creeping under the ill-fitting door. What had happened to him? I wondered. Dead? Abroad? In prison?

Life in that little room was difficult at first, often irritating. There was much to learn, I discovered. I was appalled by the price of food; eating out had to be strictly limited, even in greasy Indian restaurants or the filthy cafes and cafeteria chains dotted around London. Cooking on the small gas ring in the one battered saucepan Miss Craig had supplied proved messy and troublesome. Washing was a problem too: the laundrette served well enough, but shirts needed ironing. I bought an iron and managed to overload the fuses (or so Miss Craig insisted) one night when everyone seemed to be using their appliances. The overhead light, I found, wasn't strong enough to read by. So a reading lamp had to be added to other expenses. I saw my scholarship money melting away even before I had started working in earnest.

In time, however, these annoyances and inconveniences became routine. I was turning, retrospect tells me, into a Londoner. The small parts of the huge city that formed the site of my daily life became familiar. I began recognising the elderly man in a dun-coloured dustcoat who was usually arranging newspapers on a rack outside his shop in Great Russell Street at about the time I was walking from the tube station to the British Museum. I wondered what had happened to him when I noticed that for a week or two someone else was tending the rack. It was a relief to see him back at his post.

I began to learn the rhythms of life in and around Molyneux Street. The noisy rows Mr Gotts and his daughter conducted in their first-floor flat could be anticipated with some accuracy, even though their cause remained a mystery. The old lady who ran the small grocery grew to recognise me as one of her regulars. After a while she treated me to bits and pieces of gossip. Did I know that the people in 17 were moving out, emigrating to Australia? Obviously she didn't pick me for a colonial. And what about the young couple across the road? Mostly, I did not have the faintest idea of what she was talking about; but I felt that I was beginning to belong.

And I was beginning to belong in more subtle though much more satisfying ways. It is difficult to account for a vague, halting process that took time to unfold, but I began to realise that I had the measure of London—or at least of those parts I had come to know. As autumn turned to winter, I was enthralled by the way the gathering mists and fogs, mixed with the acrid smoke of coal-fires, shrouded the long stretches of terrace houses and imposing monuments in a strange, often glowing beauty. The trees in the parks and in small gardens surrounded by wrought-iron pikes shed their leaves, leaving behind a fragile tracery of branches. The first chestnut sellers appeared on the streets. London, I came to understand, was a winter city. Walking home in the dark afternoons, the lights of the shops in Oxford Street, the crowds milling around bus stops and pouring through the entrance of the tube station, the tangle of rush-hour traffic took on a wonderful melancholy, especially when the fine, misty rain of late autumn made the streets glisten with patches of brilliantly coloured light. Life was withdrawing into smaller and smaller spaces as the cold of December began to bite; windows in the houses I passed were tightly curtained, with only small slivers of faint yellowish light peeping through. Then it was Christmas and the decorations in Regent Street sparkled and glinted as the shops grew even more crowded, and as holly and ivy—mostly plastic—sprouted everywhere.

I began to understand, too, the consolations of a life that was hard, almost deprived in comparison with the space, light and plenty which had become commonplace for me in Australia. I came to suspect that those shabby, pasty-faced Londoners in their worn macs and topcoats whom I would pass in the streets, most of them carrying string bags or paper parcels of cabbages and bottles of milk, perhaps a rubbery cake from Lyon's wrapped in crinkly cellophane, led a life in many ways richer than mine had been. I knew that it was very difficult for them to exploit the city's (to my eyes astonishing) cultural life—the theatres, concerts, recitals and operas on which I spent all the spare money I had, hearing world-famous musicians whom I had only ever encountered on the radio, seeing in the flesh legendary actors known to me only from films or by repute. I doubted whether many of them enjoyed the free or almost free wonders London had to offer: the room after room of antiquities in the British Museum, the old masters in the National Gallery, more recent art splendidly displayed in the Tate, or even the exhilarating drama of Speakers' Corner in Hyde Park, with its zealots, eccentrics and madmen.

Yet for all the misery of their lives in an England still suffering some of the effects of postwar hardship, with their cramped rooms and bed-sits, the cost of food, the long queues at post offices and laundrettes, the struggle to make ends meet in a harsh world, even the crowds shuffling along the Edgware Road seemed in some indefinable way to enjoy the benefits of living at the centre of things. They were connected by tangled but nevertheless real bonds to the power, influence and brilliance of a city which still retained much of its imperial self-confidence, though older hands said that things never recovered after the war. Life in London had a complexity which I had not encountered in the more uniform textures of Sydney. The wealth and ostentation of Mayfair and Belgravia, those discreet houses that spoke unmistakably of riches and confidence, existed—harmoniously I thought—with the plain little terraces of Molyneux Street, each divided into a maze of rooms like mine on the top floor of Miss Craig's. The gleaming Rolls Royces and Bentleys shared the crowded roadways with bizarre three-wheeled contraptions, or those deadly German bubble-cars that were becoming more popular by the day, it seemed.

From the gods high above the stage at Covent Garden I would watch as the great and the good in their red-lined boxes sipped champagne from elegant flutes served to them during the intervals by respectful waiters in white mess-jackets. Beside me, one of the moth-eaten old ladies of Bayswater would reminisce about the time when she was very young, when she heard Melba and Caruso, or about later years—when Bertie or Reginald or whoever was still alive and they could afford proper seats at the opera—when she thrilled to Lotte Lehmann, Melchior and Flagstad.

I became an expert interpreter of the myriad fine distinctions of the class system, which was still more or less intact then, despite the lamentations of those who saw themselves living in a world where people no longer knew their place. In the tube I learnt how to tell the differences between the Simons, the Jeremys, the Peregrines, the Rafes or Ralphs and the Ruperts in their expensive suits and grubby shirt cuffs and collars. I came to understand why Rafe wore a bowler with a grey suit while Simon and Rupert matched theirs with black jackets and striped grey trousers. I recognised that Jeremy was a little way below them on the pecking order because his shirts were too clean and his cufflinks too flashy. The long-faced ladies in camel-hair coats or suits, sitting ramrod straight, were, I realised, genuine *grandes dames*. I also learnt to interpret younger women's stations in life by the way they tied scarves around their heads.

I understood a little the complicated structures of exclusions and hesitations that kept people apart in that remarkably stratified society, but I also appreciated that they were bound inextricably by the great city in which they lived. London was a leveller which nevertheless allowed the most exquisite of distinctions to be maintained. I was fascinated by the way you could turn the corner in a shining Belgravia street of great houses, their windows gleaming, but without the telltale rows of buttons disfiguring similar houses in other parts of the city, which confirmed that former grandeur had been divided into flats, flatettes and bed-sitting rooms, to find yourself at the centre of the plebeian chaos of Pimlico—a Pimlico of down-at-heel pubs, fly-spotted shops and street barrows—which had not yet succumbed to gentrification. The two worlds may not have acknowledged each other, but they rubbed shoulders everywhere in the city. One day, waiting my turn at the bootmakers to buy shoelaces, I found an obsequious shopkeeper practically prostrating himself in front of a young man, no more than a boy. 'My lord' looked embarrassed, his ears and neck, I noticed, grew increasingly flushed the more the bootmaker demeaned himself. When he had finished, the young man turned round and shot me a half-ironic, half-apologetic look.

I saw the Queen, too, several times, whooshing past in a big black car. I remembered the cheering crowds lining Macquarie Street in the blinding sun; the small gloved hand; the ecstasy as we laid eyes on our sovereign for the first time. In London no heads turned when she passed by.

11

It was in many ways an unremarkable life. Nothing spectacular or earth-shaking happened. There were, of course, the usual alarms and anxieties of the unfamiliar. Sometimes, lying sleepless in bed in the early hours of the morning—for it was in my first weeks in London that my lifelong insomnia began—I would be seized by the gut-wrenching realisation that I was all but alone in a large, impersonal city. Drifting into a few hours of uneasy sleep, I would be haunted by images of illness, accidents, or worst of all, of running out of money. But in my waking hours, and on many nights too, I slipped comfortably into the patterns of living in London. I would beat a path almost every day to the tube station at Marble Arch, travel the few stops to Tottenham Court Road and make my way to the British Museum, into the Reading Room and the unvarying rituals of studying dusty words in dusty books.

I had a few friends in London, mostly people from Sydney Jim Carlton and I had known at university who had drifted to London in the great migration of the time. Gradually a focus for a social life of a kind emerged. It was a large flat in a Victorian villa in a leafy Kensington street, Melbury Road. A blue plaque affixed to the wall advised that the painter Holman Hunt had lived there.

The flat housed a population that came and went, sometimes to return, in a seemingly random manner. It was mostly chaos, unexpected arrivals, brothers, sisters, boyfriends sleeping on mattresses on the living-room floor, in the entrance hall and at times of severe overcrowding even in the kitchen. There was a permanent core of two or three women who made a living of a kind through the soul-killing drudgery of relief-teaching for the London education authority. After a week or two they would receive instructions to go to yet another grim school filled with mean-eyed adolescents, future gaolbirds and prostitutes, they used to say in those politically incorrect days. They would be harassed, mocked, insulted and often threatened by their street-wise charges. Just as soon as they managed to impose a little order and sanity, the teacher they had replaced would return—perhaps from a rest home—and they would be moved on to face another school of thugs and harridans.

Those women managed the lesser chaos of Melbury Road as efficiently, and just as ruthlessly if needed. They made sure that everyone contributed to the rent, put their money into the kitty, didn't make so much noise as to enrage the slightly demented landlady downstairs—the former leader of an all-woman dance band—that the front door was always securely shut, that lids on rubbish bins were tightly in place. Despite all that vigilance, the flat in Melbury Road was a happy if somewhat hectic place. It became a club and a salon. You could turn up at mealtimes—with a bottle or two of cheap Algerian wine, or Emu sherry imported all the way from home, or perhaps half a pound of mince to throw into the all-purpose stew or spaghetti sauce, maybe a block of cheese—to find company, conversation and, on occasions, a bit of romance.

One or two of the women had well-to-do boyfriends, in most cases dentists who had been attracted to London by the princely sums they could earn grinding away at teeth on the National Health. Most could afford to run a car. On weekends a few carloads of us—everyone chipping in towards the hideous cost of petrol—would drive to Salisbury and Stonehenge, to Windsor or Oxford, down to Sussex or to the Cotswolds, eating sandwiches and pork pies in raftered pubs or cream teas in prissy, chintz-covered tea rooms where nice ladies in aprons served us, looking a little askance when they heard us speak Australian. We would go to concerts and plays, sitting at a dizzying height above the actors' heads or in the very back row of the circle at the Festival Hall.

On two or three occasions, those of us who had saved up enough money went to Paris for a few days, flying—our hearts in our mouths—to Beauvais from a channel airport in a clapped-out DC3 and continuing to Paris by bus. We stayed at the imposingly named Hôtel du Senlis on the left bank, near Paris's own Pantheon. It was a terrible, bug-ridden doss-house where rusty tepid water gurgled out of ancient taps above cracked washbasins. But it was Paris and it was exhilarating to walk, half-washed, in the mornings to the vast student café around the corner for *tartine* and coffee.

One New Year's Eve we climbed into our dinner suits and long gowns—for none of us, no matter how short money might have been, would have dreamt of going to London without the proper clothes—and drove to a dinner-dance in a restaurant somewhere in the Home Counties, thrilled by the thought of our extravagance and the sacrifices which would be necessary in the new year to make up for it.

My day-to-day life as a postgraduate student provided few opportunities for companionship or stimulation. I was glad, nevertheless, that I had decided to live in a large city, not in the stifling atmosphere of an Oxford or Cambridge college. Some people I knew, who had been academically more canny, talked ruefully, when they escaped to Melbury Road for the weekend, about the horrors of that life. After a while I also came to appreciate Brown's indifference as a supervisor. At first, though, I was aware not so much of the lack of intellectual stimulation—for I got enough of that from books, from theatres and concerts and from the BBC's 'Third Programme'—as of the sense that I was drifting around, aimlessly perhaps, in a vast degree-factory.

In general, I saw almost nothing of Brown or of anyone in the small English Department of University College. It worried me. I did not think that I needed much guidance or supervision—for, to be honest, I could not see how I could ever coax a thesis to gush out of Shirley's dry, dry stone—but I knew the form. One was supposed to consult. And yet every attempt at consultation came to nothing. Time after time Brown would fail to keep an appointment, or when I went to find him on spec, as it were, his door would be tightly locked. The departmental secretary, a nice, well-bred lady called Miss Hedberg, was always sympathetic: Mr Brown was at a seminar, she would say, sitting bolt upright in her chair. This went on for weeks. Then one day, Miss Hedberg leant forward: didn't I know about the seminar? she asked. No, I told her, my heart missing a beat at the thought of having committed some terrible error that would disqualify me from the degree. With what was obviously an heroic effort to overcome her disapproval, Miss Hedberg gave me directions on how to find the Marlborough Arms in a short, narrow lane behind Tottenham Court Road.

The 'seminar' was held in one corner—reserved by hallowed tradition—of a brown-panelled, smelly pub. The most remarkable feature of the establishment was an innocent looking door marked GENTS. As you opened it you were confronted by a long, giddying flight of steps plunging into the deep basement of the building. Escorting members of the seminar down those steps was at times the task of the junior members, who were also expected to fetch and carry, almost like pot-boys in a Shakespeare play crying out 'Anon, anon, sir!' Brown was one of the leaders of the seminar; the other was one of the two professors in the department at University College, a dreadful individual called Hugh Smith. Smith, on a model familiar to me from Sydney, was in charge of language studies and Anglo-Saxon. He was, I learnt, the doyen of the prestigious English Place Names Society, a remarkable linguistic and historical survey of the manner in which the names of towns and villages came into being. I never saw the other professor, James Sutherland, respected editor of Alexander Pope, at those seminars, or indeed at University College except on one occasion, at a reception to welcome new students where he peered at my name tag and remarked: 'Ah, another Orstralian'.

Smith was one of the most unpleasant people I have ever known. He looked like a balding Bertrand Russell, and wore the kind of suit you see Russell wearing in photographs of him taken in his Cambridge glory days. Brown was far better tailored, and betrayed therefore his lesser social status. Smith affected the aristocratic—perhaps, like Russell, he was an aristocrat—by ignoring every canon of good manners and consideration. The subject of the seminars was invariably slander, of people and institutions I did not even know by name. As more and more beer spilled on Smith's food-stained suit, he would become more and more scabrous. No reputation was safe with him, no one seemed to measure up to his Olympian standards.

Mercifully, he paid almost no attention to me. But, at times when the conversation flagged or when one of us juniors—there were several coevals of that rank fortunately—escorted someone down the creaky steps to the urinals, Smith would direct his gaze towards me. 'Ah, you're from Sydney,' he would say for the tenth, perhaps hundredth time. 'Then you would know Mitchell.' Indeed, I agreed, I knew A. G. Mitchell, the great authority on Australian language: he had taught me. 'Well then,' Smith would announce, 'if you write to him do tell him that if he shows up here we'll string his guts right around the place'—pointing to the fake timber beams of the Marlborough Arms. I never penetrated the source of that mystery and, years later, when I saw Mitchell (who had by then become Vice-Chancellor of the newly established Macquarie University) I could see no point in asking him for clarification.

I hated the 'seminars' and attended them as infrequently as possible. It was bad enough being shy and awkward, but my difficulties with alcohol only served to convince Smith, and Brown to an extent, that I was a wimp, a wet blanket. I have never been able to drink. After the war I succumbed to every known childhood disease in quick succession—having stayed miraculously healthy during the terrible years of danger. I had mumps, chicken pox, both kinds of measles (which would have pleased Lady Bracknell, I realise), whooping cough and, worst of all, jaundice. I turned a bright copper colour and lived on mashed potatoes for months. Hepatitis had obviously damaged my liver, or made it more delicate at least. During my student days in Sydney I became expert at playing with a glass of wine throughout a dinner or a party to make it seem that I was not a wowser. Beer I could scarcely abide. So the seminars were misery, vile trials. And yet they were as close as I ever came to collegiality.

The British Museum offered slightly greater opportunities for companionship. If my scholarly and academic life had any shape or rhythm, it was thanks entirely to the North Library. I put my name down for one of the permanent desks which were ranged along the long sides of the room, at right angles to the rows of desks where casual readers worked. Being allocated one of those permanent places carried some weight in the subtle hierarchy of the place. It meant that you hadn't just blown in from the main Reading Room to consult a rare book that could only be used in the North Library, but that your work was intimately connected with rare books themselves. The privilege included a green-leather frame with your name stencilled on a piece of cardboard placed inside it. You could also keep on the space in front of you up to thirty or so books—not the treasures of the North Library, which had to be returned to the circulation desk each time you left, with a small yellow slip bearing your name on it, but the run-of-the-mill reference books and modern editions with which you were supposed to supplement your intellectual labours among the monuments of the past. From those seats the daily traffic of the North Library could be observed with something of the look of a venerable member of an exclusive club eyeing a raw recruit.

Some of those green frames bore illustrious names. At first I felt a particular thrill in my proximity to greatness. But the celebrated scholars were rarely seen. Their desks, piled high with books, remained unoccupied week after week, month after month at times. I learnt that there were even more privileged scholars working in the North Library, those who had been given small private rooms to pursue their researches without distraction. The practice was being discontinued by that time, though. The infamous T. J. Wise had once occupied such a room. He used his privilege to cut pages out of priceless copies of old books and to paste them, with the skill of a virtuoso surgeon, into copies of the same editions in his private library, which he had bought very cheaply because they were, in the jargon of the trade, imperfect. The word 'imperfect' now appears in many entries for the British Museum's holdings of sixteenth- and seventeenth-century books, principally the plays of Shakespeare's age. For 'imperfect' it is usually safe to read 'mutilated by T. J. Wise'. No one knew who the few remnants of that great privilege were; nor even where those cubicles were located. To all intents and purposes, the famous and largely absent scholars at the permanent tables of the North Library represented the apex of that hierarchical world.

They took no notice of anyone, except perhaps the few up-and-coming scholars of ambition—almost always North American—who sought their attention with the elaborate refinement and cunning of courtiers. I noticed Schoenbaum talking to one or another of them on rare occasions. He would also talk to me sometimes, so acting as a link in an essentially feudal chain. I got to know, as well, one or two other people who were, like Schoenbaum, at the point where their careers might take off into some glorious stratosphere. Nothing of the kind had happened, it seemed to me in later years as I glanced down the title pages of respected journals in which Schoenbaum's name was appearing more and more frequently. They probably sank into the kind of comfortable obscurity into which I settled after my return to Sydney: the accolades, the great books, the fame were not to be their (or my) lot.

The rest of us were postgraduate students. I remember some extraordinarily driven Canadians, suffering (I was surprised to realise) an even more virulent strain of cultural inferiority than Australians, for they had constantly to look over their shoulders at their rivals across the forty-ninth parallel. Conversation with them was impossible, unless you took a deep breath and asked them about their work. Then the floodgates would open. One grey-haired woman, considerably older than the rest of us, was 'working on' Victorian children's books. I now realise that she was a trailblazer in a field that was to become very chic some two decades later. At the time, however, she was regarded as slightly eccentric. The consensus among her compatriots was that she was not up to 'serious' work.

After a while I learnt that it was unwise to ask her anything about her research. If you were foolish enough to do so, she would launch into a seamless monologue, like a character in a tiresome Elizabethan comedy, harping on the one theme: her life was misery because she kept finding more and more children's books in her 'period'—another magic word in the British Museum Reading Room. Towards the end of my time in London I realised that I had not seen her for some weeks, months perhaps. Had she submitted? No, someone told me, she was in a clinic somewhere. Gossip said that she had been carried out of the women's residence where she had been living in a straitjacket, but that was only malice most of her acquaintances insisted.

In the long run, I made only two friends in the British Museum. Alan Brissenden had gone through the English Department in Sydney a few years ahead of me. Before I left Australia I had heard of him, but we had not met. Occasionally in London I saw him and his wife Elizabeth. Mostly, though, Alan and I would spend a little time in one of the grimy cafes around the museum. Even that became less frequent when the Brissendens' first child—my godson—was born. Alan found that much of his spare time was taken up with helping to look after the baby, shopping, and making ends meet. I envied him. His life seemed to have a pattern that mine lacked, even though a part of me was glad of the independence, the opportunities I had to see plays, listen to music, and travel to the Continent whenever I had saved up enough or—as was more often the case—my parents sent me a little money. But I envied Alan principally because he was obviously engaged with his work. He had chosen to write a thesis on sexuality in John Webster's plays—a rather bold topic in those prudish days before the academy's infatuation with anything and everything to do with sex. The rumour-mill had it that he was doing significantly original work, whereas I was bogged down in James Shirley, whose plays came to seem increasingly mindless the further I got into them.

The one new friend I made in the British Museum gave me my first glimpse into the textures of a kind of English life that came to seem very attractive to me, despite its dowdy ways and the hardships and miseries that often accompanied it. Curiously, given what seemed to me the Englishness of her way of life, she was Czech; her parents had left Prague in 1938, just before the Munich Pact, when she was four or five years old. This was Ann Keep. She worked as a translator on series of books dealing with the arts of the world. She was extraordinarily gifted with languages—translating from French, German, Italian and Spanish into English, and from English into French and German. Because Czech was her first language, she had a little Russian too. Her husband John Keep was a well-regarded Slavonic expert in the University of London.

The marriage had hit a rough patch at the time Alan introduced me to her. After that Ann and I would see each other almost every day, spending more and more time smoking cigarettes on the portico of the museum, as the pigeon droppings plopped down from the pediment above us. She was looking, I think, for companionship with someone for whom there were no associations with their circle of friends and acquaintances. Perhaps our similar backgrounds attracted me to her, though we rarely spoke of our early lives, apart from filling in the briefest, most sketchy details. It was a desultory friendship which took place mostly on that portico covered in pigeon-droppings. Increasingly, the insufferable James Shirley was driving me to distraction and in need of distraction. I would walk along the narrow passage connecting the North Library to the main Reading Room, find Ann at the seat she usually occupied, and we would chat over a cigarette or two, or sometimes a cup of watery coffee in the slop-covered café in the basement of the museum, or in one of the slightly cleaner establishments nearby. Sometimes we would have lunch in a spaghetti bar a few blocks away.

I did not meet her husband John for some time. He was in America on exchange. It emerged from the odd hint I picked up that he had accepted the offer not merely to advance his career but to place some distance between them—though I never learnt what problems the marriage had struck. As was the custom among many people in those days, we put up a wall between us, marking off the limits beyond which friendships of that sort must not stray. So it was two or three months after my friendship with Ann developed that she invited me to have dinner with them in their South Kensington flat.

That was the first time I saw how people like the Keeps lived. They had bought the leasehold of an apartment in a classy row of terraces called The Boltons. When they negotiated the agreement there was no more than ten years, fifteen at the most, left on the lease. That is how they could afford it, Ann confessed, adding that she was concerned about what would happen when the lease reverted to the superior landlord and they would have to find the capital to renegotiate or somewhere else to live. It was a tiny flat. The first thing I noticed about it was how much furniture, how many pictures, books and lamps had been crammed into the small living room. The kitchen was no larger than a galley. There was only one bedroom, I think, with a kind of box-room leading from it, where more books and a desk were kept. John had his room at the university of course, Ann said, but she had to do everything at the museum, even if she happened not to need to consult anything.

I was surprised, even a little shocked, when I walked through their front door—embellished with an extraordinary array of security locks, bolts and latches. The carpet was slightly worn, the wallpaper faded, with the odd brownish patch revealing a history of leaks and burst pipes. The furniture, to my eyes, was higgledy-piggledy, certainly not like the carefully decorated homes of some of my Sydney friends, with their Queen Anne or Chippendale suites. Nor was the place particularly tidy, especially because books were lying around everywhere, much as in Brown's study at University College. The pictures on the walls were mostly busy eighteenth-century prints, some of them delicately coloured in fading pastels. I don't remember much china, but what there was seemed old and even perhaps grotesque. The other thing I recall is that there was no overhead light: the room was softly lit by three or four table lamps that cast a warm, pinkish glow. These impressions are trivial, but they were my first exposure to the way the London intelligentsia lived. Until then I had seen nothing but those flats, such as the one in Melbury Road, where my shifting circle of acquaintances settled for a year or two at the most.

Ann introduced me to her husband. He was like the flat—short, as short as I am, I realised. He wore a threadbare suit of very good cut much in need of cleaning. The conversation chugged along awkwardly while Ann left the room to prepare dinner. The food was unpalatable but they had very good wine and a fine cognac—Ann said she had brought it back with her last time she visited her sister in Paris. We drank coffee out of little china cups so old and brittle that I was terrified in case mine turned into powder in my hands.

We talked about plays we had seen, about books we had read—or rather Ann and John had read, for I soon realised that I was an innocent where literary and intellectual life was concerned. John spoke amusingly about American brashness. Ann described the difficulties she was having with a Swiss author whose book she was then working on: he

A Sentimental Education

would neither accept nor reject her English version; the publishers were losing their patience, she said, and if they cancelled the project she would receive only a small fraction of her fee. What else we talked about I have long forgotten.

At about ten or ten-thirty at the latest I picked up a few signals suggesting that it was time to leave. It was a fine night, cold but bracing. I decided to walk home instead of rattling around in the tube. John said he would walk part of the way with me. From the coat rack he took a scarf which indicated that he had been to a famous college in Oxford or Cambridge. We walked out into the dark night. He shivered slightly but said that he couldn't be bothered climbing the stairs again for his topcoat—perhaps he'd only come as far the corner. But he walked with me for ten or fifteen minutes. He wanted to thank me, he said, for being so kind to Ann while he had been away. I began to wonder what he meant. She was having a difficult time, he went on, as she herself had said, with her author. It was all very vexing. That's why it was so awfully kind of me—I remember that word 'awfully'—to see her through that rough patch. He went on like that for a minute or two longer, then abruptly shook my hand, saying how much he had enjoyed the evening, and walked briskly away.

In later years I came to know a number of people who belonged to the same world as the Keeps, people who possessed a certain style which I found alluring, seductive even, although with them, too, I often had difficulties reading the codes, penetrating beneath the layers of subtle politeness to guess at their meaning and intentions. I realised at the time that such a world had severe limitations. Most of those people were beset by endless financial worries—as I was to be throughout my life. But the poverty they often spoke about did not seem to rob them of opportunities that I found wholly enviable. The Keeps might have been preoccupied by that lease on their flat, by the stinginess of Ann's publishers, but they travelled widely. He would be off to America one month, then to lecture in Germany or Sweden for a week. She would spend a couple of weeks between books with her sister in Paris, and while she was there, they would visit friends in Spain or in Florence, or else just get in the sister's car to drive around Provençe for a few days.

And there was their London life too. I didn't hear much of that because it became obvious that they were at the time leading largely separate lives. Yet there was the flat in The Boltons, the books and prints on the walls, the large bunch of keys to operate the row of locks on the front door, the assortment of good furniture, concerts, plays, recitals and the occasional opera (always in cheap though not the cheapest seats), the new showing at the Tate or the Courtauld, and the friends whose names Ann occasionally dropped into the conversation, which I recognised from by-lines in quality magazines and the Sunday papers. It was a little, huddled life, snobbish in many ways and not in the least disinclined to make outsiders such as me faintly uncomfortable. For all that, the Keeps gave me a glimpse of what it might be like if some miracle occurred and I managed to finish my thesis, get a degree and be offered a job in London. The little flat in South Kensington became an icon of a possible life—it suppressed thoughts of the seminars at the Marlborough and the impasse which my struggle with James Shirley had reached at the end of six months or so.

12

No-one had looked at Shirley for years, Schoenbaum had said that day in Brown's room at University College. In that, at least, he was perfectly correct. The large catalogues of the British Museum Reading Room revealed almost nothing, apart from a study published by an obscure American scholar in 1914. The learned journals were equally silent, except for one or two minor notes on bibliographical questions. Nor were many plays available in modern editions. The collected edition was published in 1833, the work of a scholar of minor repute. He was another clergyman. As I read play after play I began to feel sorry for the long-dead gentleman. His colleagues had obviously beaten him to the best prizes; all that remained were the pickings. I imagined him filling out his days in a comfortable benefice, writing the occasional sermon, preaching at a few services, visiting the sick no doubt, and then escaping from the boredom of his life—and perhaps from troublesome fellow-clergymen and a querulous family—by immersing himself in James Shirley, just as I was doing more than a century later. And, increasingly, I was feeling sorry for myself too.

Shirley, who was born in 1596, arrived late on the scene in the great age of Shakespeare. By the time his first plays were performed in the 1620s, Shakespeare had been dead for almost a decade but was still a presence, though even in his lifetime he had been displaced by the more sensational plays of Beaumont and Fletcher, the Tweedledum and Tweedledee of Renaissance drama. Since that kind of melodrama was all the rage at the best theatres, Shirley tried his hand at it too. He was a little more talented, perhaps, than the nonentities who survive only as names and in lists of titles, but it soon became obvious to me that his talent was not particularly large. He could turn his hands to a decent blood-and-guts melodrama, a 'dignified' tragedy about the conflict between love and honour, a few mildly amusing comedies— but that was all.

He seemed to have been a thorough professional. But professional playwrights came in their dozens by his time, and Shirley was never able to secure more than a toehold in the competitive and intrigue-ridden London theatres. At one stage, indeed, he fled to Ireland, to try his fortunes setting up a theatre in Dublin. It was not a particularly successful venture, for he was back in London within a few years. It did produce, however, an unintentionally hilarious play about St Patrick, complete with the obligatory love story for a subplot and culminating in the great scene of the good saint's driving snakes out of the Emerald Isle. After that his career chugged on for a while, but the only notable thing about it was that his last play, *The Court Secret*, was in rehearsal in 1642 when Oliver Cromwell's parliament ordered the closing of all theatres because of their ungodly lewdness. Or so conventional wisdom had it—I began to suspect that those dour puritans were exercising, perhaps, refined literary judgment when they put Shirley and his colleagues out of business. And I was to spend at least two years of my life with such mediocrity, trying to coax enough out of it to be deemed worthy of a doctorate.

At first my task was simple enough: I sat day after day in the library reading Shirley's plays and then, as I discovered to my horror, the substantial body of work on which he was supposed to have collaborated with his contemporaries. This was an age when most plays, even Shakespeare's at times, were cobbled together by several hands, like film or television scripts in our time. Sometimes I cheered myself up by remembering that I was reading texts no one had looked at for generations. Nevertheless, by the time I reached the end of what I pretended was a preliminary investigation, I did not feel any wiser or more inspired.

Brown was not at all interested or helpful when I tried to tell him about my difficulties, but perhaps I had put them so obliquely that he did not realise their extent. Whatever the case, after three or four months I thought I had reached an impasse. What to do next? The 'life' of course.

Strangely, it seemed at the time, Brown became animated when I mentioned to him during a quiet moment at the Marlborough that I should see if I could find out anything new about Shirley's life or career: there was, after all, the rumour of recusancy, that is, of being a covert Catholic. His eyes lit up: yes, some real research for a change—a remark that both puzzled and alarmed me. It was the first inkling of something I was to understand fully only months later: that Brown had little liking for literature, that he was interested in books as physical objects, in the process of their manufacture, the accuracy of texts contained in them and—at some greater remove—the people who wrote the texts which compositors, printers and booksellers had promulgated. He had the true scholar's disdain for aesthetic and cultural values. For him *King Lear* was of as much interest as one of those anonymous, often vacuous plays I had found in the slim volumes of the Malone Society. That was to account for the strange fact which burst on me after a few sessions at the Marlborough that for Brown and his colleagues having the privilege of living at the centre of great culture was of little consequence. They never went to plays, concerts or exhibitions. Their lives revolved entirely around their research and their drinking—and presumably around their families, about whom they never spoke. For that reason it was a matter of indifference to Brown that I should be persuaded to change my thesis topic from Brome to Shirley, even after I had said that I hadn't found Shirley particularly interesting. Both were good research-fodder.

Research he could understand. I must spend some time, he announced, at the Public Record Office. He would arrange a reader's ticket. And he was as good as his word. A few days later a small brown card arrived in the mail, a six-month reader's ticket for the great repository of secrets, scandal and gossip in Chancery Lane. So, for two months I abandoned the North Library for a submarine world under a shallow dome of greenish glass.

In Sydney, at the time when I dreamt about becoming an academic, I often entertained fantasies of the scholar's life. I saw myself in a handsome panelled library with thick leather-bound folios propped on stands in front of me, and smaller, squat quartos and octavos in neat piles. I imagined that I would spend time happily looking at a word or passage, thinking, considering, discriminating and reaching decisions about the meaning or significance of whatever I had been sifting through with patience and dedication. In the British Museum I saw, indeed, one or two people doing just that: absorbed in front of a large book on a stand, occasionally jotting a word or two in a small notebook, but mostly engaged in what could only have been thought. The reality of the scholar's life, I was to learn, was very different. It was mostly chaos and frustration, at least for me. Any piece of research, no matter how straightforward it might seem, must begin with preconceptions. You have to set out looking for something, and you must have at least an inkling or an intuition of what that might be—otherwise it would be impossible to take any step, make any move. Yet once you embark on following an intuition, doubts and contradictions assail you on all sides. The evidence is almost always ambiguous—only the most fortunate will come upon something so startlingly clear as to put all doubt to rest. Instead of greater clarity there is in most cases increasing fog: the possibilities and leads branch off in all directions, threatening at times to invalidate the whole endeavour, at other times to convert the original concept into its opposite. And all the while the matter on which that research is based—in the case of literary scholarship primary and secondary sources and documents—multiplies, bringing further possibilities of chaos and despair. For that reason there were few serene people around me in the North Library. Most of us seemed to be drowning in a sea of books, vainly attempting to hold back the tide. We flitted like butterflies from possibility to possibility, and from one arcane source to another where confirmation of our *idées fixes* might be found.

The British Museum Reading Room was nevertheless orderly and calm compared to the hectic industry in the green-bathed world of the Public Record Office. I often mistrust my memories of the place; it sometimes seems as if I have superimposed on it one of Phiz's illustrations for the chaos among which Dickens's characters battle against a hostile and irrational world. Yet what I remember of the Public Record Office is precisely such an accumulation of papers, of enormous volumes of manuscripts and portfolios with their ties flapping madly, papers almost spilling out of them, being carried everywhere by pasty-faced men and women weighed down by the load of history. I remember that even on the brightest days such was the underwater gloom in that great space that the little lamps above the desks shed only the faintest illumination, a small pool of light into which the high piles of documents cast crazy shadows. Not only were the desks overburdened with those tottering piles. Everywhere great wooden shelves on castors were wheeled about by dust-coated attendants. The circulation desk was buried beneath stacks of papers, as if they had been left there by a child grown tired of a game. It seemed a world on the brink of disintegration, the readers straying backwards and forwards from the rows upon rows of reference books on high shelves around the walls as if they were wandering galaxies in a perplexing universe.

I was appalled, I remember, at the thought that it was here that I would be searching for something about the wretched Shirley. Where to begin? How to begin? How to enter that maze of a thousand years or so of official suspicion, malice, intrigue, slander, the reports of diplomats, crown agents, spies and informers, the terrible machinery of a cumbersome state?

I was paralysed for the first hour or so. I had strayed into a world without bearings. I watched the people scurrying about with their piles of documents and notebooks. They seemed to know exactly what to do: I had no idea where to begin. It was not, after all, as if I were searching for something connected with the great affairs of state preserved in notes, memoranda, reports or personal accounts. I was not looking for material about Henry VIII's divorce or the plans for a penal colony at Botany Bay. My task was to find something hitherto unknown about a wholly obscure individual who had lived three hundred years earlier, enjoyed tiny fame as a writer for the London stage—no better than a vagabond in the eyes of many contemporaries, therefore—who may, just may have come to the notice of the authorities because he had refused to abandon his Catholicism. But even if that were so, I reminded myself unhappily, he was small fry, unlikely to be the subject of ream upon ream of sensational documents.

I began to suspect that if I were to find out anything about him in that bizarre place I would need either extraordinary luck or years of patient sifting of catalogues, abstracts, abstracts of abstracts, lists, genealogies; the great framework, in short, that supports historical research. I was not inclined to believe in luck; nor did I have much more than two or three months, or the patience if it came to that. Yet I did not like the prospect of reporting to Brown that I could find *nothing*. I could imagine him turning on me as King Lear does on his daughter: 'Nothing will come of nothing, speak (or in this case "try") again.' So I had no choice but to try to discover some atom of possibility that might sustain that 'contribution to knowledge' which was one of the conditions of a doctoral dissertation. The many volumes of the Abstract of State Papers lining the walls of the Public Record Office would be a place to begin, I decided.

I thought it best to start looking in the years that coincided with Shirley's career as a playwright between the early 1620s and its abrupt end in 1642. Those twenty years filled many volumes: the suspicious efficiency of the state, as is the habit of all states, seemed to have overlooked nothing, no matter how trivial. The index to each volume produced, as I might have expected, epidemics of Shirleys in the usually relaxed attitude to spelling conventions current at the time—Sherley, Shirly, Sherleigh, Sharlie, Shorly, Chorley, an infinite process of mutation in which you might imagine Shirley turning into Shakespeare or Queen Elizabeth. Again, the hopelessness of my task struck home. I realised that I would have to adjust to a finer focus, concentrating on the more plausible versions of the playwright's name, knowing all along that twentieth-century notions of plausibility were among the least of the age's priorities. But I learnt then the other great tool of the researcher's trade: cutting your cloth according to the measure, for even the entries under the conventional modern spelling of Shirley's name—as it appeared on most though by no means all of his published plays—produced an epidemic of James, Jas., Jacobus (and also, of course, Iames, Ias. and Iacobus), not to mention the non-committal and infinitely teasing 'J' and 'I'. And the other vagrant spellings of the surname produced their own crops of Jameses and first names that might stand for it.

The next task was a quick scan and sifting of those entries for each volume, darting between the index and terse, heartless summaries of interrogations, investigations, calumny, innuendo and malice. Most, of course, could be discarded. I learnt, to my great distress, that a certain James Shirley who featured in several summaries of a dispute over the succession to a minor title turned out to be twelve or thirteen years old at the time the playwright made his debut on the stage—and even ingenuity could not make Shirley's ploddingly decent grown man's work into the brilliant flashes of precocity. It went on like that: excitement, the racing of the pulse followed by disappointment, until at the end of two or three weeks I had a list of forty or fifty possibilities.

That was only the beginning, for those summaries gave no more than the briefest hints about documents which were likely to be, I thought with a sinking heart, many pages long. Next came the time-consuming business of requesting the relevant files from the bowels of the Public Record Office. Research work, I began to understand, consists mostly of waiting, like travelling by air. Two, three hours would go by before the first of the documents arrived. And there were the disappointments, too—the cancelled flights: small slips announcing that the requested document could not be located. Nevertheless, by the afternoon of the day I first put in the maximum requests slips allowed at any one time, several bound volumes and loose leaves in stout cardboard folders were waiting for me on the collection shelves.

I lugged the pile of documents back to my desk. There was a particular thrill, I remember, as I undid the ties on a blood red cardboard portfolio. Inside, sheets of yellowing paper were covered in a small, spidery hand. It was an odd moment. Much more so than with the old books in the North Library, I had the sensation of touching the past. Here were words written three hundred years or so before I opened that portfolio, by people about whom I knew nothing, whose lives seemed impossibly remote from mine—creatures in a costume melodrama. Yet they had left behind those carefully composed, though at first sight illegible, sheets of paper which perhaps no one had looked at since the day they disappeared in the great maw of seventeenth-century English bureaucracy. And here was I, holding them.

The documents were not easy to read, but because most of them were official depositions of one kind or another they proved somewhat less intractable than some of the material I had practised on in Sydney when learning the vagaries of sixteenth- and seventeenth-century handwriting. And in any event, most consisted of endless repetitions of a few banalities. Someone had placed a complaint with the authorities about a certain Jas. Shirley's failure to observe the Lenten fast. Jacobus Sharly was in trouble for not paying the poor tax, or for keeping unruly apprentices. None of the documents I read seemed to contain anything particularly relevant or significant—and besides, I discovered that these people were only members of a large cast of walk-on characters in the great dramas of state with which these often massive documents were concerned. There was, inevitably, considerable frustration, but also the excitement of the chase, and most satisfyingly a sense of structure to the task. Day after day I saw the material I had decided to consult diminish—unlike my thesis itself which seemed to balloon out in all directions, stretching to infinity, I sometimes feared.

Admittedly, when I reached the end of my cull and decided that I could not spare any more time if I were to finish my thesis before my scholarship ran out, I had not found much. There were all sorts of trivial details which might have pertained to James Shirley the playwright—but by the same token they could just as well have been referring to dozens, perhaps hundreds of his contemporaries with similar names. What is more, none of that gossip about tithes and unruly apprentices seemed particularly relevant. I was discouraged, but there was at least one scrap I could use. A certain Jacobus Shirley had been detained and questioned at Folkestone after crossing the Channel. What had he been doing in France, the authorities wanted to know. Whom had he visited? Was he bearing any letters, messages or commissions? The document was not very precise about the cause of suspicions or indeed the answers the traveller gave, but it seemed likely that Shirley—if indeed it had been he—had aroused suspicion because of his reputation for being a covert Catholic. He must have satisfied the authorities, however, because the document recorded that he had been released and allowed to travel to London without further surveillance. Just as well, I thought, since if he had ended up in the Tower or on the Folkestone gibbet, it would have put paid to any possibility that this Shirley was the same man who went on to write more of his dreary plays.

Brown proved uncharacteristically interested and sympathetic when I told him what I had found—or rather failed to find. A contribution, he said, definitely a contribution. Minor, admittedly, but it filled in a little of the picture. I was pleased but found myself wondering what it was exactly that I was filling in. I had no time or inclination, however, for that kind of speculation. I took up permanent residence once more in the North Library.

I have never been back to the Public Record Office. But those few weeks acted, I now realise, as an indication of where my interests and sympathies were to lie: in scholarship or research, rather than in the pretentious pomp of academic literary criticism—a craft I nevertheless found myself obliged to practise for thirty years or so because that, after all, was what a literary academic was supposed to do. But my heart was never in it. Yet at the time I was trying to cobble together *A Study of the Life and Works of James Shirley* I knew that if I had any prospect of gaining a doctorate and a job in a university I must engage with a critical examination of a body of work which seemed to me, if not exactly worthless, of very minor importance indeed. No matter how many fantasies may still have been in the air around me, I realised that the best I could hope from my thesis was a meal ticket.

I wished, nevertheless, that the prospective meal ticket had been more interesting. As time went by I increasingly came to regret that I was not working on Brome. He may have been intellectually no more challenging or poetically refined, but he showed a freshness and energy that were lacking in Shirley's carefully calculated politesse. Without having the least theoretical awareness—of the sort that was to dominate literary studies in my last years as an academic—I was sorry to have missed out on the chance of doing 'research' on a writer far more 'connected' to his society and his age than the pallid, proper Shirley. Yet even Brome could not have satisfied, I came to suspect, the other great lack in the academic and scholarly patterns my life was following. There was almost no intellectual context to my work, just as there was nothing but gossip and backbiting at the seminars in the Marlborough. It was not so much that I was aware of this lack as that my professional and academic life seemed to run in entirely different grooves from the great cultural and in a way intellectual stimulation London of the early sixties offered. Hindsight makes me recognise that if I did become a good academic, it was thanks as much to the education of a kind I received as a result of my decision to do my postgraduate work in a university many people in the Sydney department considered not quite top-notch, which happened to be located in what I became convinced was the most exciting city in the world.

13

There was unpleasantness at Molyneux Street. Miss Craig caught me on the stairs one morning. I was taking too many baths, and so was Mr Carlton. She tried to run a friendly place, she went on, without too many rules and restrictions, but surely a bath each night was not necessary. She couldn't afford it. Either she would have to install a meter in the bathroom for the gas heater, which would be unfair to the other tenants, or she would have to raise both our rents. And while she was about it, why did I always insist on disinfecting the bath? I didn't have the courage to tell her that I used to slosh it out with Dettol because a frequent user of the bath was her dog. Miss Craig and her friend would drag the protesting beast, its legs stiff with resistance, by the stout chain around its neck. It would yelp and whine as they lifted it into the sudsy water for its twice or thrice weekly wash. And besides, I had the deepest suspicions about the hygiene of the person responsible for the acrid-sweet smell that crept under my door almost every night. I told her I would mention it to Mr Carlton.

Jim and I had been thinking of looking for a flat for some time. We had done nothing about it, however, partly through inertia, but largely because neither of us wanted to leave Central London—even Kensington seemed the end of the world—and we knew, or thought we knew, about the impossible rents people were asked to pay there. Miss Craig's complaint tipped the scales: there was no harm in looking. Because my time was more flexible, I decided to begin first thing the next morning. It was a relief to have a legitimate excuse (to myself, for Brown did not care) to escape Shirley for a few days.

I had heard many hair-raising stories about flat-hunting in London, so I was prepared for a long, possibly fruitless trudge. I decided to begin in Baker Street, where I had seen several estate agents on my way to Selfridges or the Everyman cinema. I did not hold out much hope: they looked like the kinds of establishments that dealt in luxury maisonettes in posh buildings with polished brass door-knockers and liveried doormen. Within ten minutes, however, I had struck gold.

I couldn't believe it when the supercilious individual who had received me said that he had just what I might be looking for. Should we inspect it now? I was in a daze. It was not far, the agent went on, so there was no need to find a taxi; we could discuss the arrangements on the way. He took me to a short street a few blocks away. Called Wyndham Place, it starts at the northern edge of Bryanston Square, ending in front of a handsomely proportioned Georgian church, much favoured for weddings by the lower echelons of London's social elite. The agent and I stopped outside an unadorned terrace house, only slightly larger, it seemed, than Miss Craig's, but by then I knew enough of the arcane discriminations of the class system to be aware of the difference a few feet of street frontage could make. The door was not locked; nor were there rows of buttons next to little metal slots with names scrawled or neatly typed on them. I was beginning to get suspicious of what kind of flat I was being shown.

We climbed a carpeted staircase—slightly wider than the stairs in Molyneux Street—to the top floor, where the carpet gave way to linoleum. There were three doors on the landing. One led to a long, rather narrow room running from the front of the house to the back, with windows at either end. A set of free-standing shelves marked off the rear portion, with two beds placed at right-angles to each other along the walls. The front part was the more surprising: it was furnished with 'pieces' that reminded me of the Keeps' flat in Kensington: a sofa, possibly late Georgian, a Victorian wing-chair, a pleasant table, more chairs, a hideous but very English standard lamp and a lovely, intricately veneered escritoire. The floor was covered in good, thick carpeting.

After I had been gazing in amazement at the room for some time the agent said he would show me the kitchen. It was a large, linoleum-covered space in the front of the building with a good stove and—most astonishing of all—a large and expensive collection of cookware, mostly in enamel, and all manner of other utensils. Were the furniture and the fittings to stay, I asked. Oh yes, furnished, of course—the agent stared at me as if I had put my knife in my mouth or committed some even more ghastly solecism—why don't we look at the bathroom? It proved more than adequate. The flat was perfect— our chances of renting it were nil, I decided.

On the way down, still dazed, I made an effort to take in more of the place. White doors without locks or numbers led off each landing. It was quiet, but you could hear the clatter of typewriters behind several closed doors, muffled conversations, someone talking on the telephone. This was obviously no rooming house or warren of tiny flats. Solicitors' offices, the agent told me, guessing my puzzlement: at night we would have the place to ourselves—though the owners were very particular about keeping the front door locked after five in the afternoon and about turning off the lights on the stairs. He was beginning to talk to me as if I were already the tenant. Was I interested, he asked on the stoop. Of course, I said without hesitation. Well then, he suggested, we should go back to the office and discuss the lease.

The rent turned out to be high: ten pounds a week, as well as electricity and gas charges, and the telephone—I had noticed a white handset on a small round table. I did a quick reckoning in my head. My rent at Miss Craig's was three pounds, with electricity and the disputed use of the bathroom, though the gas for heating and cooking had to be paid for by endlessly feeding the monster in the corner. Jim was paying a little more for his larger, more comfortable room on the ground floor. I felt fairly sure that he could afford the difference. As for me, I was in so much of a muddle already in trying to survive on my scholarship that I was convinced I would sink sooner or later with or without the extra expense. So I told the agent that we would take the flat. He looked pleased. We would need references, of course, he said, and the owner would like to meet us—that evening if possible, or the next morning. And there was another thing. The lease was already drawn up; we must agree to move in within a week at the most after it was signed.

I walked away from the agent's office with my head spinning. I couldn't believe my luck, and yet there was something not quite right—surely, I thought, people would be killing each other to get hold of that flat; why would the agent be so eager to let it to the first comer, especially an Australian student? All sorts of lurid and bizarre fantasies were racing round in my mind until Jim got back from work in the late afternoon. We telephoned the agency, expecting everyone to have left by then. But the agent was still there; would Mr Carlton like to inspect the flat? We could meet the owner at the same time.

The owner turned out to be the head of the firm of solicitors that occupied most of the building. He was in his early thirties, pink faced and well barbered, wearing pinstripe trousers and a black jacket. Jim and I sat in front of his imposing desk, which had the air of a surface on which no work was ever done. 'Were you up at Oxford, Mr Carlton?' he asked—for Jim, who had been in England for the best part of three years by then, had learnt to mimic perfectly upper-middle-class argot. 'No? I thought I recognised your face, or perhaps your tie,' he added enigmatically. To me he paid little attention. Jim had some references with him. I said that I would ask the supervisor of my thesis to write one. But the man who obviously already saw himself as our landlord gave an elegant wave, rather like the little wave of a gloved hand I saw inside the big black car in Macquarie Street in Sydney as it drove past the cheering crowd in the sunshine. Everything was moving with great speed—too fast, I started thinking, feeling that gut-wrenching alarm that comes when you've arrived at a decision that cannot be undone. We would move into the flat in two or three days' time.

Miss Craig was *désolée* when I told her we would be leaving. She said *'désolée'* because she was an actress, although an out-of-work actress, and knew that it was proper to speak like that. Perhaps she had been too tactless. She only *mentioned* the matter of the bath—speaking in italics was also one of her accomplishments. Surely we could work something out. I began to feel sorry for her: losing two lodgers at one blow could not have been easy. But I told her as gently as I could that we had taken a flat, though of course we would pay out the week's rent. We moved into the new flat in time to meet the deadline the owner had set. I was both elated and disturbed—disturbed because it had all happened so suddenly, in such a curiously casual manner, when conventional wisdom had it that finding a flat in London you could actually afford was to spend a season in hell. And I wasn't entirely sure that I could afford the luxury. But above all, there seemed something unsettling, sinister in a way about the whole business. Why the insistence on our moving in immediately? Why had the solicitor been so little concerned about the references I was supposed to present? Why was no word spoken about other prospective tenants, who might, for all we knew, have been prepared to pay a higher rent? These questions and the luridly alarming answers to them played on my mind as I was packing my belongings in readiness for the move. As we learnt eventually, we were not about to take up residence in a sinister den of evil but in a pleasant little flat which had been, and was indeed to remain, no more than the stage set for a bedroom farce.

We should have realised that there was something very odd going on as soon as we began hauling our belongings up the narrow flight of stairs. An elderly woman in a shapeless floral apron, the archetypal English charlady, was mopping the linoleum on the top landing. The door to the main room of the flat was ajar. We noticed that it had no lock, not even a keyhole. The two envelopes the agent had given us when we signed the lease contained one key each, for the front door. The charlady looked us over with a characteristic mixture of suspicion and deference, but she knew her place and went on with her mopping. It was accompanied by a curious, muttered lament about 'poor, poor Mrs —' the solicitor's wife, or mother perhaps. Had she died, I wondered, or suffered some terrible calamity?

It took three or four ascents before we got all our belongings upstairs. The charlady was still on the landing, obviously taking immense care to make sure it was spotless. Her lament, like the grieving queens' in *Richard III* or more accurately perhaps like Juliet's Nurse's, seemed to consist of an elaborate assembly of sighs, exclamations and cries of distress. 'The poor, poor lady, poor Mrs —; 'e wouldn't want them to have a key now, would 'e; poor Mrs —, the poor, poor lady.' I was all ears, but I'd grown sufficiently familiar with the rituals of English life to know that you were supposed to pay little heed to the lower classes.

Miss Gilchrist—we called her that in private, though we never found out her name—was not to be discouraged. Her monologue seemed endless, as was her intention to clean every nook and cranny on the small landing. But she obviously had something in mind. Finally she came out with it. She knocked timidly on the door we had left half open. She did the offices downstairs every day, she told us with a sullen, embarrassed uncertainty. She could do us as well a couple of times a week for a few shillings. We leapt at the offer. Her mood brightened, but as she was saying that she'd come the day after 'tomorrer', she sank back into her tragic vein: she would do it for 'er, poor, poor thing; but we wouldn't catch 'er dead doin' it for 'im, now would we?

For a moment or two we wondered what all that might have been about, then we became distracted by the business of settling in. Once or twice that day and for a few days afterwards I found myself worrying that the flat, at least the main room, couldn't be locked. But the place was orderly enough, the solicitor seemed a decent chap, and anyway, neither of us had much worth stealing.

In the next few weeks I revised my opinion of the solicitor. He seemed decent enough, it was true, but he was also a twit. Specifically one of those slightly upper-middle-class English twits, all blather and hot air, whom you'd hear in the tube telling Simon and Jeremy (usually at the top of his voice) about his marvellous weekend in an oast-house in Kent or over in Deauville—and if a woman were included in the conversation, you could count on her to say, 'Super, absolutely super'. The solicitor was like that. He had not abandoned his conviction that he'd known Jim at Oxford. 'Were you up at Balliol, Mr Carlton?' he'd ask whenever they met on the stairs. 'Or Magdalen, perhaps?'

He entertained no such fantasies about me, but I too came in for my share of obtuseness or leg-pulling—I could never decide which— after he saw me in the entrance hall one Friday carrying a small suitcase. 'Off to the country for the weekend, Mr Riemer?' 'No,' I told

A Sentimental Education

him foolishly, 'Paris.' After that whenever he caught me with a suitcase or an overnight bag I knew exactly what to expect: 'Are you travelling to the Continent, Mr Riemer?'

He was irritating, but harmless—and we had hardly anything to do with him. His legal practice seemed a well-run, quiet affair. Besides him there appeared to be a clerk or two, or perhaps a junior solicitor, and his secretary, a stunningly beautiful Eurasian woman. There did not seem to be many clients, but it obviously didn't matter too much: we had learnt from Miss Gilchrist's monologues that 'Poor Mrs —' was a wealthy woman with a place in Dorset, where she spent most of her time. So we forgot the irritation of being unable to lock the flat. And at any rate, since (miraculously it seemed) *A Study of the Life and Works of James Shirley* was beginning to take shape, I found myself spending more and more time in the flat writing drafts, sketches, eventually sections and chapters on the small portable typewriter I bought shortly after arriving in London.

By contrast, Jim was away from home for most of the day. He had progressed sufficiently in the firm he worked for to be given a company car. Every morning he drove off at about seven for the factory and its offices on the outskirts of London, not returning until six in the evening, or even later. One day, however, as he tells the story, he began to feel ill and was unable to concentrate on his work. Probably flu, he thought. By lunchtime he decided that it would be wise to go home to bed. It was a dreary, bone-aching winter day. Wrapped in his overcoat, hat firmly on his head, he somehow managed the long drive through tangled traffic on slithery, treacherous roads. Luckily he found somewhere to park in Wyndham Place almost straight away. He dragged himself up the stairs, opened the unlockable door, put his hat on the coat-stand, and caught sight of the solicitor on his bed, pinstripe trousers bunched around his ankles, beneath him the shapely legs of the secretary. For one of the very few times in his life, Jim says, he was nonplussed: what to do? The only thing that occurred to him was to mutter 'Oh, sorry', replace his hat and spend a few hours half-comatose in a cinema.

Word of the misadventure was obviously whispered around the office, because the next time I ran into Miss Gilchrist she gave me a lengthy and reasonably lucid account of the situation in Wyndham Place. Our flat had been the solicitor's love nest. He had been able to make good use of it because his wife spent much of her time in Dorset, and he could legitimately claim that it was more convenient to sleep over at work rather than go home to an empty house in Holland Park. His wife must have suspected, however, what sleeping over at work really meant, for according to Miss Gilchrist she had caught him at it—just as Jim had—and delivered her ultimatum. The flat must be let immediately, to the first comer, or else she would stay in Dorset permanently and he would not see a penny more of Daddy's money. The threat had obviously worked.

Miss Gilchrist let on something else as well. The solicitor was convinced that it had been I who had caught him with his trousers around his ankles. It made sense, after all. So after that I found myself wondering what might happen when we bumped into each other on the stairs or at the front door. But nothing happened. Twittish as ever, he'd say good morning or good evening, ask whether I was off to the Continent or if Jim was sure he hadn't been up in Oxford. The man seemed to have no shame. Was it, I wondered, bravado, pluck? Or was it something else, the would-be-aristocrat's disdain for the rabble when caught exercising a kind of *droit du seigneur*?

It was probably all of these, and something else besides, it occurred to me many years later. He probably didn't care; it wasn't important. Having to put up with usurpers in the flat was, perhaps, a far greater nuisance. At least the money was safe for the time being—unless of course Poor Mrs — got to hear of this escapade, which no doubt was one of many. And, in the great scheme of things, the incident and the peccadillo were trivial enough. Far more spectacular decadence was going on all around us, under our very windows, indeed, without our suspecting it in the least.

But not quite. One of the two rows of all-but identical terraces that lined the short stretch of Wyndham Place was broken by an archway leading to Wyndham Mews, directly opposite the front windows of our flat. A very cultivated family seemed to occupy the house to the right. On fine mornings I would sometimes catch sight of a gentleman in a well-cut suit, watch-chain draped across his waistcoat, standing on the narrow first floor balcony, enjoying the sunshine. Sometimes a young man, no more than a boy, would be standing with him, his chain also glinting in the sun. When Britain was shaken by the prospective sale to foreign interests of a great national treasure, Leonardo's cartoon of the Virgin and St Anne, a poster for the campaign that raised enough money and influence to save that superb example of England's heritage (or spoils) was prominently displayed on a ground-floor window of the house. It was no doubt occupied by a wealthy and cultured family. That would have explained the large shiny cars—Rolls Royces, Bentleys, Daimlers, the occasional Cadillac—that you could see squeezing into the mews, especially on late afternoons and evenings.

We would remark from time to time on that cavalcade of gleaming metal. Perhaps a high-class prostitute lived there, I suggested. Jim, who was always far more level-headed, and usually right, pooh-poohed the idea. The mews was where the millionaires of Bryanston Square and Montagu Square garaged their cars. Yet he was wrong, at least in that instance. A few years later, as I was following the unending saga of the Profumo affair in the Sydney newspapers, I learnt that it was precisely there in Wyndham Mews that Dr Ward maintained one of the establishments where those legendary *femmes fatales*, Christine Keeler and Mandy Rice Davies, entertained the good and the great, among them John Profumo, Her Majesty's hapless War Secretary, as well as a succession of less exalted clients: financiers, captains of industry and at least one Soviet spy.

14

Afterwards, and for a long time to come, that sordid little incident in our top-floor flat remained no more than the source of a good story. Yet even that evening, as I listened in disbelief to Jim's story of our landlord's erotic adventure—amused and offended too, almost soiled by the invasion—I was beginning to sense that it was just another illustration of my growing ambivalence about the nature of English society.

The solicitor's peccadillo was as far removed as you could get from the images of imperial greatness and cultural supremacy which had formed the staple of clichés dished out to us at school—the empire on which the sun never sets (even though by then it had become the rather more pussy-footed British Commonwealth); the glories of Shakespeare, Wren and Nelson; the peerless excellence of English justice; the benefits of British civilisation which we enjoyed in the farthest corner of the globe. Of course, such simple-minded slogans found no place within the shadow of Edmund Blacket's loving exercise in pastiche and imitation. There the tone was too ironic and sophisticated to tolerate a kind of patriotic sentimentality which one associated with American kitsch: hand on the heart, Stars and Stripes forever. The people in black gowns who lectured so learnedly about Ben Jonson and Milton, Pope and Jane Austen would have considered it vulgar and naive to state the obvious. And yet no part of that education took into account anything like the double-edged significance of what happened on that afternoon on the top floor of a small terrace house in Marylebone. Thelma Herring discussed often enough the sexual imbroglios of Restoration comedies, where unsuspecting husbands, fathers, friends or complete strangers are, indeed, in the habit of coming upon gallants with their britches around their ankles. It was all grist to her mill; she could discuss (as befitted the true scholar) the most titillating material in the most objective, least prurient manner. Yet nothing in those lectures I endured on Wycherley and Congreve, and the whole succession of bawdy and randy playwrights and versifiers—even the Earl of Rochester, who earned a brief mention somewhere in the syllabus, though the censors would not actually allow us to read his verse—suggested that being so caught was as much part of an admirable civilisation as Canterbury Cathedral or the works of Alfred, Lord Tennyson.

For all its vulgarity and exploitativeness, the farce played out in Wyndham Place was particularly English, and shared many of the salient characteristics of English life so admired by those who professed its culture and civilisation in faraway places. Even at the time it struck me that there was something attractively decadent about the seduction in the upstairs flat. Here was no hurried assignation in a seedy hotel room or a quick grasp on prickly grass, or even full-blown sex on the floor behind the filing cabinets. I had heard of such things in Sydney, and there were those among my acquaintances at university who claimed to have had precisely such a proposition put to them by a young lecturer or sex-crazed senior professor. The seduction in Wyndham Place had far more style.

It took place, after all, in the solicitor's own domain, in that cosy well-furnished upstairs flat. I began to understand how much it must have galled him to be forced to let it to us, of all people, colonials, and one of us far worse than that, a colonial of very dubious standing. I tried to imagine, too, the little signals, the prearranged code which would have passed between him and his secretary before she got up from her desk, sauntered over to the filing cabinet perhaps, and then slipped out through the door. So after the initial surprise and annoyance, I began, in a curious way, to admire our landlord, while all along my contempt for his posturing ways increased. If you were going to be sordid, I decided, you might as well do it with some aplomb. And there was something particularly English about that.

Around that time I realised that decay—that is, the physical manifestation of decadence—also enhanced the attractions of England. I recall clearly the first time I saw a proper Gothic cathedral. Westminster Abbey, with the traffic of a huge city swirling around it, failed somehow to make a strong impression. One wintry day, when I had driven with some friends to look at Stonehenge and then went on to Salisbury, catching sight of the great spire against the mist of an early afternoon sky, I experienced with an almost tactile immediacy the presence of something very old. Then, as we strolled around the building, that sense of antiquity became even more pronounced. There was something fragile, and therefore moving and in a way beautiful, about that crumbling structure. You could see how bits and pieces of it had worn away throughout the centuries—the featureless woman's head on a boss, a prophet without a nose. And you could see too where attempts were being made to shore it all up, to put off, no matter how provisionally, the inevitable work of time, rain, snow, sleet, smoke, the exhaust gases of thousands of cars and buses, which one day would reduce the cathedral to rubble. Except that in those days everyone expected destruction to come far more swiftly from the nuclear conflict many were convinced would visit us in the very near future. Inside, too, amid the jumble of monuments and memorials, under the high ribbed arches holding up that wonderful structure, there was a poignant sense of decay, of a world not frozen still in time but one constantly in flux. It was Sunday, I remember, and as we stood in the entrance we could hear the choir, from somewhere far away it seemed, though you could see nothing, no priest or congregation, an evensong of ghosts perhaps.

So it was a romantic impression certainly, much enhanced by the evidence of age all around us, of ancient, unseen ceremonies too. It made that sandstone Gothic university where I had learnt about this world seem gimcrack, a risible imitation precisely because it was so new. Of course, in that world everyone deemed it to have the patina of age—yet it was, I came at length to realise, not merely new, but also perfect and harmonious. Every detail—every chimney, doorway, window and gargoyle—had been designed and conceived with a great plan in mind, an act of homage and commemoration. Nothing was out place because even the building's asymmetries were studied, with an eye to effect, rather than the products of chance or accident. And for that reason the building—and perhaps the ideals it represented—were dead, as imitations are always dead: too solid, too substantial.

As we walked away from Salisbury Cathedral that afternoon, we took one last look at the building. It seemed all the more real and substantial because its appearance constantly changed at the whim of the mist that was beginning to form and when the late-afternoon clouds parted briefly to allow weak sunlight to illuminate now one little turret, now a part of the stone spire. The cathedral looked as if it had taken root in that place, and with this had come growth and also, inevitably, decay. In such ways I began to appreciate and respond to the nature of that much-admired English antiquity which had formed the figured bass of my education in Sydney. The most significant lesson was, perhaps, that the past was not frozen in its own eternal contemporaneity, as it tended to be for us whenever we tried to understand what Shakespeare's world 'meant' by something—or Chaucer's or Pope's—but lingered, altered admittedly, forever changing, yet connected to our present despite the tyranny of time. What had been no more than an historical pageant, with its great figures walking on and off in a succession of ever-fresh tableaux, was now revealed as a living history, with the inevitable sense of decay that the notion of succession implies.

I felt that most poignantly in small, impressionistic ways during those years in England, not from any deliberate intellectual or scholarly exploration of the past. The British Museum Reading Room certainly offered greater access to the literary remains of that past than the well-stocked library of Sydney University could hope to rival. So there was some benefit, as I was to find, in reading the original printed versions of Shirley's plays in those jealously guarded copies which could only be inspected among the green leather appointments of the North Library. There was, for a while at least, some magic too in handling those old books, the sensation of the soft, aged leather between your fingers, the peculiar aroma of old paper and old ink. But, to all intents and purposes, a faithful photographic facsimile would have done as well, whether in Sydney or San Diego. Reading the originals in London was merely a matter of necessity: the British Museum, together with a small handful of libraries in the English-speaking world, was the only place where the few surviving copies of those old books were housed. The same would have been true even if I had been writing my thesis on Brome or Shakespeare or Ben Jonson. In itself, the endeavour did nothing to illuminate the world which Shirley's plays reflected.

Nor did it come from the few attempts I made to visit famous literary or historical sites. Stratford told me nothing about Shakespeare. I went there dutifully, inspected the quaint half-timbered house—sloping floors and ceilings, not a right-angle to be seen anywhere—where he was supposed to have been born, but it was just another old house turned into a museum and souvenir shop. I stood on Clopton Bridge to watch the eddies in the water below. Caroline Spurgeon had taught us many years earlier that Shakespeare had drawn much of his most characteristic imagery from doing precisely that. All I was aware of, however, was the brownish river and the roar of cars and charabancs behind me. On another occasion I drove with friends to Canterbury, along the choked highway that followed the old pilgrims' route. It seemed to have no connection with Chaucer, though there was a momentary thrill when we came upon Thomas à Becket's tomb.

The most important illumination came from the gradual, and always ambiguous, realisation that the past continued to live on in the everyday existence of ordinary people. It could take many forms. I realised, for instance, that some, though probably not many, of the people who worked in the offices around New Oxford Street and High Holborn, a short walk from the British Museum, would spend their lunch-hour in the great exhibition spaces, looking at Greek marbles, Assyrian lions, Egyptian funerary monuments. As James Shirley became less and less tolerable for me, I grew into the habit of slipping out of the Reading Room for a while, walking through the narrow streets of Bloomsbury and Covent Garden to Trafalgar Square and the National Gallery, to stand in front of a painting or two, no longer exhibits in a gallery you 'do' conscientiously, but almost familiars, old friends whose acquaintance it was nice to renew. Sometimes I would go farther afield to look again at the Turners in the Tate Gallery down by the river, or to the Wallace Collection or, if time were short, to the Courtauld Institute near University College—it was conveniently close to the rear entrance of the British Museum.

Yet the most powerful stimulus came from people, and from my few glimpses of how they lived, or at least wished to live. It was, moreover, by no means free of worrying ambiguities and paradoxes. I gradually discovered that English people of a certain class and level of education were obsessed by the past, burning to be surrounded by its remnants and mementos. It took some time, for instance, for the import of something Ann Keep had said early on in our acquaintance to sink in: the row of terraces in Kensington where they lived was only Victorian, she remarked, but very comfortable. It struck me that she too yearned to be living inside walls older than those raised during Victoria's reign. By that time, though, I had seen enough of English life to understand how much discomfort and inconvenience people were prepared to tolerate in order to live somewhere 'old', especially if that place had a history, no matter how humble.

That was in direct contrast to my experience of Australia of the fifties. Then everyone's dream, it seemed, was to live in a brand-new texture brick, double-fronted house on a perfectly bare, recently levelled block of land. All over Sydney turn-of-the century houses, and some older ones too, were being torn down to make way for the modern. That spirit was not altogether unfamiliar, for before the war, and in a rather different key, as it were, my parents worshipped the modern, especially American modernity. The three places where they lived from their marriage in 1935 to our departure for Sydney in 1946—excluding of course cellars and air-raid shelters—were two newly constructed apartment blocks and a Bauhaus villa on the outskirts of Budapest which they considered the last word in ultramodern chic. They would have found it as strange as the denizens of the rapidly spreading suburbs of Sydney that anyone should choose to live in a poorly constructed eighteenth-century terrace house with tiny, inconvenient rooms, narrow staircases, ill-fitting windows and slapdash attempts at providing such modern amenities as plumbing and electricity. Or, indeed, that living among such surroundings would have been a source of pride.

And yet that is precisely what I began to discover among the few people I came to know. For some the allure of antiquity became an irresistible passion. They would spend their time, money and energy in searching for remnants of it to cram into their small flats or bed-sitting rooms, scouring stalls at fairs and markets for a chipped piece of Chelsea ware they could afford, or a foxed early-nineteenth-century print of a sentimental rural prospect, ancient coins, a Jacobean spoon perhaps, and if they had the means, more substantial pieces of furniture or oils by minor English painters. They seemed intent on keeping the modern world at arm's length, to build a protective wall around themselves with mementos of history.

15

I also discovered that the mania for antiquity reached its climax in the countryside, among the stockbrokers and wealthy lawyers I would overhear in the tube on my way to the British Museum, when they would discuss (much more loudly than they needed) the fourteenth-century mill or barn in Kent they might buy, or the gate-house of a long-vanished priory in Somerset. With one family I met, the quest for antiquity seemed to have become, indeed, the source of tension and disaffection.

They had spent many years in Mexico. When the family was repatriated after the husband, who (as was the custom) had retained the title Captain from the First World War, retired from his post as the head of the Mexican branch of a large British concern, they set about looking for a suitable place in the country. When I knew them they lived in Herefordshire, on the Welsh border, in a pleasant though

A Sentimental Education

entirely unremarkable nineteenth-century farmhouse. It had obviously once been the centre of a thriving farm, but over the years, in hard times, parts of it had been sold. By the time the Davies family—the Captain, his wife Bea and two adult daughters—bought the house it was surrounded by no more than a large garden and a small, overgrown copse. It was there that they entertained visitors from what they resolutely insisted on calling the Empire; a charitable task they undertook, I began to suspect, because after their many years abroad they found it difficult to gain entry into what might have passed for society in that relatively isolated part of England. Jim Carlton was introduced to them by some organisation or other when he was convalescing from appendicitis the year before I arrived in London. On two occasions I went to one of their house-parties with other young Australians and Canadians—and one lone, very white South African—to experience English country life.

It seemed to consist mostly of quarrels between Captain and Mrs Davies. Almost invariably, those quarrels had their origin in the behaviour of an old horse called Humphrey, very much the property of Mrs Davies, which the Captain detested with undisguised passion. Humphrey's villainies seemed chiefly to concern his habit of gnawing away at the bark of several fine beeches growing on the periphery of the garden, but on one occasion he enraged an already irate Captain Davies by marching through the open kitchen door, attracted perhaps by the odours of Mrs Davies's indifferent attempts at cooking hearty country meals—she was a terrible cook, or perhaps she had been making or at least supervising the preparation of chilli con carne for so long that she had forgotten the delicate technique required for steak and kidney pudding or toad in the hole.

Humphrey was merely the immediate ground for disputes that would sometimes continue for hours on end, the Captain grumbling about his inability to understand women, even though he'd been forced to spend his life among them, their irrational ways, their stubbornness as, for example, Bea's refusal to send that dreadful old horse off to where he belonged, the knacker's yard. He would go on and on, from morning till night. Mrs Davies tolerated it all with ill-disguised irritation, saying little apart from a ceremonial 'Oh really, Arthur' or two, thrown in for form's sake, you felt. It became clear soon enough that the source of the quarrel was that rambling, gloomy farmhouse rather than Humphrey's intolerable habits or the way they were indulged, though these grounds for recrimination were by no means unconnected.

One of the ceremonies a newcomer had to endure was the Captain's minutely detailed tour of a small part of the house: all that remained of a fourteenth-century structure around which the rest of the building had been wrapped by its nineteenth-century owners. To my untrained eyes there was little difference between that pair of wainscotted rooms and the rest of the place, but it was more than one's life was worth not to agree with the Captain's irate assertion of their superiority over the rest. And to think, the recital would conclude, that they could have lived in a genuine fifteenth-century house, had it not been for that wretched horse.

Mrs Davies was a dedicated rider. Indeed, on a summer morning, as her guests trickled down to the dining room for the bacon, kidneys and sausages which had been slowly stewing and drying out since the previous night in fine silver dishes on an electric plate warmer, she could be seen returning from her first ride of the day. The house just beyond Staunton-on-Arrow, a little village on the Welsh border, had been bought chiefly because of its stable—the customary plural would have been quite inappropriate for the small shed where Humphrey would flee of his own accord whenever the Captain found him at the beeches again. On the whole it had nothing to recommend it to the Captain: it was neither practical nor old enough to be interesting, just another dark, damp farmhouse. Indeed, there was something about the place that brought Seth, the flowering sukebind and *Cold Comfort Farm* to mind. The Captain would have much preferred a house a few miles away near Old Radnor, on the other side of the border. He would take parties of guests in a large, beautifully maintained old car to look at it from the outside. It seemed like most other houses in that part of the country, but in the Captain's eyes it had the inestimable beauty of age—fifteenth century, almost unaltered. And the church at Old Radnor had its glories too, one of the best-preserved rood-screens in the west country, whereas the church at Staunton-on-Arrow was a wretched affair with an incompetent organist. 'No more than a florin, mind you!' the Captain would order his embarrassed guests, in a voice that would have penetrated the worst barrage on the Somme, as the plate went around on Sunday mornings, when we all felt obliged to turn out for church parade. I had been warned before my first visit: I arrived armed with several two-shilling pieces to distribute among those whose extravagance had prompted them to set half-a-crown aside for the purpose.

It would be difficult to parody the Captain and Mrs Davies; they parodied themselves in their endless squabbles and disputes. Nevertheless, beneath the Captain's laments about the house at Staunton-on-Arrow, his yearning for the fifteenth-century place at Old Radnor, there ran a significant current of English life. Perhaps the years he had spent in Mexico had sharpened his desire to be connected with what he may have seen as unbroken traditions, as they were preserved in stone and mortar, old houses and rood-screens. In the same spirit, I began to realise, the people in Sydney who hung nostalgic etchings of Winchester Cathedral and Windsor Castle on their lounge-room walls, and filled their houses with toby jugs and china plates depicting misty rural prospects, were also yearning for that sense of continuity which revealed itself in the worship of the old. I, too, felt the allure of antiquity, for that was something missing from the life I had led in Australia. There everything seemed so new. It lacked texture and resonance—an unformed world.

In Australia we paid no heed to the antiquity around us, for it had nothing to do with our way of life. Behind the row of houses lining one side of the dusty street in an outer suburb of Sydney, where my family lived for a few years, thick bush fell away to a deep gully. A waterhole at the bottom was surrounded by massive rock outcrops. It was a menacing, unsettling place. Occasionally, and wholly against my parents' prohibition, some of the local boys and I used to climb down the steep path leading to those rocks. They showed me some faint scorings on the surface of one of the rocks: the Aborigines made them, they told me without much interest or enthusiasm. And to tell the truth, I found nothing particularly interesting about those shallow marks: they did not seem to have anything to do with our lives or the world in which we lived.

The house in Herefordshire had one saving grace for Captain Davies. One afternoon he led a party of us through the little coppice at the end of the garden. It was as overgrown and untended as the bush behind that nondescript suburban Sydney street. After climbing a gently inclining path, we came upon a long, grass-covered mound. Beyond it the ground fell away sharply, towards Wales. Roman earthworks, the Captain announced, one of the limits of their empire, he added with some pride. We stood silent, impressed, around that very ordinary hillock which seemed nothing other than a natural feature in the hilly landscape. But its antiquity endowed it with an emotional charge. We were standing on history, a substantial evidence of continuity, a testimony to the unbroken occupation of the countryside. The rocks beside the pool in Sydney were farthest from my mind as I stood there taking in all that antiquity. And yet that faint evidence of the impact of human beings on an apparent wilderness in the suburbs could well have been far older than the earthworks near Staunton-on-Arrow—if that is what they were, for Mrs Davies, we learnt, was scornful of her husband's one treasure: it was only a mound, she said.

Sandstone Gothic

The earthworks were, nevertheless, impressive; the rock carvings in Sydney were not because, if anything, they spoke of a disjunction, of a world incomprehensible to my own. The mound in Herefordshire, on the other hand, was yet one more guarantee of English civilisation, as it were. The Romans had been there and had brought with them their skill, their technology, the organisation of a complex empire. And England, in the Captain's eyes, was a direct heir to that advanced civilisation, as witnessed by the nondescript mound on the edge of his otherwise unremarkable and undesirable property. He too had a stake in his nation's proud history.

I remember marvelling at that commonplace spot, just as I marvelled at the booth beside the abbey church at St Albans where you could buy for a pittance battered Roman coins that had been unearthed around the nearby amphitheatre. There I came to own my piece of history, and felt the thrill of being connected with it. I grew to understand the respect of the English for their past. It was, after all, merely a more tangible and visible immersion in their history and civilisation than the endeavour of preserving the literary monuments of that civilisation in the lecture halls and classrooms where I learnt of Lord Bacon's connection with the place where I bought that tarnished coin.

Nevertheless, as time passed and as the antiquity of the world in which I lived—even the noisy metropolis of Central London—became familiar and unremarkable, I began to sense something suffocating about that respect for history, for England's glorious past. I remember reading in one of the Sunday papers about a lady whose hobby was to cultivate plants and flowers known to Shakespeare's age in order to preserve a vital part of England's heritage. Many years later, I visited her garden in a side-street in Stratford-upon-Avon. Bound by richly aged brick walls, the garden had been arranged by its owner, a frail, transparent-skinned old lady, as rows upon rows of brightly coloured annuals, briars laden with tiny, compact roses or large, floppy varieties, in colours, she told us, that would have been known in Shakespeare's time. We would not find in her garden, she added, the result of any modern experiment with cross-breeding, or species introduced since the early seventeenth century. It was, she said, an English garden. As she spoke, the rumble of traffic, the sounds of thousands of feet walking around the small Warwickshire town on a fine summer afternoon sounded much more than a few streets away: they came from another world, one which those old walls sought to exclude, it seemed.

That was in the eighties, a time when the England the old lady tried to preserve or revivify with such dedication seemed even more distant and hypothetical than it had two decades earlier. By the time I saw the garden, Mrs Thatcher had transformed London into a city of sharp-suited young men hurrying around wearing two watches—one showing the time in New York, Tokyo, Hong Kong or wherever their attempts to make money (and pots of it) were concentrated. It was the era, too, of the Falklands War and the wedding of Charles and Diana: bread and circuses, smokescreens to hide the reality of what England had become in the post-industrial world—crumbling cities, rusting shipyards, choked motorways, greed, poverty, squatters in abandoned terraces or in Centrepoint, the hideous skyscraper that had remained untenanted for decades because its owners found it more lucrative to leave it that way. The walled garden of true English flowers, the pretty villages in Kent and Sussex, ancient cathedral towns where not a coloured face could be seen, all seemed irrelevant to the England of the last decades of the century.

Twenty years earlier I was not so aware of the dead hand of the past. When we stood respectfully on Captain Davies's own piece of Roman heritage I was still enamoured of a world that seemed enriched by its long history. You could come upon the textures of that past in the most ordinary and unexpected ways, even in London where, tucked away at the end of a short blind alley or behind an apparently unremarkable Victorian building, you could sometimes discover a remnant of the fifteenth or sixteenth century that had escaped fire, war or development: a genuine half-timbered façade, for instance, instead of the garish pastiche of Ye Olde Curiosity Shoppe. In those ways I sometimes felt that I was coming into contact with the physical attributes of the intellectual and cultural tradition to which I had been introduced in Sydney in a setting appropriately mimicking that past. But even in those years I was beginning to experience an unease, the suspicion that the infatuation with the past that manifested itself in all manner of ways in English society was somehow to turn one's back on the present, to keep at arm's length a less than glamorous or noble reality.

It was precisely the respect for arcane hierarchies that proved more and more distressing the better I came to understand English society. It was evident enough even in London, that polyglot place which was not entirely Britain or England but enjoyed considerable extraterritoriality in a way that only a great cosmopolitan city could. I was appalled at the thought of what life might have been like in Oxford, where tradition had been enshrined with religious zeal. But even in

London I was at times brought up sharply by patterns of behaviour that seemed entirely at odds with a bustling, confident city in the second half of the twentieth century.

I never stopped being amazed by the arrogance of those who saw themselves as a cut above others: loud, florid men who would bulldoze their way through a queue at the cloakroom of a theatre; elaborately coiffed women ordering shop assistants around in their high-pitched voices on which elocutionists had obviously been hard at work. In the early sixties the class system remained largely unchanged despite almost two decades of the postwar welfare state. As remarkable as the arrogance of the upper orders was the respect paid to them by those who regarded themselves as their inferiors. A substantial portion of the population seemed devoted to their own subservience. Jim Carlton liked to tell the story of a young man in his office who was passionately devoted to music but would never consider attending a concert because he didn't own a dinner jacket and, what is more, thought it would not be appropriate for him to wear one. Those were the years when very casual dress began appearing at concerts and theatres—dinner jackets seemed entirely the preserve of one or two people you could see in the boxes at Covent Garden who would, in many cases, be fast asleep by the end of the first act. But Carlton's young colleague knew none of that: for him concerts, even in the 'democratic' Festival Hall, were not for his kind.

Of course, much had changed since the war. I grew accustomed to hearing all kinds of lamentation about the disintegration of society, the loss of values, about too many tourists in London, far too many black faces, the usual complaints of people incapable of accommodating change. There was evidence also of an insularity which had never disappeared from English life, but was becoming defensive rather than glorying in imperial might. My years in England coincided with the first round of negotiations between Britain and what then was known as the European Common Market. There was much outrage and anguish, especially since sinister plans were unveiled at around that time to attempt once more to dig a tunnel under the Channel. Where would it all end? Michael Baume, then working as a financial journalist in London, shuttled between London and Brussels reporting on the rapidly stalling negotiations for the Australian press. He would be gone for days and then reappear one evening, motorcycle helmet in hand, at the flat in Melbury Road, depressed at the way things were going. The British were too suspicious, he would say, too wrapped up in their increasingly unviable nationalism to seize their last opportunity to regain economic and political influence in Europe. They were too respectful towards traditions that were, in many cases, no more than empty shells. Though he did not say it in so many words, he also seemed aware of the dead hand of the lingering class system, which served to prohibit individuals and society as a whole from fulfilling their potential.

Once more our fool of a landlord, the pinstriped rake, provided the focus for that memorable lesson. Early in the winter of 1962 a great sulphurous fog descended on the city. Gradually life came to a standstill. Cars and buses disappeared from the streets; because of the extreme cold, rails and points froze on the Underground where it emerged from its tunnels. Within a day or two the system was brought to a halt. Yet day after day the cleaning lady somehow managed to turn up at Wyndham Place. One night, as I went downstairs to make sure that the front door was locked and the lights had been put out, a faint yellowish glow warned me that a light had been left burning in the broom cupboard. Inside, I found Miss Gilchrist huddled with her knees around her chin in that tiny space tucked in underneath the slope of the staircase. She looked startled, then confessed that she had been unable to get home. Why was she huddling in the cupboard? I asked. There were several chaises longues in the waiting room on the first floor. I offered to get her some blankets so she could bed down for the night. But she refused, embarrassed and alarmed. It wouldn't be right; what would Mr — think?

There was no persuading her. Eventually she agreed to accept the pillow, blanket and cup of tea we took down to her, muttering her gratitude and her conviction that it wasn't right to put us gentlemen out. She stayed there the whole night. I was appalled, guilty that we hadn't been more insistent and forced her to lie on one of the comfortable sofas in the waiting room. Yet even then, during a disturbed night when I couldn't help thinking about her growing stiff with cold in that cubbyhole, I began to realise that she was acting with considerable, though no doubt instinctive, prudence. The solicitor would not take kindly to such *lèse majésté*. It was one thing for him to use our beds, quite another for the charwoman to bed down on his sofa.

By that time I had decided more or less conclusively to return to Australia. Almost three years in London had taken the shine off my yearning for a world with a history. I had some misgivings about this decision, however, and thought that given the appropriate circumstances I might change my mind. In the meantime the decision was purely hypothetical for there remained the matter of my thesis, that other exercise in attempting to live within the confines of a perplexing and paradoxical tradition that seemed to value the past far more than it was involved in the present.

16

Half way through my scholarship I came to realise, with that hollow feeling you get in the stomach when a situation seems entirely without hope, that I could no longer afford to temporise, that I must try to fulfil the stringent requirements for a doctoral dissertation by engaging in a critical discussion of Shirley's plays.

Until then I could skirt around that impossible task by burying myself in the 'scholarship' I had been carrying out for almost eighteen months. After my stint in the Public Record Office I discovered several diversionary tactics. One was the venerable scholarly pursuit of hunting for source material. Playwrights of Shakespeare's age were great bowerbirds. They seemed to have a remarkable reluctance to invent plots for their plays, or perhaps they lacked the skill. But they displayed enormous ingenuity in finding stories and anecdotes in unlikely places, sometimes mixing two or three together in heady brews. Identifying sources for a play of the period was long considered a *sine qua non* for the expert. I remembered Thelma Herring, on whose shoulders so much of the teaching of the drama of the period fell in Sydney, lecturing endlessly (and to most of us incomprehensibly) about the dusty histories, collections of short stories, anecdotes and jests, creaking plays and the like which Shakespeare and his contemporaries raided and appropriated. I was never sure what relevance there might have been to such erudition. Of course, you could get a lot of academic mileage out of the fact, for instance, that Shakespeare's version of the story of King Lear and his three daughters is unique in allowing that domestic squabble to end in disaster with the death of the old king and his maligned daughter. But that was an exceptional case. Mostly, hunting for sources seemed a self-justifying activity, a branch of the world of learning which you did not question, only followed.

So I set about reading the mercifully few scholarly books and articles on Shirley to find out what had been said about his sources. I soon discovered an alarming possibility, a Pandora's box opening in front of me which would take a lifetime, it seemed, to close again. Unusually in his age, Shirley had some knowledge of Spanish. What is more, one sadistically unhelpful scholar claimed, he had made some use of Lope de Vega in several of his plays—without giving any further hint. I knew little about Shakespeare's Spanish contemporary apart from one terrible fact: he had written hundreds of plays. If, as the author of that learned essay suggested, one took into account two further Spanish dramatists whose work Shirley could have known, Tirso de Molina and Calderón de la Barca, the list of candidates probably stretched to a thousand plays or more. How could those Spaniards have been so prolific? I remember asking myself in despair.

I needed help. Brown was ill with the flu, Miss Hedberg, the secretary, told me with a strange look on her face. He'd be laid up at home in a suburb near Blackheath for a good few days. Schoenbaum seemed the next logical port of call. Sorry, he said, outside his period: nowadays he stopped in 1616, the year of Shakespeare's death. I couldn't decide whether he was being bloody-minded or whether he had managed to compartmentalise his professional life to such an extent that the year 1617, for instance, held as little interest for him as would 2017. I read a few of Lope's plays—only a fraction of his immense output had been translated into English—without becoming any the wiser. In a fit of bravado or desperation I bought a teach-yourself Spanish language book and began practising sentences about boys giving sweets to their sisters and mothers cooking delicious things for Sunday lunch. None of that brought me any closer to the great scholarly discovery I felt awaited me in those hoary Spanish entertainments.

Eventually Brown rose from his sickbed. I went one afternoon to the seminar at the Marlborough Arms: I'd learnt by then that you had a better chance of finding him there than in his room at University College. He seemed quite cheerful and refreshed. As on an earlier occasion, the suggestion of anything 'scholarly' immediately engaged his interest: he knew exactly whom to consult, mentioning the name of a scholar at Emmanuel College, Cambridge, a world authority on the drama of the Spanish Renaissance. He would arrange for me to see him.

Once more, he was as good as his word. Within a few days a postcard arrived from the eminent personage—to my shame I have forgotten his name, but I fancy it might have been Wilson—telling me that he could spare an hour or so one morning the following week. It was in such circumstances that I had my one professional contact with either of the great universities, Oxford or Cambridge.

I set out very early, just after daylight. It was one of those watery days when a fine mist softens the outlines of even the ugliest of railway yards, and turns a flat and unremarkable landscape into a prospect of shimmering beauty. Weak sunshine was dribbling through the mist as the train drew into the station at Cambridge; a few spires and odd corners of massive stone structures could just be discerned in the gaps between the commonplace buildings surrounding the station. I remember a feeling of nostalgia and regret as I made my way, map in hand, in the direction of Emmanuel. Had I been right in turning my back on this world?

The farther I got from the station, the lovelier Cambridge became. As I walked among the great buildings, with delicate carved tracery and massive gateways of time-worn oak, young people on bicycles swept past me, their glows billowing out behind them (just as I'd seen at the pictures in Sydney), and I had an irresistible sense of missed opportunities, of what seemed for the moment a great miscalculation. Perhaps here, surrounded by calm and beauty, I might have found something more satisfying than the struggle to make something out of Shirley's dreary plays, the soporific world of the North Library, or the pools of spilled beer that gradually covered the tables at the Marlborough. I remember arriving at Emmanuel College in a state of depression, and also conscious of my inferiority when the porter, inspecting a typed list, confirmed—superciliously I fancied—that indeed the eminent scholar had an appointment with someone from London. He lifted the telephone receiver to warn him of my arrival. I recall walking across a quadrangle, up a narrow, twisting flight of stairs to a landing where I found the appropriate door, then knocking gently.

The expert on Spanish Renaissance drama received me in a friendly enough way. I think he made some tea but I may just be imagining it, because that is the kind of thing you would expect in a place such as Cambridge. His room looked much like Brown's study: jumbles of books, folders, loose sheets of paper everywhere. I noticed that the ceiling bulged in a crazy way, vouching for the authenticity of that environment. The window overlooked the quadrangle I think, but I was too nervous to take much in. The celebrated scholar tried to put me at my ease. He gave a short disquisition on the differences between Spanish and English drama of the sixteenth and early seventeenth centuries. I recounted the main plots and situations of those of Shirley's plays for which no sources had been discovered. He shook his head: no, they rang no bells. But he suggested some books on Lope de Vega I might consult. And that was that; it was time for his next appointment.

I had arranged to visit an acquaintance who was living in digs in the suburbs, one of the young men who haunted the flat in Melbury Road during vacation time. He seemed in a particularly disheartened mood. He hated Cambridge, he said: so stuffy, so boring and so bloody cold when the east wind blew. He could hardly wait to finish and move to London.

I pressed on with Lope and the other Spaniards for a week or two but soon realised that it was a hopeless task. I imagined myself as one of those eccentric nineteenth-century gentlemen scholars who could devote their lives to tracking down every botanical reference, for instance, in Shakespeare. But I had a thesis to write, so I began looking in more accessible places for the elusive discovery that would allow me to claim that it incorporated original material. I was lucky. By chance almost I came upon a passage in a wordy sixteenth-century translation of Machiavelli's history of Florence which had been, beyond doubt it seemed to me, the inspiration for one of Shirley's best-known plays, a lurid blood-and-guts melodrama *The Traitor*. It was not much, but at least all that threshing around had produced something. Brown was pleased again. Once more he said that it was a contribution, and would arrange for me to publish a short note in the prestigious *Review of English Studies*. I was inordinately proud when it appeared, some time after my return to Sydney, even though it had been set in small type at the back of the journal among all the other minor 'notes'.

Nevertheless, trying to patch a thesis together left me feeling cynical and deep in gloom. Was the world of scholarship all sham? Were those dedicated people around me, the celebrated scholars too, chasing after rainbows, deluding themselves about their perceptiveness, the logical and irrefutable grounds on which they were proceeding. Or was I alone among them the con-man, the illusionist? I began to fear the truth of that. Yet some voice of reason inside my head suggested otherwise: surely the enterprise itself was questionable, or at least trivial and meretricious. Again, I tried to cheer myself up in the way I had done months earlier in the Public Record Office: I was learning a craft, almost a trade; there would be time enough in the future to apply what I had learnt to something worthwhile. The trouble was that I couldn't imagine what that might be. I was turning sour, crabby. The shine had been taken off the romance of old books, old worlds where, I had thought only a year or two earlier, I could find a way of life to sustain and satisfy me—just as the wonder of living in England had been replaced by the commonplace and the familiar and also the occasional bouts of irritation they brought.

My depression had a curious effect. It confirmed me in the determination that I must finish my thesis as quickly as I could in order to find a job and earn some money. Not for a moment did I consider chucking it all in and living in a garret or joining the Foreign

Legion. And I was still convinced that I wanted more than anything else to teach in a university. It was all, I realised, a tissue of contradictions, but my calling, such as it might be, was to teach. As for the rest—scholarship and criticism, the claptrap of academic preening—they were necessary evils.

So I set about stitching the bits and pieces I had gathered into what I hoped would pass for a thesis.

I did not commit any of the cardinal sins of the scholarly and academic life. I did not lift slabs of other people's work; I did not invent evidence in the hope that no-one would be perspicacious enough to prove me wrong. In short, I observed all the forms and ceremonies. And yet I constructed a largely illusory edifice, as I had done in a way during my student days in Sydney. I believed in the truth of the thesis which—I found to my horror and delight—was more or less writing itself, as little as I believed in the 'truth' of that revue sketch about a collection of Chekovian caricatures or the man who announced the time on the telephone. Both they and *A Study of the Life and Works of James Shirley* were essentially parodic. For my thesis I adopted a suitably learned tone of utterance and tried to construct as plausible a simulacrum of a genuine thesis (whatever that might be) as I could manage.

In one way it proved remarkably easy, especially when I came to that substantial part which I had been dreading and putting off for far too long: the critical discussion. Earlier, that had seemed to me the impenetrable barrier to my success. How could I discuss critically—that is to say according to the conventions of academic discourse then current—something as transparent and undemanding as those occasionally entertaining, often dull plays? I had no room to move because the emphasis in those days lay very much on the difficult and the intractable: the more obscure or contorted a text, the more respectable academic fodder it seemed to offer. Nowadays I would be in a happier situation: I could turn Shirley's inanity to my advantage by pointing out how his complaisant heroines, always subservient to fathers or lovers, were products of patriarchal repression; the obsession with personal honour an unconscious glossing over of a cruel and exploitative social order; the absence of common folk (except as the occasional comic servant or yokel) a sign of the marginalisation of all those who fell outside the hegemonic hierarchies of the court and the rapidly burgeoning mercantile classes. But such options were not open to me: those elements in the plays were merely instances of the seventeenth century's *Zeitgeist*; to draw attention to them would have been regarded as solecisms, an unwarranted stressing of the obvious fact that the period's view of the world was different from ours. Having realised that there was nothing vital to be said about those undemanding plays, I started finding that there were, after all, things I could say, even though very little seemed to me either important or inevitable.

I went on, therefore, to construct some sort of shadow-theory of Shirley's significance for the drama of Shakespeare's age. The fundamental point of my thesis depended on the fact that the last of his plays was in rehearsal in 1642, just at the time when the God-fearing Long Parliament ordered theatres to close. I discovered that I could make a great deal out of that little fact—or enough anyway to present Shirley's plays as compendia of characters, situations, theatrical tricks and devices, even turns of phrase that had contributed to the popular success of Shakespeare and some of his contemporaries. The plays emerged as affectionate but mechanical imitations of earlier, more robust ways. And to my great surprise my 'theory' was beginning to make sense—enough at any rate to allow me to trace a line through the twenty-odd years of Shirley's career as a playwright to demonstrate how efficiently he had worked over the spirit if not the actual contents of famous plays by older writers and responded to changes in taste and fashion. Towards the end of my writing, I began to suffer from that most pernicious of academic diseases: self-satisfaction.

Brown, I discovered, had no interest whatever in my attempts at writing a critical commentary. By then he had more or less given up acting as a supervisor—placing in me the first seeds of the suspicion that however my thesis turned out, I would be awarded my doctorate because it would prove too embarrassing to him otherwise. At the same time, I began to regret that I had been frustrated in writing about a much more interesting figure, and about plays which, while no more demanding than Shirley's, were at least unusual, thus justifying the business of critical commentary, an activity that came to seem more and more dubious as I worked away at a thesis for which I had less and less regard as the weeks passed.

The detachment and indifference helped, nevertheless. In the autumn of 1962 I found, a little to my surprise, that the main body of the thesis was finished. All that remained was to gain Brown's imprimatur, prepare a bibliography and have my messy, much annotated typescript turned into more or less professional-looking work. Several times I tried to encourage Brown to read the draft; at last he decided that he would like to look at the final typescript, reminding me that the rules of the university allowed a certain number of ink corrections on each page. I suspected that this was his ruse to gain time, to put off the business of reading something which he probably thought of, quite accurately it seemed to me, as a tedious chore.

I rented a bulky Underwood office machine from a supplier a few blocks from Wyndham Place. I staggered the short distance to the flat with the wretched thing cradled in my arms. By the time I reached the top of the stairs I was ready to drop from exhaustion. I bought massive quantities of typing paper, boxes of carbon paper, and little strips of tipex for the inevitable corrections. Prue Page, a friend who made a living as a relief teacher, needed time away from classrooms and hooligans. She was—still is no doubt—an excellent typist. For the next month or two she spent days in the flat clattering out *A Study of the Life and Works of James Shirley*. She couldn't work at home, she said, there were too many distractions in the flat she shared with her sister and several friends from Sydney. So I thought it best to keep out of her way, leave the place to her to get on with the job. I had time on my hands.

17

I spent my last months in London in a curious state of indecision. Just as I was putting the finishing touches to my thesis, I received a disturbing letter from Milgate. He had decided to retire early as the Challis Professor of English Literature. The letter was evasive, with a sinister undercurrent of levity: he had grown tired, he wrote, of all the administration, the mindless, repetitive tasks a professor was called on to carry out. It was all too much; so he resolved to call it a day.

Wilkes wrote too. Everyone expected him to succeed Milgate; the common wisdom in Sydney was that he had become the unquestioned heir. His letter certainly read as if he had expected to be the next incumbent of the chair. It said little about Milgate, except for what I already knew. But he did mention that a lectureship would be advertised shortly, and urged me to apply. When it appeared, the advertisement called for applicants with expertise in sixteenth- and seventeenth-century drama. It would have been foolish not to apply. I assembled the requisite referees, including (with some misgivings) Schoenbaum, whom I had begun to mistrust. I kept on remembering the afternoon in Brown's study when he steered me away from Brome into the arms of Shirley. Where was the definitive study of Brome which he had insisted was on the point of being published? I put my suspicions out of my head and completed my application. I wasn't entirely certain, however, that I wanted the job, that I wanted to return to Australia. The aimless weeks during which Prue was typing my thesis provided wonderful opportunities for brooding and indecision.

Now that the possibility of leaving behind England, London and the British Museum Reading Room had arisen, I found myself looking at what had become familiar and commonplace with sharpened eyes. As I wandered around in the autumnal city, something of the first thrill of living there returned. The days grew shorter. The leaves on the trees turned a dusty brown-grey, then fell, forming great squashy piles in parks and gardens. Old stone and warm, red brick took on a watery shimmer. Great landmarks—Big Ben, Nelson on top of the column in Trafalgar Square, the Duke of York on his, the dome of St Paul's glimpsed from a bridge across the Thames, the Albert Memorial rising above the bare trees in Kensington Gardens—and also everyday, domestic places were transfigured by the rising mists. The lights in shops and windows came on earlier and earlier. The weather turned cold. I experienced a marvellous sense of well-being as I walked through the doors of an over-heated cafe or a Lyon's Corner House. The last of the tourists left. London was returned to its true owners, among whom I now counted myself.

I realised how fond I'd grown of the city. Fondness led to tolerance. I discovered some pleasure even in the seminars at the Marlborough. Perhaps I had grown used to their rituals, or perhaps I had been accepted. Even Smith's vileness seemed somehow less objectionable. That too, I came to suspect, was part of the tradition, of the layers of the past that gave substance and charm to life in the city. It may not have been the most attractive experience London or England could offer—as indeed our landlord's amours or the Davieses' endless squabbles were not—but it was part and parcel of a life that came to seem increasingly civilised as the prospect of leaving it behind became likely. It was an aspect of the mellowness, from which decay was never far distant. I wondered what it would be like to return to Sydney's pitiless sunshine and to the sharp corners and raw edges of life it revealed. I thought ruefully, too, about the textures of suburban life, having enjoyed the many blessings of living in the heart of a great city, despite all the inconveniences which now seemed almost inconsequential. Even the Simons and Jeremys braying in the Underground had a certain style, I persuaded myself. They were preferable to the beery creatures in ill-fitting suits I used to see in trams and trains in Sydney with folded copies of the *Mirror* or the *Sun* tucked under their arms.

My premature nostalgia embraced, naturally enough, the British Museum. The echoing rotunda, the eccentrics, the shabby scholars, the rituals of the North Library had become part of my life. I would miss them if I left, even though I was sufficiently self-aware to know that if I were to stay in London, I would not have the patience and dedication of those around me—Ann Keep, for instance, who worked day after day at her translations; the red-faced Russian, reputedly one of Ottoline Morrell's minor lovers in his youth, who had been trying for decades to establish some collateral link with the Romanovs; the old lady, swathed in shawls summer and winter, who was writing a life of Byron. I knew that I would grow restless and disconsolate, shutting my books more and more frequently to stand besides one of the brass ashtrays fixed to the wall just outside the entrance to the museum. And yet to grow impatient in such a place seemed a privilege to be treasured, not to be abandoned lightly.

Staying on had become, as it turned out, something a trifle more than a daydream. Brown and even Smith dropped the odd, ambiguous hint over slops of beer in the Marlborough. Nothing definite, certainly nothing they could be held to, but they suggested that perhaps, if things worked out that way, they could use someone who knew about the minor dramatists of Shakespeare's time, a field that was fast becoming neglected. But then, their hints seemed also to suggest, things might work out otherwise.

I realised that I lacked adventurousness—or perhaps my reserves of risk-taking had been used up during the war and in my far less threatening career as a mimic and parodist in Sydney. When I received a telegram from the Registrar of the University of Sydney announcing that I had been appointed to the vacant position, subject to the success of my thesis, I wired back the next morning accepting the job.

18

As the world seemed on the brink of destruction during the Cuban missile crisis, Prue Page finished typing the thesis. All that was required was for Brown to give it his seal of approval. I left the bulky typescript with Miss Hedberg one morning. She promised to get it to him immediately—I impressed on her that it was essential to have it examined in time for me to sail for Sydney at the end of December.

A long silence followed. Day after day I would go looking for Brown at the Marlborough or at University College. Miss Hedberg was embarrassed and evasive: he was home with the flu, she didn't know when he would be well enough to come to work. After a while she relented. Handing me a folded slip of paper, she suggested I should ring Brown at home, adding that she wasn't supposed to give his telephone number to students. With my heart in my mouth I dialled the seven digits. Brown sounded slurred and breathy. Perhaps I'd come out to pick up the manuscript, he suggested.

The great smog that was to imprison poor Miss Gilchrist in a broom cupboard had just begun to hang over London: British rail advised that suburban train services were prone to long delays and suspensions of timetables. I borrowed Jim's car and drove through the chaos and murk towards Blackheath. At first no-one seemed to be at home in the nondescript semi-detached villa where Brown lived. Then the door opened, and there he was, red-eyed and not entirely steady on his feet. Frightful flu, he said, would I like a drink? I refused as politely as I could. He led me into a large, untidy room, almost a replica of his study at University College. It took him an eternity to find the typescript among the piles of books, folders and papers littering the floor. Finally he came upon the two volumes, finding each under a different pile. 'Very good,' he mumbled, adding that I could submit—he'd made a few suggestions in the margin that I should look at.

I drove back to Central London in a fog so thick that the lights of the car were thrown back into my face. It was only good luck or providence that guided me home intact. In my flat, shaking and exhausted, I riffled through the pages to find Brown's annotations. There was almost nothing.

The viva voce followed a few weeks later. It was, I realised, merely a ceremony: Brown made almost no contribution to the ritual. His co-examiner asked a few questions, and then I was told to wait outside while they conferred. It must have taken ten minutes, fifteen at the most, but to me it seemed a lifetime. Finally the door opened and Brown called me in. Perhaps it was time for a pint at the Marlborough, he said, going on to mention, in the most casual way imaginable, that I would be granted the degree provided I corrected a few typographical errors and a couple of inaccurate dates. That task took me two or three hours; then it was over.

All that remained was to get my affairs in order and set sail for Sydney. The university had booked a passage for me in the splendour of first class on the new superliner *Canberra*, the pride of the P&O fleet. In a sense I cut myself adrift from London, from my life in England, as soon as I had escaped the Marlborough on that winter afternoon. There was too much to do, too little time to be plagued by those second thoughts that had come to me when I accepted the job in Sydney. I was looking forward to a three-week holiday on the boat and then to the beginning of a new life, my part in the great endeavour of civilising a raw and unformed world. I packed my belongings, which were to travel in the hold of the ship; I attended to the paperwork required by the two universities—one for the corrections to the thesis and arrangements for having the deposit copies properly bound, the other for my new academic post.

Then it was Christmas. A group of us had been invited to spend the holidays in Herefordshire. We set out for Staunton-on-Arrow early in the morning of Christmas Eve. It had started snowing by the time we reached the Cotswolds. A nice White Christmas, I thought, remembering the searing heat of Sydney at Christmastime. It was dark by the time we arrived. Approaching the Davieses' house, we had driven through tunnels of snow piled high on either side of the narrow road. We hurried with our bags along a roughly cleared path at the side of the house. A biting wind from the east made my skin tingle, then lose all sensation. Mrs Davies, showing us into the living room, said that she expected we could all do with some tea. One of our friends, who had been working for some time in Paris as an au pair, got very excited. It would be wonderful to have real tea, after those dreadful teabags the French insisted on using, she announced just before she caught sight of a couple of tags dangling out of a fine silver teapot. Then, when we had thawed out a little, we were shown to our rooms.

My farewell to English life could not have been better arranged. The next few days turned out to be a mixture of charm, eccentricity and high farce, encapsulating in that large, poorly heated farmhouse both the most attractive and civilised aspects of Anglo-Saxon attitudes and their troubling undercurrents.

A dinner party had been arranged for Christmas Eve. It would be an informal affair, we had been told: we need not bother to bring dinner jackets. In the early evening, as the wind grew stronger and the snow began to fall again, the guests arrived. First to come was a girl of twenty or so, Hermione, dressed as I remember in one of those stiff-skirted taffetta affairs women wore to parties and dances in those years. Because the skirt did not reach the ground, Hermione was, strictly speaking, informally clad. She was accompanied by a middle-aged gentleman in a clerical collar. Captain Davies made the introductions. Then Mrs Davies appeared. The vicar would be staying for dinner, she assumed. Ah no, the gentleman—whose parish of Eardisland adjoined Staunton-on-Arrow and its wretched church and incompetent organist—reminded her that he had only one eye. It was difficult enough driving Hermione over in the dark—he'd better be getting back seeing that the snow was falling heavily. Yes, he did have time for a glass of sherry. But there was one thing: how would Hermione get home?

A short conference took place. Jim Carlton offered to drive her home; he knew where to go. The Captain put his foot down: no, it would be unsafe in Jim's small Vauxhall. Hermione must stay the night. Hermione looked pleased, but then Mrs Davies put her oar in. Michael would take her home, she announced, in his Landrover. And that was the last word. The vicar finished his sherry and said goodbye, wishing everyone the compliments of the season.

Michael, the owner of the Landrover, arrived as the Captain and Mrs Davies were farewelling the vicar at the door. 'Go in and introduce yourself, Michael,' we could hear Mrs Davies saying to him. A tweedy young man with a small moustache, just a few years older than we were by the look of him, walked into the room. Then, glancing round, he announced: 'Mmmmmichael Kkkkking Kkkkking'. Over drinks we discussed the weather and Hermione's plight. Michael wasn't sure whether he could drive her to Eardisland: he lived in the other direction, down in Wales, it turned out. But Mrs Davies pressed on; from some reason she was reluctant for Hermione to stay the night. Finally Michael King-King (for such indeed was his name) agreed. But he musn't be late, otherwise Mmmmother would be worried.

We went into dinner. After the customary smoked salmon and capers, Mrs Davies produced the first in what proved in the next few days to be a succession of tough, undercooked turkeys. We hacked and chewed our way through our portions in near silence. The effort had rendered conversation difficult; and besides, it turned out that despite his impediment Michael King-King was a compulsive talker, a dedicated anecdotist. I have long forgotten the subject of his monologues: you were so intent on waiting for the words to come that their sense or sequence became almost a secondary consideration. Then the plum pudding arrived, with brandy that refused to flame properly, and brick-like hard sauce. We would have coffee in the drawing room, the Captain announced, leading us to a seldom-used room correctly furnished with uncomfortable chairs and sofas. We sat in tense near-silence. The Captain, perhaps sensing the awkwardness, launched into reminiscences of his years in Mexico, which some of us had heard several times already. Then he declared that it was time to unveil his wife's Christmas present—he wanted her to enjoy it now rather than to have to wait until the next day.

He led the party into the kitchen where we waited while he disappeared into the pantry. A moment later he was back wheeling an object on castors, covered with a sheet. Whipping the sheet off, he stood proudly beside a small dishwasher of a kind I had seen in several London flats with tiny kitchens. There was a round of applause. Then the Captain began loading the machine with the fine, transparent china and old silver they had used in honour of the season.

We watched in silence, realising that he hadn't remembered to scrape the plates before stacking them or to connect the hoses to the taps. I wondered whether something should be said, but thought better of it. None of my business, I decided with extreme cowardice. When the machine was filled, the Captain plugged in the electric cord and the contraption began wheezing and rattling, and sliding slowly across the kitchen floor. A moment or two later it started emitting dense smoke and then, with a crackle, the lights went out. The Captain felt his way around the walls of the kitchen until he came on a flashlight on top of a shelf. He rang the local electricity board. The operator apparently told him that burnt-out fuses were not regarded as an emergency, especially on Christmas Eve and particularly when the road from Leominster was treacherous, if not impassable. Jim and I offered to look at the fuse box. I held the torch while Jim soon had the power restored. Back in the kitchen Mrs Davies opened the lid of the dishwasher with a teatowel wrapped around her hand. Inside, pieces of turkey, stuffing, potato, peas and gravy had congealed into a hideous, nauseating mess. There was nothing for it, the Captain declared, but to fetch Mrs Beddoes.

Michael King-King, suspecting perhaps that his Landrover would be called into service, said that he must be going, especially if he was to take Hhhhermmmmione to Eardisland. She, who had spoken hardly a word all night, smiled sweetly. The thought occurred to me that Mrs Davies might have been indulging in a spot of matchmaking. So off they went in the Landrover. The Captain, rugged up against the cold, said that he would drive down to the dairy. He was gone only a few minutes, coming back with an ancient, bent crone, a figure out of a gruesome folktale or a Gothic romance, obviously Mrs Beddoes. And like all creatures of legend, she was muttering dark imprecations about newfangled gee-gaws. I wondered whether she had put a curse on the Captain's present. She set about scraping the congealed muck from plates and dishes and washing them in clouds of suds.

Later that night, while trying not to freeze to death in bed, I was struck by something that had come to me often during my first weeks in England, and kept returning when London became a familiar and even a cherished place. It was, I realised again, hard to believe sometimes that the English were real. There seemed something fundamentally theatrical about them, as if they were acting out roles, or constantly playing to an audience of outsiders. I sometimes wondered whether the braying in the tube was for my benefit alone or, when I eavesdropped on my neighbour at the opera expounding a very approximate version of the action of *La traviata* to his wide-eyed girlfriend just before the curtain went up on the Egyptian temple where the first scene of *Aida* is set, whether the rest of the public in the theatre were his real audience. There was Brown's snuff-rag too, besides a thousand other, insignificant instances. And now Mrs Beddoes. Had the Davieses arranged the whole charade as a Christmas entertainment for their colonial guests? Perhaps Mmmmichael Kkkking Kkkking, and the one-eyed Vicar of Eardisland, the sweetly smiling Hermione, Captain and Mrs Davies and Humphrey in his stable were also fantasies, chimeras.

So those Christmas days in Herefordshire took on the qualities of an improbable farce. Yet I have also retained memories of beauty and mellowness. I remember the golden glow of the low-lying sun as it struck the drifts of snow around the house. The delicate, almost heartbreaking beauty of bare branches against a pale, grey-blue sky. We visited a frail elderly couple in a small manor house protected from gales and sheets of snow by low, bare mounds—hills or prehistoric barrows, you could not tell which. Inside, fire crackled in the grate and pieces of old Chelsea and Rockingham reflected the leaping flames. At church on Christmas Day, where the Captain roared his usual injunctions about the collection plate, it was hard not to be moved by some sense of the numinous and the miraculous, no matter how much a rational or cynical self might have mocked that improbable tale of a virgin birth. And it made curious sense when we sang 'The Holly and the Ivy' or even 'Good King Wenceslas'. The traditions, as much as the theology, of those old rituals might have been questionable, outmoded in the contemporary world, and yet they made connections with richly textured experiences and possibilities of life for which—I came to realise—the mock-Gothic splendours of the University of Sydney were no substitute.

We left for London the day after Boxing Day. The trip was long and hazardous. Because of the condition of some of the roads, we were forced to make a detour by way of Oxford. In the failing light of afternoon we caught a glimpse of spires and domes rising above a misty horizon. At that moment I felt again a pang of regret that I had turned my back on that world. In the evening, we stopped at a pub somewhere in the Thames Valley. The snow crunched under our shoes as we made for the door. Inside, the warmth and the mingled smell of beer and food were welcome and comforting. We sat far too long over our half pints and veal and ham pies, reluctant to hazard snow and ice once more. When Jim and I got back to the flat in Wyndham Place we found a long, tapering needle of ice suspended from the ceiling-height lip of the cistern, reaching almost the whole way to the red linoleum of the bathroom floor.

It snowed hard on my last night in England. At first it seemed as if the trains to Southampton would not be able to run. I waited for many hours in an angry, desperate crowd at Waterloo. Eventually the trains left, arriving at the docks many hours after sailing time. We were relieved to see the ship still at its moorings. A few days later, after calling in at Naples, the *Canberra* caught fire in the middle of the night. We were told that we would have to stay on board the smoke-filled vessel until tugs could be sent from Belfast to tow it into port. This could take weeks, perhaps a month, we were informed. Then the ship's engineers managed to get one screw to turn at half-speed. We limped into Malta. After several days of confusion and skulduggery from bloated, pink-faced and wholly inept officials of the shipping company, who had flown out from London to deal with the emergency, I managed to convert my fare into an aeroplane ticket to Sydney. A few days later I caught sight of Blacket's clock tower, the Great Hall and the Quadrangle as the 707 I had been travelling on from Rome, for an eternity it seemed, broke through a thick cover of cloud on its final approach.

PART II

CULTURE AND ANARCHY

1

In accordance with a custom that probably went back to the university's earliest days, members of the academic staff arriving from abroad were usually met at the dockside by a senior representative of their discipline. Though I was returning to my own university, I too would have been met by someone, Wilkes no doubt, at Circular Quay had the *Canberra* docked there, as scheduled, in the last week of January 1963. As things turned out, when I arrived at Sydney airport early one morning, only my anxious and relieved parents were waiting. I had managed to telephone them from Rome, after several unsuccessful attempts as the line fell out at Aden or Colombo, and a heavily accented voice announced that the connection with Sydney could not be made. Should they tell the department, my father asked over the whine and crackle, when I managed finally to get through, but I thought there would be little point to it: they would all be on holidays.

I discovered, nevertheless, that almost everyone was in Sydney in that sticky January. Two or three days after arriving, when I had caught up on sleep and spent some time with my parents, I made an appointment with the Registrar, Miss Telfer, and left a message with Wilkes to say that I had got home safely.

Miss Telfer welcomed me and listened with amusement to the tale of my adventures at sea. I mentioned to her that a refund from the shipping company would arrive in due course. I wasn't to worry about that, she replied. Why not regard it as danger money? We shook hands, and I went off in search of Wilkes and whomever else would happen to be around.

I arrived in time for morning tea. That proved the first tiny inkling of a changing world. The department no longer assembled, I discovered, in the Muniment Room, but in an alcove that had been partitioned off from the landing at the top of a staircase. Inside this small makeshift room members of the department sat around a large polished table. There was no space for them to stand in small groups, as had been the custom in the Muniment Room. My first impression as I looked at the gathering was of a committee or a board meeting. It was, perhaps, an early sign of the bureaucratisation of the university that was to creep up on us in the course of the next three decades.

I saw many familiar faces that morning, and also some people I had not met before. In the two and a half years I had been away from the department, the university had grown. Those were the palmy days of generous funding, which allowed all manner of innovation: for instance, a comprehensive system of weekly tutorials in all three years of the basic undergraduate course in English, as well as a slight reduction in the monstrous load of teaching most academics had to endure in earlier, more parsimonious days. A large number of new appointments had been made in most faculties. Three decades later that was to result in the university's becoming top-heavy with senior people at the higher end of salary ranges, a cause of some anguish to younger academics who saw their own prospects of promotion blocked, and a golden opportunity for increasingly suspicious and hostile administrators to demolish the well-established system of tenure.

I remember being a little apprehensive on that first morning. The transition from student to colleague had begun during my half-year as a teaching fellow. But now I was a fully tenured member of staff, entitled to greater familiarity with people who seemed at one time to have dwelt on an exalted plane. I was unsure of what tone to adopt as those were still the days of some formality. My worry was how to address certain people, whether I should take the initiative in the first-names stakes or wait for the appropriate signals. Fortunately, the one person who had shown me any ill-will, Harold Oliver, had left to take up the foundation chair of English at the University of New South Wales. He had left, I heard, because he realised that he stood no chance of beating Wilkes to the Challis chair. I got the impression that no one missed him, and I was certainly relieved that I would not have to deal with him.

That morning, and for several weeks afterwards, my colleagues went out of their way to be friendly and to help me through the difficult transition to a new life. I had no doubt that their goodwill was entirely genuine; there remained at that time a measure of collegiality among most academics, a matter of style and *esprit de corps* no matter what personal, intellectual or even ideological differences might have divided them. If faculties and departments were quarrelsome, as the Department of English was said to have been during my undergraduate years, people took care to contain their disputatiousness within the bounds of well-established conventions. In later years those conventions came to be seen as evidence of the fundamental hypocrisy of academic life; for me they remain as emblems of a more civilised mode of conduct than the contemporary fashion for strident ideological and personal battles, which are often conducted in the full glare of publicity.

Nevertheless, my colleagues' interest in me was tinged by a certain anxiety. They knew that a few months earlier I had met the new Challis Professor, S. L. Goldberg, formerly a senior lecturer in English at the University of Melbourne. As is the devious and vindictive way of most universities, the higher powers seemed to take umbrage at the universal assumption that Wilkes would succeed Milgate in a smooth transition of power from reigning monarch to heir apparent. No doubt they had decided to spike such presumption and to teach the underlings a thing or two about power by appointing the outsider. It had happened before; it was to happen again. Goldberg's surprising appointment was merely my first experience of the quixotic way in which many senior academic posts are filled.

Most of the people in the Sydney department were apprehensive. Some, no doubt, were secretly pleased that Wilkes had been taken down a peg or two. Yet a small and enclosed society like a university department is always fearful of change: universities, even in their most radical phases, are profoundly conservative in spirit. Members of the Sydney department had further cause for anxiety. There had always been suspicion and rivalry between the two oldest universities, which usually manifested itself as their ignoring each other. But Goldberg's hostility to the style and aspirations of the Sydney department was known to be far more extensive and deeply rooted. People feared for their future as much as for their discipline.

I was the harbinger, the one who had laid eyes on the threatening figure of power. Sitting at the highly polished table in the new common room, and in conversations throughout the weeks that followed, my colleagues came back time and time again to the nagging questions: What was he like? What did I make of him?

2

I told them as much as I thought prudent, but I was incapable of being entirely candid—with myself as much, perhaps, as with my colleagues. I felt it unwise to speak openly about my own misgivings and apprehensiveness after my first (and with hindsight disastrous) encounter with someone who would be able to exercise almost unlimited power over most of us, especially over me, the newest and rawest recruit to his empire. I fudged and finessed, but I think I fooled no one; they seemed to realise only too well that I was uneasy.

Some months earlier I had stumbled on an odd little scene in the London office of the Commercial Banking Company of Sydney, the university's bankers, where instalments of my scholarship payments were deposited. One morning, when I had called in at the bank to see if that month's money had arrived, I caught sight of a group of familiar faces—among them Ralph Farrell, Professor of German and Dean-elect of the Faculty of Arts in Sydney—deep in conversation. One of the group, standing at a slight distance from the others in a *tableau vivant*, was unfamiliar to me. I gave little thought to the incident: I was far more worried about the state of my finances and the likelihood that the monthly instalment had not arrived.

By that time Milgate had written to me to say that he had decided to retire. Another letter from Wilkes confirmed that he had been appointed acting head of the literature section of the department. Shortly before catching sight of that group in the bank I had sent off the cable accepting the position in Sydney, expecting that I would be working for Wilkes, whom I liked and admired.

Then came a more circumspect letter, saying that Wilkes had accepted the foundation chair of Australian Literature, established after considerable delay and controversy. Dr Colin Roderick of Angus and Robertson had launched a public appeal for the endowment of the nation's first professorship in its own literature. He had hoped, gossip insisted, to be appointed to the position. The response turned out, however, to be disappointing: insufficient money had been subscribed to fund the chair. Eventually the university came to the rescue by finding the amount necessary to top up the sum raised by the public appeal. It insisted, however, that certain conditions be written into the terms of appointment. Those clauses, all but ignored at the time of the chair's foundation, were to assume a role of extraordinary importance two years after Wilkes's appointment. Wilkes's letter went on to say that as Professor of Australian Literature he would remain a member of the department. The Challis chair had gone, however, to S. L. Goldberg from Melbourne. What is more, he wrote, Goldberg was currently in London on a Nuffield Fellowship.

I was alarmed by the news. I sensed disappointment and even perhaps anger beneath Wilkes's measured, businesslike words. It occurred to me that there was a warning in the remark that Goldberg was in London. Yet I still made no connection between that unexpected turn of events and the group of people I had glimpsed standing in the bank. There was far too much to preoccupy me.

Not long afterwards, I received one of those buff-coloured postcards British academics liked to use for their correspondence, the precursors, perhaps, of the e-mail or the facsimile message. It was from Goldberg. He'd heard that I was coming to the end of my postgraduate work. Perhaps I would like to have dinner with him and his wife, the note went on: it is always good to meet fellow Australians. I rang him and arranged to have dinner with the Goldbergs in the Nuffield flats opposite the zoo in Regent's Park. I was a little uneasy, but nothing in our brief phone conversation warned me that the evening might be a spectacular disaster. Nor did I tumble to the possibility that Goldberg was the man I had seen among those Sydney academics in the bank.

On my way to the Goldbergs' flat I took with me a copy of the weekly magazine *Spectator*. The issue had been out for some time by then: Ann Keep, as I recall, had given it to me because it contained an amusing correspondence about a recent cultural and literary scandal. It concerned an attack F. R. Leavis, the well-known Cambridge academic, had made on the novelist and civil servant C. P. Snow. Three years earlier Snow had delivered the Rede Lecture at Cambridge which, in its much publicised printed form, came to be known as *The Two Cultures and the Scientific Revolution*. His thesis was commonplace enough: Snow argued that in Britain no civilised or cultivated person could afford to be ignorant of literature and the arts. Nuclear physicists found it incumbent on them to be conversant with Shakespeare, biochemists with Leonardo and Goya. The reverse, according to Snow, did not hold true. A literary figure or an academic in the humanities could remain ignorant of, for instance, the Second Law of Thermodynamics with a good conscience. His lecture was, in essence, a plea for the readjustment of that imbalance.

In 1962 Snow's views provoked an intemperate response from Leavis in another public lecture—it provided the basis for the opening section of Leavis's book *Nor Shall My Sword*. Leavis's attack on Snow was peppered with the usual *ad hominem* imprecations, which are never far removed from academic disputes. Snow, according to Leavis, was a shabby thinker and poor novelist: the success of his prosaic and unimaginative novels was no more than an indication of the debasement of contemporary culture. The argument of Snow's lecture, Leavis declared, was wholly fallacious. To equate familiarity with Shakespeare with knowledge of the Second Law of Thermodynamics was to display regrettable insensitivity to the fundamental and indispensable conditions of civilisation, our only guarantees against barbarism.

And so Leavis's attack went on. It was little more than a rehashing of the science versus humanities debate of Victorian England, enshrined a century earlier in Matthew Arnold's tract *Culture and Anarchy*. Like Arnold, Leavis allowed no quarter to the scientific and technological sectors of society; and as with Arnold, Leavis's extreme reaction to Snow's lecture was coloured by deep hostilities and resentments of a kind only possible in a rigidly hierarchical, class-ridden world. When Leavis, the Cambridge don, took the popular novelist and technocrat to task, he was attacking with equal fury what he saw as the privileged position of the uncouth and the philistine in modern British society.

The issue of the *Spectator* I had taken along with me in such blissful ignorance contained a spirited defence of Snow by members of that very establishment which had provoked Leavis's ire. There were letters from notables in all walks of life, but particularly in the arts, including one, I recall, from Dame Edith Sitwell, who had been coaxed out of the reclusiveness of her last years to leap to Snow's defence. I had just enough time on the short journey to read those elegantly insulting letters; then I folded the magazine and pushed it into the pocket of my overcoat with (as I realised later) the banner announcing its sensational contents clearly visible. I gave that no thought as Goldberg took my coat from me in his cosy, well-heated flat. I was much more struck by the fact that this was the person I had seen with that group of Sydney people a few weeks earlier.

I knew nothing about Goldberg, and I was largely ignorant of the passions Leavis had stirred up even in Australia. I knew something, of course, about Leavis's criticism—that marvellous book of his early years, *New Bearings in English Poetry*—and also that he had helped to establish the literary journal *Scrutiny*. Towards the end of my undergraduate years, a new member of the department, A. L. French, fresh from Cambridge, made use of some of the principles Leavis and such sympathisers as L. C. Knights had fashioned. French was an inspired teacher; his expositions of the poetry of Donne and Marvell in particular, and also of Ben Jonson's verse, remain among the most vivid of my memories of those years. Yet such was the pluralism of the Sydney department of the time that there was no hint that the particular way French dealt with those writers represented anything other than one of several pertinent ways. His lectures and seminars were entirely devoid of the doctrinal, indeed quasi-religious zeal with which Leavis's theories and precepts—or at least as they were understood by their imitators and parodists—were to be imposed under Goldberg's regime.

For that reason, therefore, I was ignorant of the passions and enmities in other institutions. That was another consequence of the Sydney department's old-fashioned tolerance, the belief that a university should represent a broad range of views and approaches to the discipline. The few contacts I had made in London suggested that English studies there also displayed such pluralism. In my naivete, therefore, I had no inkling when I first met Goldberg, with the copy of the *Spectator* poking provocatively out of my overcoat pocket, that this act could have been interpreted as a symbol of defiance, an unambiguous declaration, even before a word had been exchanged, that I had allied myself with the forces of darkness. Yet in the atmosphere of paranoia Goldberg was soon to bring to Sydney, I had opportunity to realise how disastrous that meeting had been, how from the very first moment I seemed to have confirmed Goldberg's worst fears about a product of the Sydney old guard who, willy-nilly, would become the most junior member of his staff.

I watched him hang my coat on a hook and followed him into a pleasant though very institutionally furnished living room, where he introduced me to Judy, his wife. Goldberg was then in his thirties, a compact, well-made person with an unremarkable mien. He was mild enough, in truth, throughout an awkward evening filled with innuendo.

We played a curious game. I knew that Goldberg had been appointed to the Challis chair; he knew that I had just accepted the offer of a lectureship. Moreover, each of us knew that the other knew. Yet nothing was said, nothing could be spoken, for Goldberg's appointment had not been officially announced, and mine was contingent on the satisfactory outcome of my thesis. The halting, often difficult conversation was kept to generalities at first, the meeting of two Australian scholars who happened to be in London and would, naturally enough, wish to establish professional contact.

Of course, that was very far from the truth. Goldberg and I had almost nothing in common, as I was to discover even in the course of that evening. He was making good use of the fact that neither of us could admit that we would be colleagues very soon. To an observer his curiosity about the members of the Sydney department would have seemed merely professional. He was interested, he said, to find out how other institutions went about the business of teaching literature: after all, he reminded me, his experience had only been with Melbourne. His years in Oxford did not really count, for he was preoccupied by his research work, as no doubt I had been while writing my thesis.

Something put me on my guard. I had no reason to distrust him. I was distressed that Wilkes had not been appointed to the Sydney chair and so, inevitably, I thought of Goldberg as something of an interloper. But I had no grounds to suspect him of malice or enmity. It seemed natural, moreover, that he should wish to find out something about his new colleagues. And his demeanour was friendly enough. Yet, as the evening went on, I became increasingly troubled. I began to notice a curious undercurrent. I suspected that he was trying to manoeuvre me into indiscretions, into a tacit admission at least that I had not received the best or most enlightened teaching in my undergraduate years.

I was particularly uncomfortable with the way the conversation kept returning to Thelma Herring. Other people were also mentioned, but Goldberg constantly brought her name up, and as we talked I began to sense a discomforting intent beneath the apparently casual pleasantry. Thelma provided, in some way, an obvious target. Her delivery, those complicated gyrations of her neck, and her infuriating habit of running over time in her lectures did little to endear her to students. Like most of my contemporaries I found her irritating and tedious. I also resented the relentless way in which she dealt with the ranks of minor writers and their work, most of which I had not read and had little intention, or indeed opportunity, of reading. Yet even before I had come to know her well and to admire her remarkable accomplishments, my mockery was tinged with respect. She was extraordinarily erudite. Her knowledge, and not merely of English literature, was comprehensive and authoritative. I suspected that there were substantial virtues behind her apparently indiscriminate embracing of all literature. I had an intuition of a generosity of spirit and intellect, of a genuine enthusiasm for writers and their work masked, sadly, by those quirks and mannerisms which made her lectures into trials of endurance.

Goldberg had obviously heard something about those things. He tried to draw me out. Would I not think, I remember him asking, that there was great impropriety in refusing to tailor one's teaching to what students could reasonably be expected to absorb? Wasn't it slightly strange, indeed, to lecture on texts not generally available, confined to a few hard-to-come-by library copies? Of course, he was right in a way, and it would have been churlish and disingenuous not to grant the strength of his argument. For all that, I found myself growing increasingly oblique and even uncommunicative. I resented the way in which he was putting me in an embarrassing position. I felt far too much loyalty to engage in the denigration he seemed to be inviting; yet I was too cowardly to object to it as I should, in all conscience, have done. I tried to steer a noncommittal middle-course, without much success as I remember. The evening grew more and more uncomfortable as I became awkwardly aware of the bad impression I was making. I could see him assessing me as vacuous and indecisive. As soon as it was decent I stood up to say goodbye, muttering some excuse about an early start in the morning that probably struck Goldberg as wholly unconvincing. We parted politely as he helped me into my overcoat with the *Spectator* poking out of its pocket.

I was worried and on edge. Even by the most charitable of interpretations, the evening had been a fiasco. Before I had reached the front door of the building I began to suspect that my academic career had got off to a dismal start. Although it was a fine, cold night outside, I felt flushed with embarrassment and self-reproach. Why hadn't I made a more positive impression, why had I seemed so diffident? It was then, standing in the doorway, that I realised what should have been obvious almost from the beginning. I had been manipulated into a situation from which I could not possibly have emerged with credit or decency. Had I played along with Goldberg's none-too-subtle game of criticising my former teachers and future colleagues he would, surely, have had a potent weapon against me. The least rumour of such a conversation would have been sufficient to discredit me in the eyes of those people as one guilty of disloyalty and a failure of collegial tact. I realised he had relied on that, ensuring that he would have an arsenal of entirely different but equally effective ammunition against me as someone ineffectual and blinded by loyalties and allegiances. I felt so worried and discouraged that I decided to go home in a taxi — a luxury I allowed myself in only the most exceptional of circumstances.

3

In Sydney, when people asked me what I had made of Goldberg, I was circumspect. What could I have said? That I mistrusted him, that I sensed something devious about him? There was nothing really to go on. Throughout the evening, Goldberg had been a polite and considerate host. Whatever I suspected might have been no more than my own apprehensiveness, my suspicion of someone new and unknown who, nevertheless, had ousted Wilkes, my mentor and well-wisher. I thought it best therefore to say little. I went as far as to confess that the evening had been awkward, since neither Goldberg nor I could openly admit that we had both been appointed to positions in Sydney.

And, indeed, the more I thought about it, the more likely an explanation that seemed to become.

I also found that my colleagues knew almost as little about our new professor as I did. He had been a senior lecturer in Melbourne, and had done his postgraduate work in Oxford. But his sympathies had turned towards Cambridge, Downing College in particular, and the venerable figure of F. R. Leavis. Gossip had it that Goldberg was one of the leading lights of a group of ambitious and ruthless people in the Melbourne University English Department who had tried unsuccessfully for some years to impose on it their own very particular views on English studies. Now they had found a toehold in Sydney: Goldberg was the vanguard, the rest would soon follow.

None of that sounded particularly cheerful. I knew little about the intellectual battles that were supposed to have been waged in Melbourne, or in Cambridge for that matter. In fact, I began to suspect that I might have been living in a fool's paradise in the British Museum, pursuing the obscure byways of literary study without understanding that there were some who would find that kind of antiquarianism a waste of time. The trouble was that I suspected that I half agreed with them. That did nothing, however, to make me less alarmed about what might happen once Goldberg arrived. I felt exposed and vulnerable. I was at the very beginning of a career in which I had to prove myself in the first year or two.

As I thought about my meeting with Goldberg, my impressions came to be coloured by anxiety. Did I remember a sneer pass across Goldberg's face when I told him that I had just finished a thesis on James Shirley? I fancied that it had, and no matter how much I tried to persuade myself that I was imagining it, the impression stuck in my mind, establishing itself as undisputed fact.

I had time on my hands during those steamy weeks in early 1963. Officially, I was not required to begin work for another week or two, and in any event January was the one quiet time of the academic year. I embarked on a crash course of Leavis's writings. I had already read some of his critical works: the essays on twentieth-century poetry, on fiction and on the poets of the late sixteenth and early seventeenth centuries. But because my undergraduate courses had been so heavily skewed towards the scholarly and antiquarian, I discovered that I knew next to nothing about Leavis's speculative and theoretical writings, apart from what I had learnt about his attack on C. P. Snow. What I found proved deeply disturbing, despite the undeniable exhilaration and polemical verve of many of Leavis's pronouncements.

His thinking was grounded in an absolute conviction that the study of literature is central to the cultural, but also ethical and even perhaps political health of a society, and that departments of English should occupy the focal points of university life. So far there was little to disagree with, it seemed to me. After all, even in my own university, the Department of English obviously commanded great respect and it was, moreover, at the centre of the university in a very precise and specific sense: it occupied pride of place around the clock tower, secure, it seemed, in its pre-eminence. At the time I was inexperienced enough to be impressed by Leavis's more far-reaching contention about the moral and social importance of literary study. Anyone setting out on the artificial and in a sense pseudo-monastic way of life of universities would find that grand assertion irresistible. It was nice to believe that pursuing a career which many would see as useless and self-indulgent, of value only as a means of training secondary school teachers perhaps, was to follow the noblest of callings. I had entertained such fantasies when I used to dream about becoming a literary academic during my soul-killing years as a medical student. Since that time the vision had faded a little. I had come to have a small experience of the less than civilised nature of much university life, as well as the boredom and repetitive routine of many of its practices. And yet Leavis's great vision of the utopian university, where the English Department commanded universal respect and where it provided moral and intellectual leadership to the other disciplines, was entirely beguiling—despite the suspicion that it was no more than moonshine.

For all that, I found something disturbing in Leavis's brave call to arms in the name of culture and civilisation. The matter was familiar enough. It was not much different from similar pleas Matthew Arnold had made in *Culture and Anarchy*, despite Leavis's largely ceremonial attempts to distance his views from Arnold's. Yet with Leavis, more so than in the case of Arnold, there was a querulousness, an aggressive tone and a remarkable penchant for abusing his opponents. I found the attack on C. P. Snow surprisingly shocking. It reminded me of the abusive polemics of religious bigots. Leavis was not content, it seemed, merely to mount an argument against Snow's notions of the desirable relationship between the humanities and the sciences. Snow had to be demolished on moral, intellectual and cultural grounds. The imaginative poverty of his novels (at least in Leavis's estimate) was indication sufficient to discredit his cultural and educational views—as if, it occurred to me, Snow had been alone in being a poor novelist, poet, writer of tragedies or whatever, who had nevertheless propounded important ideas. Was Leavis's animus against Snow necessary? I wondered. Furthermore, what was the source of that intemperance, the sense of undisguised hostility evident throughout the diatribe? Was this an accepted or legitimate academic style, one from which I had been protected? Or did it represent something undeclared, unacknowledged, the true ground for the animosity? What would happen if that confrontational style mirrored the ideals and aspirations of the man who, in a few weeks' time, was to exercise considerable influence over our lives?

Nothing else that I came across matched the white fury that seemed to leap out of the attack on Snow. Yet even Leavis's more measured pronouncements appeared sinister in their import, concealing beneath the tone of academic discourse an arrogance and inflexibility that struck me as shocking and dangerous. There was, for instance, the curious matter of his absolute demand for applying the highest of standards to the study and criticism of literature. In one sense no one could object to that. Leavis's insistence that one must always be discriminating, vigilant against the second-hand, the shoddy, the vulgar and the merely diverting or entertaining appealed to the sense of pride, the hubris latent in all academics. It could indeed be seen as imposing necessary standards of integrity on a profession which did not command a clearly defined discipline, but remained constantly vulnerable to fashion. Nevertheless, Leavis's literary discriminations, and the unconditional way in which they were expounded, seemed curious and inexplicable to me. What accounted, for instance, for his hostility against Milton? Or the dismissive, contemptuous pages he had written on Dickens, or on Spenser and Sir Philip Sidney? Were these celebrated and much admired writers—together with the other devils in what appeared to be an extensive literary demonology—as contemptible as Leavis seemed to suggest, so lacking in merit or interest? In other words, was everyone else wrong? Was F. R. Leavis of Downing College, Cambridge alone privileged with access to truth? Was he the only legitimate literary legislator of our time?

It was then that I had the first suspicion of the intrinsically religious nature of these disputatious and inflexible attitudes, of a fundamentalism in cultural matters, predicated on absolute conviction, akin to the doctrinal certainties of Calvinism. And I felt, too, the cold wind of intolerance blowing through those pages, just as much as I had sensed similar winds during my schooldays when a particularly bigoted clergyman tried to inflame the Religious Education classes I attended. I remembered how his whole life seemed to have been consumed by his zeal to expose the evils of Roman Catholicism. Every moment of every class was dominated by that grand preoccupation, by his mission to save us, his vulnerable charges, not so much from

Satan and the blandishments of the flesh (though there were many circumlocutory diatribes against self-abuse, too) but from the pope, the Scarlet Woman, the Whore of Babylon. In Leavis I found the same intolerance, almost the same sense of a God-inspired mission, though it was masked by a considerably greater degree of sophistication.

I could discover no reason for those unconditional judgments that seemed to run entirely contrary to the carefully established body of literary opinion that had formed the basis of the teaching in the Sydney department during my undergraduate years. Of course, Leavis offered any number of explanations, some of them hugely intricate, for his opinions. He sought to demonstrate the deleterious effect of Milton's mannered, Latinate diction both on Milton's own verse and on the subsequent history of English poetry. He argued that Dickens was no more than a mere entertainer, lacking in the fundamental seriousness demanded of any great literature—that was before his rediscovery of Dickens, which led to much complicated backtracking and revisionism among his far-flung disciples, including those in the Sydney department. He mounted an elaborate discussion of why in the final count *Macbeth* 'failed' (a favourite and revealing term, as I came to find) in its last act where (as with Othello) Shakespeare allowed his tragic protagonist to cheer himself up with spurious remorse.

So there were explanations and arguments enough, although none of it convinced, or at least banished the suspicion that something quite different, unacknowledged and perhaps unrecognised lurked beneath those passionate discriminations or prejudices. I remember a nagging feeling as I read essay after essay throughout that January of alarm and anticipation, suspecting that the clue was almost within my reach and yet remained elusive. Gradually, though, clarification, or at least what seemed to me a compelling explanation offered itself. It emerged out of the feeling that so much of what I was reading had been fired by resentment—against the unfortunate C. P. Snow, and also against some well-known (though by now largely forgotten) scholars. Here, I guessed, was someone deeply wounded, who felt an irresistible need to challenge privilege and ingrained power. Leavis's was the lone voice of the prophet crying in an academic wilderness, shaking his fist against Babylon, against the Sodom and Gomorrah that had promoted Milton and Dickens, Thackeray and Sir Philip Sidney to their unearned niches in the great literary pantheon.

That was clear enough. Yet it took some time for the cause of that resentment to come into focus. After all, to an outsider, to one whose first exposure to the study of literature occurred among nostalgic memories of the great temples of learning in Oxford and Cambridge,

Leavis seemed one of the fortunate, the blessed of the academic world. I was familiar with the respect accorded by many of the people who had taught me to anyone privileged enough to follow the university teacher's calling in those hallowed places. I also knew the barely disguised resentment of those such as the unspeakable Smith, or even Brown himself, who saw themselves as exiled to an institution in London, when their natural habitat should have been an ancient college in one of the two universities worthy of that name. I could understand, in other words, that envy could manifest itself in a provincial red-brick university, or even among the plebeian colleges of the University of London. I could not imagine why one of the privileged should feel such bitterness against a world he was fortunate enough to enjoy.

The most substantial clue came when I read Leavis's remarks on D. H. Lawrence, with their reiteration of his contempt for Bloomsbury, Virginia Woolf, E. M. Forster, Lytton Strachey and their friends and associates, vapid aesthetes, enemies of true genius intent on blocking and frustrating anyone whose accomplishments seemed to challenge their stranglehold on cultural and literary life. I had not found a great deal to admire in Lawrence when I read as much of his work as I could find—or endure—during the third year of the undergraduate course. I thought that his books were overblown, confused in their dank sexuality and worryingly infatuated with those lawless figures who saw themselves, and were seen by Lawrence, as incarnations of the Nietszchean Superman. I was inclined to agree with the view that there were fascist tendencies in Lawrence's persistent habit of setting the exceptional individual's vision of society and human relationship against those conventions which were usually dubbed, with a sneer, as bourgeois. But above all, I found most of his books tedious and muddy and at times even laughably sentimental in their celebration of dark loins and snakes shedding their skins. Only *Sons and Lovers* spoke with a genuine and candid voice: the rest, I thought, were largely hot air. When, during my time in London, *Lady Chatterley's Lover* became available after a spectacular court case, I too bought a copy (already wrapped in brown paper) from Boots the chemist. It struck me as sad, pompous and ultimately boring.

But for Leavis Lawrence towered above every one of his contemporaries. In him, Leavis's book *The Great Tradition* and his later study of Lawrence assured us, the English novel found its triumph and fulfilment. In his praise of Lawrence, Leavis constantly stressed Lawrence's quintessential Englishness, a kind of Englishness which had become compromised in the postwar world by the many opportunities for travel—to the Costa Brava mostly—by transistor radios and by long-playing records, according to the more bizarre of Leavis's apocalyptic pronouncements. In Lawrence the fundamental strengths of English culture were preserved against cosmopolitanism of a kind at which Bloomsbury excelled. The failure of conventional literary academics to acknowledge Lawrence's pre-eminence was another instance, according to Leavis, of the straitjacket the powerful and the influential had imposed on a vital and living culture.

So there it was. It all came back, as everything English inevitably did, to class. I was sure that I understood the source of the deep and ugly resentment that disfigured most of Leavis's writing, bubbling up like an noisome eruption in the attack on Snow. In particular, Snow was the enemy because he had remade himself, wormed his way into the esteem of those who saw themselves as his superiors. Leavis's privileged position as a fellow of a Cambridge college, I came to understand, might seem the pinnacle of achievement from the perspective of someone in Sydney, but in Cambridge he was as much trapped by hierarchies and exclusions as if he had spent his life in the most obscure of provincial—or colonial—universities. Downing College was not King's, St John's or Trinity. It was one of the lesser colleges, a fit place for one of humble origins (such as Leavis) to try to upset the apple cart, but hardly to be taken seriously, except perhaps by other malcontents.

I thought that I was beginning to make sense of the increasingly querulous tone of Leavis's more recent writings. The eccentric and idiosyncratic pantheon he had erected—excluding Milton and Spenser, making room for only a portion of Shakespeare's works, and promoting such misfits as Blake, Lawrence and (in a different way) George Eliot, the profoundly un-English Joseph Conrad too—was a means of cocking a snook at the establishment, at those powerful and influential people who may well have mocked his lack of sophistication, the remnants of working-class diction in his speech, and even perhaps the way he held his knife and fork. His very existence, it appeared to me, was defined by his sense of victimhood: everything he wrote seemed to be coloured by a compulsion to affront an invincible intellectual and academic oligarchy. Struggling against the forces of darkness was an intrinsic element in everything he uttered; the certainty of defeat seemed to sustain him, for without the devil he lacked identity or purpose. Like seventeenth-century puritans, whose diction and attitudes his polemics resembled, everything he wrote, everything he did seemed directed to the one end: the establishment of a New Jerusalem of the intellect where Lawrence would be esteemed and valued unquestioningly, where there would be no doubt that Milton's verse represented a perversion of the accents and rhythms of true English, where there would be no tin-eared Americans teaching English lovers of their own literature their business, where all would be amity and co-operation around the holy of holies, the English Department of every university. Out of this department true knowledge and enlightenment would issue to illuminate even the farthest reaches of the world—the School of Physics, for instance, where something as fundamentally unimportant as the Laws of Thermodynamics were taught. Yet, just as with the Levellers, Leavis's yearning for the blessed state was predicated on its never being achieved. The good fight would have to go on until the end of time, for only by fighting it could the elect identify and comfort each other.

When I reached these highly unoriginal conclusions early in 1963, I was still living, so to speak, in England. Sydney remained to an extent strange and unfamiliar, almost exotic. In a sense I was still reading Leavis in a small flat on the top floor of a house in Marylebone, or at my green leather desk in the North Library, surrounded by the ceremonies and rituals of an elaborately stratified world. From that perspective, much of what I came across in Leavis made sense, despite the querulousness, the disturbingly confrontationist stand. I could understand how Lawrence, the son of a coalminer who had refused to gentrify himself (just as Leavis resisted gentrification by never wearing a tie), would appeal to one who also felt excluded from the centre of power in a small, incestuous university town. Lawrence had suffered at the hands of the Cambridge great. He got his revenge by his venomous portrait of Ottoline Morrell in the Hermione of *Women in Love*. Leavis had been scorned and insulted by the same spirit, the same people. He got his revenge too, promoting the coalminer's son against the well-connected Virginia Woolf or that Cambridge idol, E. M. Forster.

Perhaps there was much justice in that, I remember thinking. But what did those parochial disputes have to do with the sun-drenched, much less hierarchical world where one of Leavis's disciples seemed about to establish a far-flung colony? My years in England had taught me that the sentimental, almost naive worship of Australia's English heritage found no room for the complicated networks of class that accounted for Leavis's resentments and ill temper, and of course for much else besides. Surely, I kept thinking, no one, no matter how dedicated or fanatical, would consider even for a moment imposing those very local and particular preoccupations on a world that shared almost none of those characteristics.

4

As we waited for Goldberg to arrive and the academic year to begin, there were, I found, many adjustments to be made. In one sense, my transition to a full member of the department was rendered a little easier by the presence of several new or relatively new faces. The expansion of the department had begun even before I left for London. By the time I returned it had become clear that the small, in some ways inbred institution I had come to know no longer existed. The department now embraced two or three people with American second degrees, as well as some who had no previous connections with the university. The place was becoming more heterogeneous, less confined within predictable patterns of professional progress—which I too had broken, of course, by my decision not to follow the well-beaten path from Sydney to Oxford.

Being more familiar with the ways and conventions of the university and the department than some of the newcomers gave me an advantage. Unlike them, I was a repository of a kind of race memory. I realised too that I had another advantage. Sydney had become my own town, I had friends beyond the university and enjoyed, therefore, a life which was not entirely confined by my profession. It was nevertheless strange to be back in a place where so many of my earlier experiences had occurred. I noticed how new it looked—not much more than a hundred years old. Some of the glamour and romance had gone. I was no longer so confident that within the magical confines of the Quadrangle a world of English civility could be nurtured.

I also felt some disappointment because I had been excluded from what remained for me the centre and jewel of the university. The expansion of the department meant that various colonies had been established around the university grounds. I had been allotted a room in a newish, multi-storey building on what was then the eastern edge of the university, adjacent to the noisy, polluted artery, City Road. The building was—and remains—a utilitarian structure which had been intended for use by the scientific faculties. Everything in it was subjugated to function and practicality. No decorative feature was allowed to intrude, to conceal structural elements or to diverge from the tyranny of right angles. This was in accordance with the architectural aesthetics of the time, but the chief impulse behind the design was obviously to build it as cheaply as possible. It was a soul-killing place of a kind that became only too familiar in Australian universities over the next two decades—a collection of mean cubbyholes wholly inadequate for the purpose for which they were intended after it was discovered that the standard module (laid down by some bureaucratic fantasy or other) could not contain the number of students required to constitute a class.

Each of us who formed the small enclave of the English Department which occupied a part of one floor in that building had been assigned a curious amalgam of office and laboratory. We occupied the western side of the building. Following, no doubt, the precepts of European and North American architects, those rooms had been designed as highly efficient sun-traps. And because the building had been commissioned to house scientists with their flames and stinking and volatile substances, each door was fitted with a heavy closing device. In summer and autumn, and even on sunny days in winter and spring, the afternoon sun streaming in through the plate glass heated the rooms to unbearable temperatures. There was no ventilating system, not even blinds on the windows. We tried to make life a little more bearable by propping our doors open with several stacking chairs placed on top of each other. But fire regulations were rigorously enforced: an attendant could always be counted on to make his way down the corridors ordering us, by virtue of the great responsibility placed on his shoulders, to remove those offending chairs and endure the solar ovens the architects had provided for us. The awfulness of those rooms was sardonically emphasised by the side-on view of the main building each of us could glimpse from our windows.

A particular camaraderie soon developed in that colony. We were all relative newcomers. The veteran among us had arrived in the university about a year earlier: Jim Tulip, one of the remarkable generation of Queenslanders, including Rodney Hall, Tom Shapcott and David Malouf, who were to play an increasingly important role in the cultural and literary life of the next decades. Tulip came to Sydney via Chicago, bringing with him a type of intellectual rigour very different from the emphasis on antiquarian scholarship that had been the norm of the Sydney department in the past. One of the ironies of the attempts Goldberg and his associates were to make in the next two years or so to mould the Sydney department into their own image was that people of very different temperaments, accomplishments and scholarly inclinations were equally scorned and sidelined, driving them into uneasy alliances in the common cause of seeking survival in a dangerous climate. However, when friendships began to develop in that building on what was then still the edge of the university, our common cause was far more mundane: proximity and a mild resentment at our uncomfortable working conditions. The heart of the department around the massive clock tower seemed much further away than the two or three minutes it took to stroll over there for meetings or for the ritual gatherings of morning and afternoon tea. It was remote from us because of the symbolic gulf between the high, cool rooms and our sweltering boxes, each an identical copy of the others.

I became friendly with the person in the room next to mine, a striking, tall woman with brilliant eyes who had recently moved to Sydney to pursue her postgraduate studies, before setting off for further study in England. Her strong personality, simultaneously beguiling and alarming, was sufficient to make her fascinating. The fact that she had known Goldberg in Melbourne gave her added allure in those anxious weeks when many of us were waiting to discover what our fortunes would be under the new dispensation.

Her name was Germaine Greer. Though we shared a paper-thin partition for almost eighteen months, I never got to know her very well. We saw a good deal of each other, it is true. Sometimes Germaine would ask to use my telephone—as a tutor she was not entitled to that privilege but had to make do with the emergency telephone in one of the lifts, on which she would conduct conversations while travelling up and down, until the stern guardians of the building put a stop to that infringement of sacred rules. On one occasion I drove her to hospital in a minor emergency. We also had a few conversations of more than practical or mundane nature, mostly about music. Literary or intellectual matters, however, were seldom mentioned.

The reason for that had a good deal to do with the uneasy climate of the department and, later, with the wedges Goldberg managed to drive between people. Greer, who was even then the last person in the world to follow fashion or precept blindly, seemed nevertheless to have considerable sympathy for the principles on which Goldberg and his associates based their practices. In the complicated political networks of the department which emerged in the course of that year there was no particular benefit for her in that. Unlike some of her colleagues, she had no inclination to flatter or mechanically to repeat the mantras which became increasingly obligatory for anyone wishing to gain favour. Eventually she was as much frowned on as those—myself among them—whom Goldberg came to see as encumbrances, people to be discouraged in the hope that they might eventually go elsewhere.

That, however, was not how I saw things. I became increasingly wary of Germaine because I regarded her as one of 'them'—such was the paranoia that came to dominate the department in the months after Goldberg's arrival. I did not trust her because, ultimately, you could not trust anyone in that poisoned climate. Nevertheless, the gulf between us was more fundamental. It had a great deal to do with the very different way each of us looked at ourselves and the world around us. I was more complacent and satisfied with the possibilities of life Australia offered, even though I found myself longing more and more for London and Europe—and also to escape from the intolerable atmosphere of the Sydney department. She, by contrast, was much more restless, I think, much more questioning and contemptuous of the narrowness of the world around us.

I think she was the first intellectual I had known. There were enough people among my friends and acquaintances who proclaimed themselves as intellectuals, just as in later decades I was to discover many in the public literary and cultural spheres ready to assume the title on the strength of a book or two, or even a collection of newspaper articles. Yet none of them revealed the kind of intellectualism I encountered in Greer. It consisted in part of an extraordinary assurance, verging perhaps on the arrogant. She had pronounced opinions, as I discovered (in staff meetings mostly) and an acerbic, uncompromising way of articulating those opinions. She did not suffer fools gladly: her contempt could be scathing and withering. I did not realise fully at the time the courage all that must have required, for the last thing I would have thought was that her sex had put her at a disadvantage. Often there was a disturbing edge to her confidence, something which she probably saw as intellectual honesty. I remember overhearing some hectic classes through the thin partition separating us. Germaine's voice would grow louder and louder, her words muffled and indistinguishable but her anger wholly unmistakable. At times you could hear a curious scurrying and then footsteps retreating along the corridor when hapless undergraduates found themselves ejected for some crassness or stupidity. I witnessed one of those performances. As I was passing her room the door was flung open. A young man, his face glowing with embarrassment, emerged with a nervous backward glance over his shoulders. Behind him, Germaine, her eyes ablaze, was holding the door to prevent it from closing before she had finished her diatribe. Then, as the young man scurried along the corridor and Germaine relaxed her grip on the door, I thought I caught the faintest of smiles playing around her lips.

She was a consummate performer, much given to wearing leather skirts and knee-length boots at a time when such accoutrements were considered almost pornographic. The outbursts about her students' stupidity (and also at times that of her colleagues) were as carefully stage-managed as her stunning performance as Mother Courage for one of the university's drama groups. Yet in the midst of the bravado and outrageousness there was a very different passion, one intimately connected, I think, with her intellectual gifts. She could seem as ruthless with herself as with her victims, examining her ideas, views and theories with a detachment that struck me on occasions as almost unnatural. Her impatience with the easy, the commonplace or the clichéd led her at times into the eccentric. But even at her most outrageous, there was a pressure behind her pronouncements that was both impressive and alarming. For her, literature was not cut off from other areas of speculation or possibilities of scrutiny or analysis. I am aware now of how much in advance of her time she was (at least in the context of the Sydney department) in bringing all manner of concerns—aesthetic, political, sexual—to bear on what many of us regarded as the confined and limited world of 'literature'. So, inevitably, some of us resented her, suspecting her of mere showiness, of shallow exhibitionism. She did not conform to the patterns of the Sydney department as they still existed when I met her in January 1963, just as she found it difficult to accommodate herself to the different orthodoxy that emerged a few months later—even though she had a comprehensive command of its jargon.

I did not find it easy to be in her company. Her energy and frequent disputatiousness were entirely contrary to the more detached and relaxed Sydney style. It was not good form, I thought, to carry on like that; proprieties and conventions should be maintained, even in one's dealings with less than dedicated or gifted students. Time has made me see that discomfort in a slightly different light. I am still convinced that politeness and even a degree of indifference are useful, even perhaps essential facets of academic life. They are ways of registering that undergraduates are adults who have chosen freely and without constraint to attend a particular institution or to take a particular course. The duty of university teachers is certainly to teach in the most efficient and sympathetic manner possible, but the kind of recriminations in which Germaine liked to indulge still seem to me just as questionable as the intimacy that nowadays exists between academic and undergraduate—a false and dangerous intimacy because it tends to distract attention from the simple fact that the academic, no matter how sympathetic or altruistic, is still required to judge a student's ability and accomplishments, despite all the rhetoric of caring egalitarianism. Yet my discomfort with Germaine, as I overheard her berating embarrassed students, some of them close to tears at times, or observed her needling her colleagues, had much deeper roots that were intimately bound up with the particular kind of intellectualism she displayed.

Everything that I had learnt during my undergraduate years, as well as the kind of research work I had stumbled into in London, was predicated on isolating the academic study of literature from that messy, at times contradictory and unsettling world of ideas which Germaine seemed to import, improperly I thought then, into her professional life. I had been trained, in a sense, to disregard my likes and dislikes and even the way in which certain writers or their work impinged on personal experiences, feelings and preferences. A dislike of a particular writer or lack of sympathy with a certain literary movement or phenomenon did not, in terms of such attitudes, oblige one to deny that writer's significance or achievement, or to declare a movement or phenomenon lacking in value. Such principles were deeply embedded in the practices of the Sydney department. Indeed, a diversion from them could seem bizarre and idiosyncratic. Implicit in my perhaps naive commitments was the sense that the reading and enjoyment of literature were isolated from its formal study, just as the study itself was largely self-contained, divorced from questions of ethics, morality, politics and the like.

It was that sense which Germaine was the first, in my experience, to challenge. For her, literature was not shut off from the rest of her intellectual or even perhaps emotional life. Rather it lay at the centre of a questing and uneasy existence, forever teasing away at meanings, significances, implications. In that respect her teaching was profoundly different from the professional standards of the day, if by professionalism we understand the assumption of an impersonal mask of the kind which had been the norm in my experience of university life. I do not believe that in those relatively early years she always knew where her inclinations were leading her—perhaps she still doesn't. There was much that seemed to be unfocussed, even perhaps wayward in her thinking, or at least as far as I could gather from snippets of conversation and overheard harangues. I recoiled from her ideas because they seemed to me unstructured, lacking in the objectivity which I believed—still believe—to be necessary for the academic scrutiny of literature. Yet, even then, with all my prejudices firmly in place, I found myself admiring her vigour and boldness, which always stood out in sharp relief, no matter how rough the edges seemed.

I knew that I could never follow her down that path, even if there had not been powerful cultural disincentives against it. At the time I thought this was merely a matter of professional probity—that was not the correct academic way of going about things. Now I know that my inability and distaste went much deeper, reaching down into that adventure of refashioning myself in my early years in Australia. I imagined that those days were long past; of late I have realised that their effects were with me then, and may be still. As a teacher of English literature I could not be anything but impersonal, conventional in the fundamental and not entirely dishonourable sense of the word. To have allowed my personality to impinge on my professional life would have seemed an impropriety, for it would have introduced experiences and ways of looking at the world alien to the communal experience of our students. To teach English literature, according to the academic canons in which I had been nurtured, was to locate yourself within an English sensibility, at least linguistically. There was no possibility of acknowledging those parts of my experience and perhaps personality that existed—or at least used to exist—in another language, a language remote, moreover, from the traditions and habits of mind that had become the area of my professional expertise. The disjunction in my life, which had imposed on me the task of becoming a mimic and parodist, could not be admitted into my professional activities, for to do so would have meant inevitably detaching myself from the enterprise, built on consensus and shared values, which I had recently joined. And besides, irrespective of whatever idiosyncratic prehistory one might have brought to the profession, to stray from the relatively narrow confines of the world of consensus and agreed values would have seemed to me the gravest infringement of professional propriety.

I think that I said something like that one day to Greer as we were walking over to the main building for a meeting. She was contemptuous, snorting. She did not need to say much: everything she did, everything she said indicated that she valued individuality and the questioning, indeed the subverting, of conventions and agreed principles. In that she appeared to me no more than an eccentric. I remember comparing her in my mind to the department's one true eccentric, a quirky Irishman who had joined the staff towards the end of my undergraduate years. His name was Gustav Cross, a great raconteur, drinker and allegedly a scholar of considerable accomplishments. But to me he seemed merely undisciplined and wayward. I remember enjoying his wit and irreverence, but in his course of lectures ostensibly concerned with pre-Shakespearean drama I fancied I discovered a fundamental shallowness. The six or eight weekly classes were filled with deliciously salacious anecdotes about the vagabond actors of the mid-sixteenth century, but they omitted almost all mention of the plays of Lyly, Greene, Kyd and Peele which we were supposed to be studying. To me, Germaine was tarred with the same brush. I could not understand that her apparent eccentricity burned with some intellectual fire, no matter how undeveloped it might have been in those days, because of my incapacity to distinguish between shadow and substance. Nothing in my sentimental education or in my project of self-fashioning prepared me to make such a distinction. And besides, the dark days of the department that were to follow shortly after we met revealed how closely allied intellectual ambition and megalomania could become.

5

A week or so before the beginning of the academic year, Wilkes called a meeting to make arrangements for the year's teaching. We gathered in the Muniment Room. The place had hardly changed in the years I had been away. Perhaps it looked a little more neglected since it was no longer used for the twice daily tea ceremony. Otherwise, it was familiar and comforting. The cardboard boxes containing the material for the edition of *Piers Plowman* members of the department had been preparing for years were still stacked on top of the tall bookshelves, looking just as forlorn as they always had. We sat at the varnished tables which were arranged, as always, around three sides of a square. Wilkes began the meeting by formally welcoming me, wishing me every success, adding that he was pleased to see a graduate of the department joining its staff. Then he got on with the business of the day.

On the surface everything seemed brisk and efficient. There were preliminary enrolment figures, estimates of the number of tutorial classes that would be needed, a glitch or two over the timetable and the availability of rooms. I looked around: everything appeared normal, calm, routine, and yet it was more than fancy, I thought, that made me detect a certain tension in the air, and sadness too on the part of some people. I was not alone, the conviction came on me, in suspecting that this was the last time the department would be meeting in this familiar way. There was a sense of finality; an era, perhaps a world, was coming to an end. Wilkes's easygoing, almost casual manner—the old Sydney style—seemed sadly out of kilter with the passions and resentments of the kind which (gossip insisted) Goldberg would be bringing with him. As the morning wore on that old-fashioned, genteel collegiality struck me more and more as attractive and valuable.

It occurred to me, though, that not everyone in the room was as beguiled by the atmosphere the meeting generated. I had known that during my undergraduate years the department had been racked by strife and dissension, but the few months I spent on the periphery, as it were, before leaving for London suggested that those disputes were personal, intimately connected with ambition, or rather its frustration. The department's mode of operation did not seem, however, to be questioned by even the most fractious or dissatisfied. Now I became aware of irritation and resentment at the structures and procedures themselves.

Wilkes moved on to the arrangements for teaching, and I felt a touch of panic when he came to my allocation. Would I take the course of lectures on Shakespeare's contemporaries and successors for the honours year, beginning in the first week of term? And he reeled off the names on the syllabus: Heywood, Chapman, Massinger, Ford and also Shirley, who had been added, of course, since I had just completed my thesis. It was a flattering offer. I knew that a particular cachet surrounded teaching in the honours year; to be offered such a substantial segment of the course in my first year in the department would, in normal circumstances, have been interpreted as a considerable feather in my cap. I remember two conflicting thoughts: would this be my only chance to teach the cream of our students? And then the alarming prospect of having to prepare such a course with one week's notice. Others were also becoming restive. Was it proper, someone asked, to make such arrangements so late in the piece; how could we be expected to teach adequately without sufficient preparation time? The discussion was good natured enough, but I became aware of irritation and impatience, followed by the suspicion that some of my new colleagues were anxious for change.

In the mythology Goldberg and his supporters promulgated after his attempt to remake English studies in his own image ended in disaster, the Sydney department was depicted as hostile and obstructionist from the moment of his arrival. We were hopelessly conservative, stuck in our outmoded belletristic practices, resistant to change and suspicious of anyone who deviated from the narrow and retrograde academic habits which had remained practically unaltered for half a century or more. We were supposed to have been united in our opposition both to necessary reform and to all outsiders. Goldberg, the mythology went on, suffered as much from the department's overt anti-Semitism as from its academic and intellectual conservatism. We were unwilling to listen to reason or good sense, and had determined, even before he took up his post, to withstand every one of his attempts to establish cordial professional relations.

That mythology is still current in some circles. There are those who are convinced that Goldberg was hounded out of Sydney by a concerted campaign of hostility and with the connivance of the very people who had been instrumental in appointing him. Certainly, many of us were apprehensive and fearful because of the rumours of arrogance and inflexibility that had preceded him. Perhaps one or two of us might even have harboured anti-Semitic prejudices against him, though I am inclined to doubt that, partly because the department saw fit to encourage me and to find me a position, and more importantly because it appointed and welcomed A. L. French some four years before Goldberg's arrival. Yet it is patently untrue to claim that we were united in opposition from the moment Goldberg came among us. The flurry of discontent when Wilkes announced the teaching arrangements before the beginning of the 1963 academic year was only one of a number of small but telling indications that several members of the department were anxious for change and ready to welcome the arrival of a new broom.

In part that was the result of a desire for novelty and of the enervation that a settled and unchanging system almost always provokes. In part, too, it was the product of a certain malice: some thought that Wilkes had enjoyed too smooth a path to prominence, and that it was consequently time for him to be taught a lesson or two. Perhaps more respectable forces were also at work. The world was changing around us, just as the composition of the department had changed in the time that I had been away. People such as Jim Tulip and Jim Simmonds with their American training, and Derick Marsh, with his experience of political persecution in South Africa, brought to the department professional practices that did not conform in all respects to the former Sydney pattern.

These were merely the surface ripples of deeper, more significant currents. Gradually, almost imperceptibly but nevertheless surely the old cultural ties had slackened by 1963. It was no longer possible to be as confident of the intrinsic spiritual identity of Britain and Australia as it had been during my years at school and as an undergraduate, when opportunities for travel were limited and people could consequently retain a sentimental, nostalgic allegiance to 'Home' and the 'Mother Country'. People of my generation began travelling: we saw England with our own eyes and realised that it was a more ambiguous and complex world than those essentially literary images of it which had sustained our imagination and longing. The sense of an Australian identity in intellectual and cultural matters began there, in the shocked recognition some of my acquaintances experienced on arriving at

Southampton or Tilbury that they had come to a strange world, which was not, and could not have been 'home'. It was inevitable, therefore, that the certainties which had led to the erection of the main building at the university, or the sense that in matters of the intellect there was no intrinsic difference between reading Shakespeare in Sydney or Oxford could no longer be maintained. There were other models, other possibilities. Perhaps, some of the people in the department may have felt, it was time to try them out.

Accordingly, mixed in with the apprehensiveness and the inevitable suspicion that attends any large-scale change, especially in tradition-bound societies such as a university, there was considerable anticipation and even goodwill as we waited for Goldberg. Some, perhaps many, saw change as desirable, convinced that the department could not afford indefinitely to continue with practices no longer appropriate for our students or the intellectual climate. And there was even talk of the most contentious of topics: amalgamating the two sides of the department and so doing away with Sydney's unique, and to some idiosyncratic, distinction between language studies and early English literature on the one hand and on the other the large body of literature from the late fifteenth century onwards, which was the Challis Professor's domain.

When Goldberg arrived a day or two after the official beginning of the year, he seemed affable enough. There was the usual round of meetings and introductions. I reminded him, as if a reminder were needed, that we had already met. We didn't speak again for a week or two after that: Judy and he were busy setting up the flat the university had found for them; there were administrative details to attend to; and he spent many hours closeted with Wilkes and other senior members of both sides of the department. Meanwhile I began settling into the routines of a new life. Most of my energies went into writing my lectures on sixteenth- and seventeenth-century drama. As is generally the case with inexperienced university teachers, I had little idea of the tricks of the trade, assembling far too much material, overestimating the amount that could be crammed into fifty minutes, or into the heads of even the most gifted and attentive of students. I bashed out page after page on the Olivetti on which I had written my thesis. There were far too many of them, and what made matters worse, I had not reckoned with the difficulty of reading from sheets of paper densely covered with single-space typing. The lectures were not the greatest of successes; after a while students began cutting classes—as I had done not too many years earlier. But now I was on the other side of the fence: I started worrying whether news of their dissatisfaction (which, of course, I had exaggerated to myself) would get to Goldberg's ears.

He said nothing. We had the odd commonplace conversation in those first months. He seemed to go out of his way to be friendly and not to interfere. Gradually people began to relax; the optimists felt vindicated: the ogre had turned out to be benign. Others were convinced that he was only biding his time.

The first signs of trouble arose when the time came to consider the following year's syllabus. Traditionally this was no more than a matter of tinkering, a ceremony occupying a couple of days at most. When notice of the meetings to consider the syllabus for 1964 arrived, we were amazed to see the remarkable number of days, stretching over several weeks, we had been asked to set aside for considering a general overhaul of all courses. Most of us realised that Goldberg was ready to strike, having consolidated his position by assuring himself of the support of a number of key people, principally those who had joined us in the months since his arrival.

Change was obviously in the air but few people, apart from those in whom he had confided, realised the extent to which the department's life was to be overturned. Most of us had been accustomed to a gradual evolution: rapid change was inimical to our innate conservatism, to what we saw as the academic ideal of deliberation, of not rushing things but talking them over, reflecting, allowing time to consider the implications of what we were planning—indeed of procrastinating. That, we found, was not to be the case. The old ways were to be banished with one sweep. The department would no longer offer a comprehensive survey of literature from the end of the sixteenth century onwards. Instead our students were to be offered a much narrower syllabus that concentrated on a more modest selection of great works of literature. The emphasis on scholarship and literary history which had sustained the department's practices was to be replaced by concentration on close linguistic analysis of texts, on training critical faculties and on encouraging students to discriminate between the great and the second-rate. There was to be greater intellectual rigour where syllabuses and teaching practices were concerned, Goldberg announced at one particularly tense meeting.

To outsiders the changes seemed sensible enough, and most students welcomed them. The new dispensation seemed to reduce radically those cumbersome syllabuses that appeared in the Arts handbook year after year, nominating writers rather than individual texts, so that notionally at least the rubric 'Sir Walter Scott' implied that everything ever written by that prolific poet and novelist would have to be studied in order to fulfil the requirements. From that point of view the consternation provoked by the changes Goldberg proposed seemed merely intransigent and ill-intentioned, resentment against the newcomer whose ways did not conform with established practice. It would be foolish, indeed, to deny that the acrimony that took hold of the department was tinged by such venality. In those endless meetings in which Goldberg attempted to wear down all resistance to his proposals, forever formulating new propositions to put up for the vote, I had my first substantial insight into the fierce egotism which is never far from the academic sensibility.

It was understandable that people should wish to preserve their own turf. The lecturer whose lifelong preoccupation was the study of the various versions of Wordsworth's *The Prelude*, or the one whose interest in Jane Austen was focussed on the repressed sexual innuendo in her novels would resist, of course, any change in emphasis or the suggestion that someone might be better qualified to teach those writers. Goldberg did have, indeed, one rhetorically powerful weapon. Our duty, he kept repeating in meeting after meeting, was to our students, to their intellectual and critical development. Self-indulgence should find no place in our practices: our students were not there to be inducted into our latest research preoccupation. Despite my increasing alarm and despondency as those meetings stretched on, that point, I felt, had to be granted. I thought back to Harold Oliver's classes on Shakespeare's *Timon of Athens*, which he was then in the process of editing for the prestigious *Arden* series—a matter of inordinate pride for him. The two or three lectures on the play he gave and the compulsory examination question he set at the end of the year were focussed on the one peripheral issue: whether the sole surviving text of the play represented a sketch for a tragedy that Shakespeare either abandoned or was prevented from finishing.

In that way, much that Goldberg proposed was supported by good sense. His syllabuses took far greater note of practicality than the older, comprehensive tours of English literature the department had offered. Nominally, it was now feasible for our undergraduates (who were also, of course, studying at least one other subject for their degrees) to cover the syllabus properly. It would be possible, he pointed out on many occasions, to ensure that our students were following a systematic and well-organised course of study. Haphazard practices could not be tolerated in a university that prided itself on academic and intellectual excellence. His proposed scheme would provide a better guarantee that our graduates had earned their degrees rather than bluffed their way through an impossibly cumbersome course of studies.

The fierce disputes that were to tear the department apart, and which eventually came to be played out in the public arena, had their origins in those meetings in the second half of 1963. It was there that the polarisation of the department began. From that emerged a situation with desperate consequences, not merely for the university but for individuals as well: some careers were to come to abrupt ends; some lives were blighted; and the suicide of one hapless person some years later was probably a direct consequence of those troubles. To many, the sad and shabby history of the Sydney department in the mid-sixties seems no more than the product of the intransigence of a superannuated *ancien régime* intent on retaining its privileges, resistant to any change, no matter how much it may have been grounded in commonsense or academic probity. It fuelled the growing distrust of universities, especially of the humanities, in the community at large and the contempt, as well, of sectors of the academic world for 'soft' subjects such as English. Those, myself included, who were seen as the most vocal (or the most intransigent) of Goldberg's opponents are still regarded—thirty years or more after the event—as irrationally resistant to good sense and propriety. Yet the opposition to those changes which were outlined—and imposed—during the first year of Goldberg's brief tenure was provoked by far more alarming and also venal circumstances. What was presented in so many meetings as a necessary and considered reassessment of academic and intellectual priorities was driven, in truth, by the explosive combination of an inflexible and punitive ideology, promoted with religious zeal by its adherents, and a brutal, undisguised lust for power.

6

Ideology and ambition, idealism and the thirst for power were inextricably mixed in the controversies that attended Goldberg's time in the Sydney department. As opposition against his views and practices grew in the months after that initial round of meetings in 1963, bringing about uneasy alliances on both sides of an increasingly wide gulf separating the two camps, fundamental differences in academic and cultural aspirations generated much of the dissension. Some of us found the broad principles of his programme of reform attractive and timely. Something had to be done, we realised, to counter the tendency towards dilettantism in our students, who could (if they were so inclined) rely as much on lecture notes as on reading and study when addressing themselves to hopelessly generous, all-embracing syllabuses. And yet the model Goldberg was intent on putting in place seemed to us too much driven by a particular and narrow ideology, misrepresenting and ultimately traducing the multifaceted traditions of literature by imposing on them a doctrinaire definition, any deviation from which was ridiculed with dogmatic zeal. We were shocked and dismayed by the frequently repeated ex-cathedra pronouncements that no mature person could find both George Eliot and Dickens valuable, that admiring D. H. Lawrence should have made it impossible for anyone to read Virginia Woolf. We detected a degree of philistinism in the seemingly paranoid urge to discriminate, to discard and to divide the complex and ambiguous world of books into devils and saints—mostly devils.

Nevertheless, as is the way of most institutions, the intellectual and academic grounds for our disputes were often subservient to much more pressing and alarming preoccupations. As the months went by, many of us became aware of the insecurity of our position, of Goldberg's wholly undisguised contempt for most members of his department, among whom I knew myself to be the last and therefore most vulnerable recruit. His campaign consisted of a disconcerting mixture of the subtle and the crude—simultaneously blitzkrieg, casuistic flattery and seduction. The gamut of dictatorial practices was concentrated in that small, self-contained world: public humiliation; irresistible promises of a brilliant future (at a certain price, of course) murmured behind closed doors; show trials and hypocritical ceremonies of goodwill and reconciliation. One by one we were subjected to disconcerting experiences which, after a while, left us believing that there was no place for us in the brave new world of the Sydney English Department. Initially, Goldberg seemed successful: very quickly he achieved his aim of encouraging several senior members of the department to leave, so making room for lieutenants and satraps to set out on the journey, in most cases from Melbourne, to join him in the conquest of a new domain.

Goldberg's Sydney career followed a trajectory familiar to anyone who has encountered the lurid world of the plays of Shakespeare's age. He was the Overreacher, the Machiavel, the ruthless, brilliant manipulator utterly dedicated to conquest and mastery, ready to employ all means to achieve his goal. He was Richard III, Iago and all those lesser creature who (in the clichéd imagery of Shirley and his kind) blazed like comets across the sky, burning brightly, irresistible in their progress, only to disintegrate in showers of brilliant dying fragments. At first, though, that inevitable pattern of rise and catastrophic fall was not obvious to us: when you are an actor in a Jacobean melodrama, rather than a comfortably detached spectator, it is not easy to recall the consolations of art. Nothing in the first eighteen months after his arrival suggested that Goldberg's career would also end in defeat and humiliation. Only after the event were we able to see how much our experience had mirrored those creaky old stories where creatures of great imagination and skill are destroyed by their overweening ambition, their impatient lust for mastery and, above all, by carelessness when drunk with power.

Yet Goldberg followed that ancient, commonplace pattern with touching fidelity. The greatest irony of his Sydney years was that his career and fortunes confirmed the truth implicit in those naive tales of ambition and its inevitable consequences for which he had nothing but contempt and took pains to banish from our syllabuses. Every element was there: we were living out a five-act tragedy in pedestrian twentieth-century prose.

At first, just as in those roaring tales of Tamburlaine the Great and King Richard III, fortune seemed to smile on everything he did; whatever he touched turned to gold. The times were propitious. The early sixties was a period of great expansion in universities. Funds seemed limitless, lucrative positions were being created in universities both old and new. Some members of the department, whose careers were on the cusp of a delicate and crucial stage, found positions elsewhere.

Among the first to leave was Gustav Cross, the department's Till Eulenspiegel who proved a particular thorn in Goldberg's side. Irreverent and ironic, Cross used to take great delight in puncturing some of the solemnly idiotic practices Goldberg had introduced. One particularly irksome ceremony had to do with the marking of first-year essays and exercises. Everyone of us—even I, the least experienced— knew that awarding a mark to a student's attempt at literary analysis could only be achieved by careful comparison of at least twenty, ideally more, pieces of work. You cannot with any fairness or accuracy determine the numerical worth of a single piece of work: there are too many variables, too many often intangible considerations to be taken into account. Yet Goldberg insisted on holding enervating and entirely pointless meetings where sample essays were passed around, which we were expected to assess in order for our assessments to be compared. There was no educational value in the exercise; we were too preoccupied in our attempt not to make fools of ourselves. So we played the inane game, double-guessing, nervously watching over our shoulders. Except Cross; he refused to offer himself up for sacrifice.

When asked to indicate a range of marks out of twenty each of us would give a sample essay, invariably his read '0–20'. Goldberg could barely contain his fury; the rest of us smirked behind our hands like nervous courtiers at a levée. Cross's irreverence, indeed irresponsibility, which had annoyed me in the past, was a wonderfully cool draught of sanity in an overheated world of suspicion. It was nevertheless inevitable that he would be defeated too. Cross left to take up the chair of English at the University of Newcastle.

One by one, those that had the opportunity moved on. Jim Simmonds (who, like Tulip, had brought some of the hard-edged intellectual habits of American universities to Sydney's more dilettantish climate) was, I think, a sad loss when he returned to Pittsburgh. Everyone, not the least Goldberg, expected Wilkes to leave too. The chair of Australian Literature he took up when he was denied the Challis chair was regarded by many as something of a booby prize. He had no staff, no ability (or so it seemed) to mount courses, having to content himself with the occasional lecture on Australian writers slipped into the courses on literature. The almost universal expectation was that after a decent stint as the foundation professor, he would take up the chair of English in the newly established Macquarie University at North Ryde, a short distance from where he lived with his wife and young children. It seemed the logical and inevitable step: A. G. Mitchell, formerly the Professor of Early English Literature and Language, had become the new university's first Vice-Chancellor. Surely, I remember thinking as gloom and despondency gripped me more and more, Wilkes would follow him there.

Otherwise all that were left were those who saw no possibility of escape. Our plight grew even more desperate as the people Goldberg had chosen to fill those vacancies arrived. That, no doubt, made him feel much more secure. He had routed his most powerful opponents. He had won over a few remnants of the old dispensation. More importantly, perhaps, he had assiduously courted important sectors of the student body, showing affability and concern, which seemed to them far more attractive and humane than the habitual reserve, bordering at times on a suspicion of indifference, they had experienced in earlier years. And now he also had forces to back him up. Nothing, it seemed, could halt his progress. Those responsible for his appointment were purring with satisfaction at how astute they had been.

Of the new members of staff, the most loyal and significant were Maggie and Jock Tomlinson, Goldberg's allies in the disputes of the Melbourne department, faithful supporters on whom he knew he could rely without hesitation. Some of the other imports proved somewhat less pliable. In later years, when it was possible to stand back from that awful time, I came to feel sorry for some of them. They were decent people. For instance, Tim Kelly, a priest, was a person of genuine goodwill and tolerance. I suspect that he must have been deeply troubled by the way his intellectual and academic sympathy for Goldberg's ideals were harnessed in a brutal political game. Among those whom Goldberg had imported or who were in broad agreement with his principles and academic preoccupations, only Greer stood up to him: defiantly questioning his authority and judgment, even though it was clear to us that she had considerable empathy with what he stood for. For the rest, their good nature and entirely genuine and honourable educational and literary convictions were turned into weapons in the campaign Goldberg waged, without regard for the consequences such abuse might have.

The most tragic instance of Goldberg's ruthless indifference to others was a young man called Andrew Deacon. He was one of Goldberg's last appointments, made at a time when the great enterprise was crumbling, when everyone knew that Goldberg and the Tomlinsons would return to Melbourne at the first opportunity, abandoning those who had compromised themselves in the bitter disputes of the previous two or three years. Deacon was a most nervous and insecure person. Though he was academically gifted, his diffidence made him a poor teacher. He lacked, moreover, all political skill or prudence; he reminded me of a loose-limbed dog as he unquestioningly ran to pick up sticks of dynamite Goldberg and the Tomlinsons often threw for him to retrieve. I do not think that he understood how desperate the situation had become, how Goldberg's star had almost set. And then he was abandoned, obliged to remain in a department where many regarded him with contempt, where he had so alienated himself from others that even he came to realise how precarious and dangerous his situation had become. That knowledge destroyed him. I remember a dreadful moment during the tea break in a particularly stormy meeting when he vomited into the common-room sink. Eventually he left the department. His death some time later was, I am sure, prompted in part by the scars his experiences in Sydney had left behind.

There were others, too, with whom, I suspected, cordial and even sympathetic relationships might have been possible in a less poisoned environment—Wilbur Sanders for instance, whose brief time in Sydney was merely a prelude to his progress to greater glories in Cambridge. John Wiltshire spent somewhat longer in the Sydney department. I remember him, also, as someone caught in an impossibly overheated situation where his intellectual and academic inclination towards

Leavis's doctrines ran into conflict with the political demands made on him in an increasingly acrimonious climate. Indeed, Wiltshire was for a while one of the editors of a journal called *Balcony* which two relative newcomers, Michael Wilding and Stephen Knight, started together with several other members of the department, myself included. The increasingly hostile stance *Balcony* took towards the new orthodoxy eventually obliged Wiltshire to dissociate himself from it. Nevertheless, his relationships with the rest of us remained as cordial as circumstances permitted. With the Tomlinsons, however, nothing of the kind would have been possible.

Goldberg's personality was formal, remote and enigmatic. Some who knew him well claimed that he possessed considerable charm and urbanity. His was not the kind of personality, however, that would easily appeal to the student population, except perhaps to a handful of the most favoured, who were treated with spectacular partiality. To woo (and also to intimidate) the student body at large was left to the more flamboyant personalities of Maggie and Jock Tomlinson. Maggie, in particular, played a vital (and ultimately destructive) role in the rapid refashioning of the department that took place after 1964.

I remember her as a Lady Macbeth in a tartan skirt. Her personality was forceful, supported by considerable intellectual skill. There was a hard-edged arrogance about her dealings with others, colleagues and students alike, which could nevertheless transform itself into a skittish charm with barely disguised seductive undertones. In the climate of those pre-feminist days Maggie was able to exploit without compunction a repertoire of flirtatious devices—which could, in an instant, turn themselves into displays of hissing malice. It was she, more than anyone else, who raised the temperature of the department to a pitch of resentment and frustration because, or so it seemed to me, her ill-will and arrogance were entirely undisguised. Certainly the bitter lessons I had to learn at the beginning of my academic career came largely as a result of my dealings with her.

As soon as the arrangements for 1964 were completed, it became obvious that many of us were to be removed from any possible influence over those students on whom the department's resources were to be lavished. Goldberg and the Tomlinsons were not particularly concerned with the pass students who constituted the bulk of the undergraduate population. They were, of course, to be indoctrinated up to a point in what was rapidly becoming a secular religion, but such was the relative contempt in which those students were held that Goldberg's energy and machinations were largely directed at the honours students, who would form an enlightened elite among the helots. Accordingly, most of us, the remnants of the old dispensation, were employed in giving tutorials which were obviously regarded as supplementary to the lectures where the new gospel was promulgated. Yet there were not enough tutorials to go round, even in those generous days when a class of ten undergraduates could be considered crowded. For many of us therefore, some other form of employment had to be found. I was allowed to give a series of lectures in the first year, but only in the evening. The implications of that would have been clear enough to me even if Jock Tomlinson, whose indiscretions sometimes caused Goldberg great embarrassment, hadn't been in the habit of announcing at staff meetings that evening students 'didn't matter'. The other distinction I received was to teach in a series of seminars on drama in the all-important honours strand in the third year.

Or at least that is how it was presented. In reality it was tutelage under Maggie Tomlinson's watchful eyes. Because the university was flush with funds in those days, no extravagance, no matter how prodigal, proved impossible. The forty-odd students in the third year of the honours school were divided into two groups for those year-long seminars that met for two hours each week. The course consisted of a survey of drama from classical Greek tragedy to Pirandello, an attractive enough syllabus, had it not been so weighed down by ideology and dogma. Maggie presided over both groups. In the name of exposing students to a diversity of views, each of those two meetings was attended by two other members of staff, though a different pair in each case. That neat arrangement gave Maggie effective control over the course: she alone came into contact with every student, and she alone could indulge, therefore, in the highly effective rhetorical ploy, à propos Aeschylus, Shakespeare or Ibsen, for instance: 'As we discovered in the other class . . . '

The other, perhaps more subtle indication of where the real power lay was in the venue of these and other seminars. Provoking considerable resentment even before they arrived, the Tomlinsons had been among the first to overcome the university's reluctance to appoint married couples, especially to the same department. The particular cause of resentment in a department made up largely of single people, or of men with young families whose wives did not and probably could not work, came from the Tomlinsons' nice opportunity to indulge in perfectly legal double-dipping in such matters as subsidised housing loans and sabbatical benefits. Added to that, both had been appointed to senior lectureships at a time when something of a log jam was beginning to develop among lecturers waiting their turn for promotion. That entitled the Tomlinsons to two choice rooms in the main building.

Maggie's in particular was spacious enough to contain the twenty or so students and the two other members of staff at the seminars which, I found, became increasingly burdensome displays of power in the year that I 'taught' the course.

The quotation marks are unavoidable, for in no conceivable way could my contribution have been regarded as teaching. Maggie was in charge. We gathered in her room, carrying piles of books, finding somewhere to sit on rickety stacking chairs while Maggie was enthroned in a deep leather armchair, often with her knees drawn up in a half-reclining position like an odalisque. From time to time she would raise herself from that faintly seductive position to search for something on her well-stocked shelves in order to consult a book, an essay, or a footnote that had suddenly become relevant—except that the suspicion grew on me very soon that these impromptus had been carefully calculated to remind everyone of her central and indispensable role. The rest of us were obliged to come well armed with books, or to trust our memories if we wished to bring off some such coup.

I found those ceremonies galling and humiliating. I could not help comparing myself with student-teachers in Victorian novels, people trapped in an ambiguous limbo between the teacher and the taught. I had no role, no function. Maggie always took the initiative. In order to make your presence felt you had to interpose and endure blatantly explicit body language from Maggie, who would uncurl herself from her chair for the occasion in such a way as to indicate that you were becoming tendentious, boring or disruptive. She invited students to participate in her little games; she played to the gallery, seeking complicity and approval. I remember one appalling seminar on *King Lear*. I had managed to find a niche in the discussion to slip in a remark. She looked at me and then, after an intolerable pause, casually remarked that that was precisely what the Fool in the play says. A snigger went round the room. I felt enraged, but realised that I had no comeback. And so, week after week I bared my neck for the knife. I knew how damaging it was, but I was driven by the knowledge that somehow I had to prove myself in the slippery, treacherous first year or two of an academic career if I were not to sink into obscurity. Yet I also realised that whatever I said, whatever contribution I attempted to make would be mocked and scorned. I was the fall guy, the living example of the bad old ways that were never to return.

I often wished that I could have followed the example of the other member of that putative trio of teachers, who had also been consigned to a shamefully subservient position. It was Thelma Herring. Goldberg and the Tomlinsons had her in their sights, and their campaign was successful: Thelma left the university to take up a position with Harold Oliver at the University of New South Wales, only to return when the departure of Goldberg and his supporters left several vacancies in the Sydney department.

In the meantime, though, Thelma had to endure the same humiliation as I encountered. Her way of dealing with the situation may, for all I know, have been more effective than my suicidal attempts to make an impression. She turned up dutifully each week with the appropriate text and a few pages of paper covered in her small, neat handwriting. But she said nothing. She listened, politely impassive, betraying no sign of irritation, as if it were most natural thing for a person of her experience and erudition to sit there and receive instruction. Or so it seemed.

Once and once only did Thelma speak out. It occurred during a group of seminars on Aeschylus. We were reading the three plays of the *Oresteia*—in translation, of course. I noticed at the beginning of those weeks that Thelma had with her not the slender, brown-edged Penguin Classic, but a substantial book which obviously contained the Greek text. I doubt if Maggie noticed, or if she did, she pointedly ignored it. We came to the last chorus of the last play, a hymn to the superiority of reconciliation over vengeful justice. Maggie was spinning some elaborate theory about Aeschylus, about Greek tragedy, indeed about 'great' literature in general, arguing that everything in the cycle tends to the climactic moment of that final chorus, that what had gone before—the terrible story of Clytemnestra's vengeance on Agamemnon and the subsequent lust for revenge in their children, Electra and Orestes—demanded the focus and resolution of that peroration.

She went on, I remember, even longer than was her habit, making more and more all-embracing claims about the centrality not merely of the three plays of the *Oresteia* but of Aeschylus's other tragedies for the traditions of Western literature. All her comments were focussed on that last chorus. Without it, she implied, the three plays would be no more than primitive tales of blood-lust. The chorus was some kind of breakthrough, an indication of the ethical and imaginative greatness Greek civilisation could achieve. There was at one moment a brief pause, probably so that Maggie could light yet another cigarette. Then Thelma spoke. She pointed out that, according to the best scholars, the chorus was no part of the original play, but had been added by a Christian redactor, in order to make the cycle acceptable to the standards of a recently converted Byzantine society. She read out a few lines of the Greek—which none of us could understand—and commented that the Christian imagery was fully evident there.

Maggie should have been covered in shame. She had been found out, having committed the gravest academic sin: she had pontificated on a subject where her knowledge was partial and defective. I remember looking at her, wondering whether she would betray the least sign of hesitation or doubt. But I could see nothing. Without even acknowledging that Thelma had spoken, she continued, as before.

7

The Tomlinsons were Goldberg's most effective lieutenants and, like faithful retainers and henchmen in Elizabethan melodramas, they seemed entirely content to wage campaigns of attrition, humiliation and even, in a manner of speaking, assassination. Maggie was shameless, it seemed to me, in the way she made her contempt for us obvious, or refused to be cowed even when her lack of scholarly attainment was pointed out to her by Thelma's gentle but by no means innocent remark. Nevertheless, the force of her personality made her compelling, even attractive in a peculiar fashion. Jock seemed less gifted where complicated political games were concerned.

It became clear that he was capable of being something of an embarrassment. Tall and bloodless—he suffered from diabetes, as we found out—his attention seemed often to wander, perhaps because of fluctuations in his blood sugar. Sometimes he would betray a part of the master plan that the cabal had concocted. At tense moments in meetings when Goldberg was intent on playing a game of deception, throwing out smokescreens that became increasingly transparent after we had come to know how to read signals, Jock would fall into damaging indiscretions. He would mention something which, he claimed, we had 'agreed' on, whereas the only agreement that had occurred was behind closed doors, in great secrecy.

Goldberg, by contrast, was far more devious. He always claimed to be neutral and objective, without preconceptions, prepared in the proper way of collegiality to be guided by consensus. Early on we learnt the lesson of the unending meeting. Whenever some important issue came up for consideration, Goldberg announced that we would be obliged to continue a meeting at night or at the weekend. We sat in his large, smoke-filled room, endlessly going around the same matter, voting on innumerable variations on the same motion until, in most cases, exhaustion finally allowed him to have his way. I remember one extraordinary occasion. His wife was expecting their first child. At some point in a tense and acrimonious meeting Goldberg's telephone rang. He listened, muttered a few words of thanks and hung up. Then the meeting continued, for some hours as I recall. Only later did we discover that the telephone call was from the hospital to let him know that their child had just been born.

His other weapon was a characteristic mixture of flattery and intimidation. This, I found, was particularly disconcerting because the intimate tone was completely at odds with his customary indifference to many of his colleagues and their lives. He seemed to have no interests beyond his professional life. I remember running into him one night after I had just finished an early dinner in the staff club. Since we were both standing in a narrow doorway it was impossible not to acknowledge each other. Was I working back late? he asked. No, I replied, perhaps foolishly, I was on my way to the opera. I remember his eyes growing wide in genuine or perhaps feigned disbelief: he could never understand why anyone would bother going to the opera, he remarked.

Such incidents represented the gamut of our dealings. I was one of the lesser fry who could be safely ignored. It was all the more disconcerting therefore when his secretary rang one day to say that Goldberg wanted to see me. What did he want? Why the sudden need to speak? I turned up for the interview so early that I had to cool my heels in the secretary's room. I felt like a schoolboy waiting outside the headmaster's door. Goldberg kept me waiting five, perhaps ten minutes, an eternity. Then the secretary's telephone buzzed and she told me that he was ready to see me.

Goldberg could not have been more charming or affable. He offered me sherry, saying how sorry he was that he hadn't been able to have a good talk with me earlier, but there had been so much to do, settling into a new place was so demanding . . . The clichés flowed smoothly for a moment or two. I shuffled in my seat, perplexed by a mixture of suspicion and a tiny skerrick of hope: had I misjudged him, had I been seduced by my colleagues' ill-will and hostility? Anyway, Goldberg continued, he was anxious to find out how I was getting on. Was everything all right? Was I enjoying the work? He knew, he said, how difficult the first couple of years can be, so many classes to prepare, so much unfamiliar routine to get used to. I muttered something, I forget what. Then he changed tack. What did I think of the department, were we on the right course, were our students being properly taught? I did not know what to say. Obviously, any reply I made could have been compromising; to stay silent, however, would have been equally damaging, I realised. As in our meeting in London, I felt cornered. Again, I tried to say something non-committal. Then Goldberg sprang.

He started asking for my opinion of Wilkes, of Herring (again), of Ron Dunlop, of John Burrows, who had joined the department just before I left for London. He wanted to know whether I thought them capable of teaching our students effectively. He relied particularly on my opinion, he added, because after all I had been taught by some of these people. What was my attitude now that I had been their colleague for some time?

I was appalled. What could I have said? Could I have as much as mentioned our undergraduate scorn for Thelma's betoqued sing-song tours of Beaumont and Fletcher? Could I, on the other hand, have spoken as warmly as I knew I could about, for instance, Dunlop's marvellous gifts as a lecturer on poetry? To have mentioned one while remaining silent about the other would have been worse condemnation than saying outright that as a student I had thought Thelma a pain in the neck, but that I now acknowledged her great gifts and erudition. Once more, I mumbled something to the effect that I found it hard to decide, being a relative newcomer to the profession, but that everything seemed to be 'all right', or some such feeble phrase.

Again, Goldberg changed course abruptly. He began speaking about the financial difficulties of the university and the department, which surprised me given that the procession of recruits seemed unending at the time. I must think of my future, he advised, all concern and goodwill it seemed. In three or four years, when I would be ready to apply for promotion, the competition would be intense. He paused, apparently thinking deeply as he lit a cigarette. He didn't know what to advise me, he went on after an intolerable silence, during which my alarm and anxiety ballooned almost out of control. Perhaps if the opportunity arose for a more senior appointment in another university, I should consider throwing my hat in—I could count on his unstinted support. He didn't want to lose me; he was only thinking of my best interests. And besides, that way I'd be in a position of much greater strength to return to Sydney when a really good job came up, something he'd welcome, of course.

So there it was. I had been as good as given my marching orders. The interview came to a sudden end a moment or two later when, glancing at his watch, Goldberg said that he had a meeting to attend. Years later, I found out that other relatively junior people had had much the same conversation, brought to an end as abruptly by the call of duty. At the time, however, it seemed to me that I had been singled out for what amounted to a notice of no-confidence. I was in despair. I didn't dare mention the interview to anyone else, so compromised had my situation become. For weeks, perhaps months, I went about my work in a distracted state. My mind ran constantly around the one question: what to do? And I had begun, as well, to blame myself bitterly for having been so precipitate in accepting the offer of the position in Sydney.

8

That interview put the cap on my disillusionment with the dreams that had propelled me towards a career which now seemed to be lying in ruins even before it had begun. My years in London and the recognition of the tedium and repetitiveness of the scholarly life had been enough to take the shine off the bright vision I had once entertained of passing on the accumulated glories of English literary culture. That arrogance could not have stood the test of the reality, the recognition that the fantasy England failed to account for the bleakness and, indeed, philistinism of much of contemporary English life. Nevertheless, the experience of the first two or three years of my professional life, when I began to doubt whether I would even have employment much longer, made me more conscious of what I saw as the folly of imitativeness, of an attempt to replicate English ways under an indifferent if not hostile sky. That insistent suspicion came to me because of the particular flavour of the literary and cultural preoccupations that seemed to impel Goldberg, the Tomlinsons and their supporters on their grand project to reshape the Sydney English Department, and along with it, in a way, the university itself.

The rhetoric of those years, insistently reiterated in lectures and seminars, in meetings of the staff–student literary society, suggested the very opposite of the slavish mimicry of English models of which the old dispensation seemed to have been guilty. In place of a mindless worship of literary figures hallowed by a bankrupt and irrelevant tradition, the new spirit promised to offer a course of study which would be meaningful for our individual and communal lives. Books would be read not because of their often spurious reputation for greatness but as a means of throwing light on fundamental questions, irrespective of class, status or allegiance. The new order promised to justify its syllabuses and requirements by more than the Everest-principle. Certain allegedly towering peaks of English literary history—Edmund Spenser and *The Faerie Queene*, for example—could safely be bypassed because their prominence was based on an outmoded and hoary academic cast of mind, wholly out of touch with true literary value and the vital function of literary study in a civilised society.

The iconoclasm of that call to arms was, of course, attractive to most undergraduates. It promised a bright new world freed from the tedium of wading through difficult and often obscure texts of restricted interest and excitement. It answered the desire for change and justified what might have seemed whimsical and arbitrary compulsions by a rigorous logic of relevance and accountability. In that, the manner in which the new courses and their underlying assumptions were sold to the student body and the academic community prefigured the justification for later upheavals in English studies and the humanities in general. Admittedly, the ideological bases on which Goldberg's reforms were built seemed remote from the neo-Marxist politicising that spread slowly through universities in the years after 1968. What is more, some of Goldberg's former supporters and sympathisers in the university became the most dedicated opponents of such left-wing tendencies as the introduction of courses in women's studies and postcolonial literature. During the years of the Vietnam War they took, on the whole, a pronounced conservative and anti-Communist stance. I remember one very nasty incident at a staff party when two of my colleagues almost came to blows over the propriety of conscripting young men for the conflict. Nevertheless, despite this political conservatism, Goldberg and his sympathisers were as effective in challenging the bases on which the university had been established as later, more politically ambitious academics with their overt programmes to refashion intellectual life. In both cases the same call to abandon a discredited and meaningless past could be heard. Both claimed to be the enemies of mere tradition and its sanction of the worthless, the outmoded and the repressive. Only the rhetoric differed: Spenser was banished from Goldberg's pantheon because his epic did not conform with notions of organic and quasi-spontaneous greatness; its highly artificial contrivance and the battery of rhetorical and mythological devices proved insupportable to a notion of literature that came from the heart and from immediate sensory experiences, without reliance on conventional modes of utterance. Twenty years later Spenser was again to be excluded because he represented patriarchal privilege.

Yet the brave new world that was supposed to save English Studies in Sydney from unthinking imitation of distant models was itself imitation and pastiche. Despite the talk of relevance, the insistence that only deep personal responses justified notions of literary greatness, and despite the scorn for such traditional pursuits as literary history, the study of genres, conventions, and a concern with writers' biographies, the new model was content almost entirely to rely only on texts and ways of approaching them approved by Leavis and his British followers. Though Goldberg and the Tomlinsons frequently accused us, the remnants of the old dispensation, of slavishly following Oxford habits, they themselves were doing little more than replaying in their antipodean fortress the battles of Downing College, Cambridge.

Nothing else would explain some of the more bizarre developments in the syllabuses of those years. There was, for instance, the unqualified worship of Donne, or more accurately of a small portion of his *oeuvre*, the more familiar of the *Songs and Sonets*. Donne had been taught extensively in the old syllabuses, but not with the same degree of adulation, the same insistence on his absolute centrality to the traditions of English verse. The reason for this adulation had ultimately to do with an attempt to discredit the preoccupation of conventional literary scholarship with the formal, highly artificial sonneteers of Donne's age: Sidney, Daniel, Drayton and Greville. In his cynical love poems, Donne mocked that school of poets mercilessly; in their championship of Donne, Leavis and his followers attempted to affront powerful critics and academics, exponents of the traditional wisdom in literary study, whom they saw as the enemies of reason, good taste, and, of course, of their own careers.

They also waged the same war over Lawrence. After Goldberg's syllabuses became established, it proved practically impossible to avoid Lawrence wherever you turned. It seemed as if he were the pinnacle of all novelists, the yardstick by which everyone else was to be measured. Our hapless students were obliged to study the most highly esteemed of his novels, *The Rainbow* and *Women in Love*, not once but twice in consecutive years. *King Lear*, one of the few Shakespeare plays to receive unstinted approval, was the only other text I recall to be honoured by such distinction. Yet the only reason Lawrence was deemed vital to the study of English literature was intimately connected with Leavis's parochial squabbles with Bloomsbury and the improper privilege it enjoyed. This gifted, important but by no means universally significant writer's work came to have an insupportable burden placed on it. Undergraduates in Sydney were required to go through the motions of adulating someone who wrote about social conditions hopelessly alien to their experience.

The obsession with Leavis knew no bounds. Goldberg and the Tomlinsons seemed to have no interest in any writing not noticed or approved by him or his followers. They ignored entirely the flowering of Australian literature that was getting under way at the time, not because they regarded it as Wilkes's domain, but because it fell outside the approved confines. The sense of cultural dependency was as strong and even more stifling than it had been under the old dispensation. Whatever we did, whatever practices we adopted were based on models that may have been appropriate for a distant society but were not capable of wholesale importation into a very different world. As much as the people who had taught me, alert to the signals from Oxford coming by way of *The Review of English Studies* and other august journals, Goldberg and his associates were highly attuned to the word from Cambridge.

Their imitativeness and dependence had some bizarre consequences. Sometimes fancy footwork was called for, as in the case of Dickens. In *The Great Tradition* Leavis had declared Dickens a great entertainer but not a great novelist. That became the Sydney gospel: Dickens disappeared from syllabuses, except for *Hard Times*, that uncharacteristically brief and dull novel which had been approved—largely, I suspected, because it is so uncharacteristic. Our students settled into comfortable ways. Dickens was not on the side of life; his language was not organic or 'concrete' but contrived; his characters and situations had not been imaginatively realised but imposed according to dead conventions and a stultifying quest for colour and effect. All that was required for students to receive accolades for their critical skill and ability were a few examples showing these failings. And, as always, some students proved better parodists than others. On them fortune smiled.

Then the unthinkable happened. Leavis re-read Dickens, and recanted. Again, the more cynical suspected that he had been driven by the need to find a subject for another book. Nevertheless, our syllabuses were rejigged, a new unquestionable orthodoxy arose. Now we celebrated Dickens's great zest for life, the tactile concreteness of his language, its lively origins in the rhythms of ordinary speech. And, as before, our students followed suit, discovering that Dickens spoke to them with an immediacy and conviction which they, or their predecessors only a year or two earlier, had found entirely lacking in his novels.

Even more peculiar was the unthinking and wholesale adoption of another celebrated ritual of dubious use or relevance. It went by the rather strange name of 'Dating'. One of the cardinal points of the dogma that issued from Downing College was that literary history had to be understood and constructed from within the textures of literary works and the language in which they are couched. There was an absolute horror of the kind of work I had been doing in my struggles to make something interesting out of James Shirley's plays: an attempt to discover how far they mirrored or diverged from the political, cultural and social climate of his time. Classes in Dating consisted of students' being given extracts in prose or verse on sheets of paper, without any indication of title, date of composition or author. From their exploration of the language, they were expected to 'feel' their way into the text in order to identify the period in which it had been written and, in some cases, the identity of the author.

It was a profoundly anti-academic, philistine practice. It promoted the lucky guess above scholarship, and it was dangerously prone to abuse. According to some people, the Tomlinsons (who were the chief exponents of these rites) were not above giving their students extracts from Chatterton's imitations of medieval lyrics, placing an entirely improper requirement on them to identify an eighteenth-century pastiche of thirteenth-century verse. Yet even where their practices were not so blatantly devious, the enterprise itself remained wholly meretricious. There is considerable justification for urging students to read carefully and with great attention to nuances of language and usage. But the material used for these classes was, almost without exception, those significant passages which had been hallowed by the practices of Downing College and its admirers. Students were expected to recognise the 'date' of something which did not emerge from their own experience but from the preoccupations of a distant world. They were required to possess not merely sensitivity to changes in language and idiom over the centuries, a skill quite possible for them to acquire, but also a recognition of changes in incidental details of English life which lay beyond their capacities and experience.

Certain personal and professional consequences of these parlour-games were far more reprehensible, however. There was much talk of the essential bond between academics and students. That was the time when the regrettable habit of students and their teachers calling each other by their first names began. Yet the atmosphere of the department was the contrary of such co-operative mutuality. Goldberg and the Tomlinsons exercised far greater control over their students than had been the habit in the easygoing, perhaps dilettantish department of my undergraduate years. The preoccupation with continuous assessment began in those days: students could no longer afford to waste months (as I had) exploring other, equally valid aspects of university life. Under the new dispensation they were expected to clear hurdles every few weeks; the consequences of tipping the bars could be disastrous, for the new orthodoxy proved unforgiving towards those who failed to meet its requirements. Yet even when they managed to mouth dutifully the platitudes they had learnt, sometimes by rote, our students found themselves controlled, manipulated, consistently reminded of their subservient role—not least in the ceremonies of Dating, because, despite the rhetoric, their teachers had a most effective weapon of attrition: they knew the title, the date and the author of the poem or passage of prose about which their charges were obliged to make at times desperate guesses. Moreover, the contempt and mockery whenever one of them made an unfortunate or ridiculous guess were often boundless.

These unpleasant ceremonies were also the product of the indiscriminate adoption of what was, perhaps, the central tenet of Leavis's teachings. An article of faith his Australian disciples shared had a curiously apocalyptic flavour, as befits the kind of secular fundamentalism they displayed. They had to contend with a hostile and malevolent world, or at least with a philistine academic oligarchy. Because they had been privileged with a vision of the true function of literary studies and with a mission to set society on the path of cultural righteousness, the forces of darkness were (they were convinced) arrayed against them. Constant vigilance was needed to guard their precious convictions; the good fight had to be fought each day and on every side.

They displayed a characteristic mixture of ruthless arrogance on the one hand and the plangency of victims on the other—perhaps the habit had been acquired from Leavis's Huguenot forbears. There was something essentially Calvinistic in their conviction that students could not acquire critical or literary competence, but had to be born with some innate gift that could only be encouraged or nurtured by their teachers. As with Calvinist doctrine, too, those not chosen—by some mysterious process of genetics or environmental conditioning—were nevertheless obliged to play the game by the rules, even though salvation would remain invariably denied to them. Accordingly, our small world was divided into the elect (inevitably few in number) and those who would never receive illumination or grace. The latter had to be kept in strict control, for we were rebellious and liable to align ourselves with the forces of darkness.

These fantasies of persecution led to the prosecution of those who seemed enemies of progress and reason. There was a hint of the paradoxical atmosphere of totalitarianism abroad: those who exercised near-absolute power presented themselves as vulnerable, as victims of dangerous conspiracies by forces capable of toppling them. Perhaps

Goldberg believed that such was the case; or perhaps he was playing a profoundly cynical game. The result was the same: unprofessional conduct, an infringement of the ground rules of collegiate life, seemed to have been justified by exceptional circumstances. It was, or feigned to be, a question of survival. And so the atmosphere became increasingly poisoned as the months went by.

Those of us who felt most threatened became suspicious and tetchy. I remember that gradually I began to grow mistrustful. Had others struck a bargain with Goldberg? Would the isolation of those—myself included—for whom there seemed no hope increase as each week went by, while others compromised or allowed themselves to be seduced by one of those ambiguous interviews? I remember entertaining nasty suspicions. At one time I imagined that Michael Wilding, who had struck me as fierce in his nonconformism, might have allowed himself to be wooed. I also remember an occasion when I said something scathing to Germaine Greer. She turned on me like a spitfire. So she too had sold out, I thought. Several other people experienced similar suspicions, entertained the same fantasies as they tried to read signals, or sought to interpret the import of insignificant events.

Many of the students had also been caught up in the paranoia that swept across the department. Goldberg encouraged them to unburden themselves over their dissatisfaction with certain of their teachers. Some of us suspected that he discussed us with students, dwelling on our inadequacies. At times I thought that the suspicion might have been no more than the product of an overactive imagination. Others, of an even more gloomy disposition, insisted that it was no fantasy but a deliberate campaign to discredit and discourage us. Many years later I discovered that they had been right. In the early nineties I met a former student. I wouldn't remember her, she told me, she had studied English at the beginning of the sixties. It was a strange time, she said, and then, to my surprise and slight embarrassment, she apologised for having made so much fun of me behind my back. I told her that I hadn't realised. She paused for an instant and then, looking me straight in the face, went on: 'Oh, but you must have known, everyone did.'

Of course, I was not entirely honest when I found myself unexpectedly reminded of a period of anger and distress. I had guessed at the time that I shared the mockery and denigration of many of my colleagues that went on, quite openly, even in lectures and classes. I knew well enough that my history and the kind of doctoral work I had done would have disqualified me in the eyes of the new orthodoxy.

I suppose that I tried to shut my mind to much of it, but it was impossible to ignore entirely a desperate and depressing situation. I felt trapped. Perhaps Goldberg was right, I began thinking after a while; perhaps I should look for a job somewhere else.

But that precisely was the catch. Cross might have been able to walk into a conveniently vacant chair: he had seniority behind him, though I suspected that influence and networks were probably instrumental in his appointment. Obviously Simmonds had been able to capitalise on the good impression he had made at Pittsburgh, and besides, he had had several reasonably successful years in Sydney, time enough to confirm the promise he had shown as a postgraduate candidate. But what did I have to show? A thesis on an obscure seventeenth-century playwright, which even I thought of as merely an exercise in scholarly methods? It was hardly enough to make the world sit up and take note. Even in normal circumstances, I knew only too well, it would have been necessary for me to demonstrate skill and ability: by publications and by acquiring a reputation as a gifted teacher and supervisor of research work. Everyone knew that it takes years to achieve such distinction. What hope, then, did I—who had only just started my first appointment—have in persuading another university to employ me? And besides, I had produced next to nothing. Any competent authority would realise that my teaching duties reflected a judgment of my abilities. Being quarantined in evening lectures and collaborating in seminars where another member of the department was clearly in charge were hardly the signs of a competent, let alone exceptional academic. And worst of all, I knew that even if those barriers could have been overcome there remained the one essential hurdle: a reference from Goldberg. Without his commendation nothing—not even the most glowing reference from Wilkes or Brown—would have carried much weight.

Anxiety, the dreadful sense that my career had run into a brick wall even before it began, took its inevitable toll. During those months my insomnia increased alarmingly. I suspected that I was getting an ulcer. Most seriously, however, I was doing little else than teaching the few classes I had been allowed to give and offering myself up for sacrifice in Maggie Tomlinson's drama seminars—or even to Jock Tomlinson in another series of classes run on the same model, where the humiliation was slightly less painful largely because Jock was as little competent at malice as at intrigue. A worshipper of Lawrence who habitually got the novels mixed up wasn't in a very good position to point the finger at a colleague's failings. Research I neglected entirely. I did not have the heart or the stomach for the kind of fiddling, time-consuming work that requires patience and detachment. And in any event, Goldberg was scathing of those who were content with 'scholarship', instead of aspiring to the higher reaches of criticism. Yet even to contemplate critical writing in that noisome climate was unthinkable. I didn't feel ready for it; I knew that I hadn't had time to begin to sort out my priorities. All I had was a profound distaste for the mean-spirited critical practices dominating the department in those days. I realised that despite all the uplifting talk about the unique power of great literature to save the world from barbarism, few moments of insight or illumination arose. Most of the lectures and classes consisted of carping complaints about the undeserved reputation of those writers who had been excluded from Goldberg's pantheon. It was a road I did not feel inclined to travel.

I could see no solution to these conundrums. I considered giving the game away. But then the other equally desperate question arose. What would I do? I realised that I had no qualifications except for teaching. Could I endure a life teaching resentful adolescents in schools, I asked myself. And there was pride, too. I remembered the way my parents' acquaintances—prosperous clothing manufacturers, real-estate developers, jewellers and defrauders of public companies—had been scathing of my ambition to become an academic. I could not allow them to enjoy that satisfaction. Nor did I want to distress my parents: I kept from them as much of my anxiety as I could. Fortunately, they were so delighted by what they saw as my good fortune and the vindication of their support throughout the years, that they shut their eyes to the sad fact that their son's new career was crumbling around him. I realised that I would have to stick it out. The problem was how to do so.

Towards the end of my second year, I thought that I had found a possible solution. I sensed that within twelve months or so Goldberg would have accomplished his stranglehold on the department. At the time, though, everyone suspected that there were several people whom he would have liked to bring to Sydney but for whom he could find no vacancies. I reckoned that it would be in his interest to see me go. The only way he could achieve that was by giving me the kind of reference that would allow another institution to take me on board. If, on the other hand, I waited long enough for him to achieve his aims, he would be far less likely to provide that reference—for I realised by then that the considerable streak of malice in him would have relished the discomfiture of those who were trapped. He needed some exemplary figures to continue with the fantasy that he, the bearer of light, had constantly to struggle against darkest ignorance. I decided that there was nothing for it but to look for another position before it was too late.

Deciding to leave was easy enough; how to go about it seemed far more difficult. The University of New South Wales was out of the question. Harold Oliver was firmly in charge there. I did not even contemplate moving interstate: if I were to live in Australia I could think of nowhere but Sydney where life could be endurable. At least my friends were there, allowing me to lead a life not entirely constrained by the university and its problems and disappointments.

There remained the third Sydney university, Macquarie, where almost everyone expected Wilkes to take up the foundation chair of English. Yet as the time for the opening of the new institution drew near, Wilkes gave no impression of a readiness to move. He seemed content in the chair of Australian Literature, editing *Southerly* and keeping his counsel. I began to feel irritated and frustrated by what seemed to be mere inertia. He was difficult to talk to. Once or twice I tried to have a conversation with him about Macquarie, trying to read the signals, but I got nowhere. I was not at all confident that he would be able to offer me a job if he decided to move on.

George Russell, who had succeeded Mitchell as the Professor of Early English Literature and Language, was more forthcoming. A gregarious, affable man, he found the nasty atmosphere in the other and dominant section of the department profoundly distasteful. He was generous with his hospitality to those who, he felt, needed support in treacherous times. The advice he gave was hardly encouraging though. Get out, he said, and as soon as possible: every month I stayed in Sydney, he went on, would make it harder for me to find another place. I didn't thank him for that: he only confirmed what I suspected. Besides, I began to sense a diffidence in him, an understandable reluctance to tackle Goldberg head on. Several times he shied away from a confrontation, gave in to Goldberg's demands about the relationship between the two sections of the department, and thereby lost a little more influence and ability to shape the course of affairs. I knew that I could not look to him for anything other than well-meant but entirely depressing guidance. And all along Wilkes kept his thoughts to himself.

It was desperation more than good sense that made me decide to look abroad. I thought about those ambiguous conversations in the Marlborough in the weeks just before I accepted the offer of the position in Sydney. Now I reproached myself for having been so hasty. I should have waited a few days, tested the temperature of the water. Perhaps if Brown had had a week or so to arrange something, a concrete proposal might have arisen. As it was, no sooner had he learnt of the offer from Sydney than I told him of my decision to accept. It had been, I decided in retrospect, a disastrous miscalculation. I tried to find some comfort in the possibility that it might not have been too late. Brown had been courteous and sympathetic in his letters—much more so than when I had to deal with him in person. He had also helped me publish two short notes on Shirley in the prestigious *Review of English Studies*. Perhaps I should try again.

That prospect seemed particularly alluring because the experiences of the two years or so since my return to Australia had all but extinguished the foolish notions that had sustained me when I longed to become a part of the academic community. I wanted to live in Europe again. I could even make light of one of the most potent reasons I had for returning to Sydney: to be near my ageing and financially insecure parents. It was time to think of myself for a change. I decided that I would try to become what I had always been in spirit, European. I would do everything to find a position in England—at University College in London, if possible, and if that proved out of the question, I would gladly consider working in the most obscure of provincial universities or polytechnics. The only imperative was to get away, not merely from the disputes of the Sydney department, but from Australia itself—from an imitative world that could erect a parody of a great English university but never rise to emulating its fundamental strengths.

The more sensible part of me insisted that this was all sour-grapes, fantasy and wish-fulfilment. The other part kept on prompting me to try anyway, but how to go about finding a job in England proved a much more difficult problem. Then a piece of good fortune came my way. Academics were awarded a pay rise backdated some seven or eight months. There was a nice, unexpected lump sum. I decided to blow it on a trip to England in the long vacation. In those days academics' summers were leisurely. After the annual examinations had been marked by late November we were largely without duties until classes began again in March. I had three months.

There was, however, the awkward matter of obtaining permission to leave the country, something you were obliged to do in order not to jeopardise superannuation entitlements. It meant that I had to submit a formal request to Goldberg. I wasn't looking forward to that. He had made it plain enough that his authority was unlimited: when someone—I no longer remember whom—complained at a meeting about the uninteresting teaching he had been given, Goldberg looked over his glasses and announced that if he wished he could give that person no teaching whatever, merely require him to sit in his room between nine and five, five days a week. So how would he react to my request for leave? I made an appointment and again suffered agonies of anxiety and misgivings as I waited for the day to come round.

Once more I found myself sitting in Goldberg's large room, which he kept in semi-darkness most of the time. As on previous occasions he stayed behind his desk. It was not a good omen: according to an unwritten convention of collegiality you were supposed to meet face to face with your colleagues, not hide behind the authority of your desk. There was a moment's silence as he studied my letter of application. Then he looked up. What was I proposing to do? he asked. I had my answer ready: make a few alterations to my thesis, follow up one or two things I did not have time to include in it, and try to find someone who would publish it. This sounded plausible. I reminded him that I was not applying for travelling money, merely for the continuation of my salary over the three months. To my great surprise he agreed. It was an excellent idea, he said as he signed the form. Then he asked to be excused: he had a meeting to attend. I realised that he knew full well why I wanted to go to England. Perhaps he was keeping his fingers crossed, hoping that he might soon be rid of me.

9

Nothing came of that half-baked plan—and in truth I would not have known what to do if something had come of it. I had given no thought to practicalities: how I might resign from Sydney at short notice; how much money I might need to set up in London and to survive on a miserable British academic salary; what would become of my parents. Yet I went through the motions. I spent a great deal of time in the Marlborough, trying to drink as little lukewarm beer as I could decently manage, listening to Brown and Smith as they repeated their familiar litanies. I laughed at all the jokes, remembered to ask after absent members of the 'seminar' and tried in general to be a good chap.

Smith and Brown, for their part, were thirsty for gossip. The bush telegraph of the academic world had warned them long before that juicy things were going on in Sydney. Now they wanted to hear all about it from me, the first messenger to arrive fresh from the trenches. I discovered that some of their information had come from Alan

Brissenden in Adelaide, who had also applied for the same position in Sydney as I had and then accepted an offer from a university where he became a highly regarded and content member of the English Department. Well, Brown remarked, wasn't Alan the lucky one.

I obliged, of course. There was something both pleasing and unsettling about being the centre of attention, recounting choice anecdotes of folly and chicanery. I told them about a frightful weekend in a national park we had been obliged to spend with the student literary society. We hired canoes at the boatshed next door to the guesthouse, and each of us was instructed to row a student around the still, pond-like reach of the river. After all, that's what you did in Cambridge. But no-one had reckoned with the feral swans. They amused themselves by butting the boats, putting the fear of God into us, and almost overturning Goldberg as he floated with his favourite final-year student—the best graduate Sydney will ever have produced, he prophesied.

Smith and Brown enjoyed that hugely. During my recital Brown would laugh, slap the table: 'That's good, that's very good!' When I finished he hurried off to buy me another pint. I felt pleased but also a bit grubby, the role of the court jester hadn't figured largely in my fantasies.

I tried to steer the conversation around to my own difficulties, but neither seemed particularly interested. I tried another tack: I hadn't realised, I told them several times, how much I would miss having easy access to primary materials. There was relatively little research you could do without adequate libraries. It would be marvellous to be closer to the British Museum for a while, I added, realising how transparent my motive had become. On one occasion Brown almost snapped at me: there are always microfilms. I felt wounded and ashamed. I hadn't realised that he was in a sense talking about himself. I learnt much later that at the time he was already thinking of settling in Melbourne, where he spent the last years of his life. At those seminars in the Marlborough, however, all I could sense was rejection and indifference. My heart sank, but I kept returning to that grimy, smelly pub, drinking lukewarm beer and amusing the company with my tales.

When it was time to leave, no progress had been made. All that I took away with me was a strengthened conviction that I did not want to live in Australia. That brief, tantalising return to London made me ache all the more for the kind of life I had led there. I did not consider, of course, the differences between the life of a transient and the difficulties of permanency. I had not given any thought to what kind of life I would have been able to lead had the miracle come about and I had been offered a post at University College.

It did not occur to me that I could not have afforded to live indefinitely even in the tiny, dank basement flat in Kensington I had leased that winter. Despite the high rent it was an impossible place: dark, mouldy, poorly heated and airless. I ignored the question of how I would make ends meet on a lecturer's salary in London. A romantic hand-to-mouth existence seemed infinitely preferable to what was waiting for me at the end of a forty-hour flight. The awful situation in the English Department had somehow contaminated my feelings about life in Sydney. I dreaded going back to the squabbles and intrigues at the university, and also to a suburban world of dull propriety. I thought ruefully of the difference between the two lives. I could have spent the rest of my days travelling to the British Museum on the Underground, looking at the charladies, listening to the bowler-hatted twits braying about their weekends, observing the changes in the face of London, admiring the beautiful creatures of the Swinging Sixties who had replaced the pasty-faced teddy boys and their wraith-like girlfriends. In Sydney I would be sentenced to the stifling world of the outer suburbs, the whining lawnmowers of a weekend, the car-washing ceremonies, the disputes with neighbours who wanted fences removed to make our suburb look more like their fantasies of California, the snarling tangles of traffic I had to negotiate driving to and from the university.

As the plane made its way to Sydney, stopping every four or five hours in southern Europe, the Middle East, Pakistan, India, Thailand, Singapore, Darwin, I was more conscious than ever that the allure London held for me now had little to do with the myths and fantasies which had once enthralled me. It was indeed far simpler. London offered the closest possibility I could find to a way of life I might have been able to lead had not history forced my parents to leave their familiar European world for what seemed to us the strange formlessness of Australian life.

When I landed in Sydney on a blinding late-summer morning, I gave in to despondency. Everything seemed mean and ugly. The tiny, garishly coloured terraces in Botany Road, the factories and car-repair yards, the vacant lots overgrown with weeds, the fumes of the traffic, the terrible stench of the tannery that hung in the still air became, in my exhaustion and depression, emblems of a hellish place. As my father's car crawled along Cleveland Street, screeching brakes and churning engines everywhere, I caught sight of the university, its clock tower rising above the roofline of slums, warehouses and factories.

I remember being amazed at how I could once have thought that the squat turret and the buildings around it could have represented the best life could offer. I longed for that dank little basement in Kensington, the weak, watery daylight, the red buses and overcrowded tube stations and the knowledge that beyond them lay a great and exhilarating city where I would never, in all probability, be anything other than a bird of passage.

10

The new academic year promised to be a replica of the last. My months in London had persuaded me to resign myself to the inevitable, however. I felt no less frustrated or alarmed, but I had reconciled myself to the lack of any possibility of advancement or even professional satisfaction. At least I had a job—for the time being, that is. I would enjoy life as much as I could, and as much as life in Sydney could be enjoyed. I carried out my duties conscientiously (or so I hoped) but with as little exertion as I could manage. At least I was lucky in my friends, I told myself, or those that hadn't left to live abroad.

Surprisingly though, the new year brought some change. In the stories widely spread about after Goldberg returned to the University of Melbourne, it was usually maintained that he had been defeated by the entrenched power and intransigence of the Sydney department, its unqualified hostility to his timely reforms, its unanimity in opposing him from the moment of his arrival in 1963. In that legend Wilkes was cast as the silent Machiavellian intriguer, ruthlessly hiding behind a façade of indifference until the opportunity to leap had arrived. According to that version of the great dispute, Goldberg was never given a chance; the cards were stacked against him from the outset in a philistine and reactionary climate. Wilkes is supposed to have marshalled his troops even before Goldberg's arrival, demanding their unqualified loyalty.

That is not how I saw things. Undeniably Wilkes played an astute political game in the extraordinary developments that resulted for a while in the bizarre co-existence of two independent departments of English Literature in the one university. He would not have been able to find his chance, however, had Goldberg not alienated the very people who had given him power in the first instance: those high officials who seemed to have gone out of their way to block the universal expectation that Wilkes would succeed Milgate. Perhaps that image I caught sight of in London when the man who turned out to be Goldberg was standing a little to one side of that group of familiar faces had been prophetic. He saw himself as the outsider and did not realise therefore that he needed the support of those whom he also regarded as his enemies.

Hindsight reveals that he lacked astuteness. He did nothing to nurture the potential support he enjoyed among his new colleagues. On the contrary, he sowed in them a disastrous sense of insecurity, perhaps the most powerful incentive to hostility and rebellion. Yet he could have got away even with that. Those were the days of the god-professor. He was wholly unconstrained by the kinds of checks that were to be imposed on the professorial body in later decades. Had he managed to retain the support of the high and the mighty, he would have survived, and achieved his aim of refashioning the Sydney department. But that needed greater political cunning than he possessed—even though he saw himself, I am convinced, as an elegant operator with superlative skills.

Among the revered traditional critics of English literature, the turn-of-the-century Shakespearean scholar A. C. Bradley occupied a central position in Goldberg's (or really Leavis's) demonology. Bradley represented everything that was contrary to the principles on which the Leavisite literary edifice had been designed. In particular, Bradley's familiar view that the central character of a Shakespeare tragedy is destroyed by a fatal flaw, to which the protagonist is wholly blind, became one of the ritual invocations to demonstrate Bradley's imperceptiveness. And yet, though it might have been poor literary analysis, Bradley's notion of the fatal flaw represented the intrinsic quality of at least one individual. Goldberg's fatal flaw was his impatience, a determination to build his New Jerusalem overnight. He was driven by a thirst which may have been prompted by misplaced idealism, but was more probably the product of ambition and a lust for power. It was that, much more than Wilkes's consummate political skill or the support Wilkes found among the academic establishment, that brought Goldberg down. None of the weird doings of the department, which provided a preoccupation far beyond academic circles for a while, would have arisen had not Goldberg become an embarrassment and a liability to the same forces which had placed him in his position of power. He did not realise that those manipulators needed to keep face, to maintain the fiction that their choice of the outsider had been in the best interests of the university.

They were not averse, of course, to his stirring the pot. As is inevitable in all institutions, they realised that the Sydney department had generated considerable resentment among some students and also in other departments and faculties, which regarded it as an overblown, arrogant institution in command of far too much influence. Perhaps the fact that many of us occupied the symbolic centre of the university, in those handsome rooms fanning out on either side of Blacket's clock tower, contributed a little to that sense. In any event, the powers-that-were seemed to have welcomed the discomfiture not merely of Wilkes himself but of those who were seen as his supporters and allies. They were nevertheless aware, I am certain, that conflict and dissension needed to be contained within politically tolerable boundaries. Any practised operator is aware of the critical point beyond which strife of that kind must not be allowed to stray. Once members of an institution or profession—no matter how misguided or even incompetent—seem to become victims, denied natural justice, the reformer is likely to be perceived as the oppressor. That, as the power-brokers of the university knew well, could not be tolerated.

There were signs that the administration of the university was becoming concerned with the speed of change within the department, with the discontent that manifested itself in the eagerness of senior and respected members to take up positions elsewhere. Perhaps they were also worried by the relative lack of qualifications among some of those whom Goldberg had chosen to replace them or promoted in their place. In short, because of its instability, the department was becoming a liability to the university's self-promoted image as an efficient and harmonious institution unswerving in its pursuit of excellence. People were gossiping about us—even in London. Those were danger signals the authorities could not afford to ignore. The speed with which Goldberg was intent on turning the department upside-down had become an embarrassment.

For all that he might have been able to survive, at least much longer than the three years during which he exercised control, had not his miscalculation and arrogance offended one powerful individual in the most direct and intimate way imaginable. There the Overreacher, the creature of insatiable ambition blinded by his lust for power, revealed his fatal flaw as surely as Bradley thought that Macbeth and Othello, King Lear and Coriolanus, not to mention the indecisive Hamlet, betrayed flaws which led them to ruin.

It happened in 1963, at the end of Goldberg's first year when he was still relatively isolated, not yet having managed to find enough places for the faithful and enlightened. In that year he had to endure syllabuses and practices he was determined to discontinue. It was the year when I, the newcomer, had been given the privilege of teaching a considerable portion of the honours course—a situation Goldberg was intent on bringing to an end by the following year. For such reasons, it became obvious that he had written off the final honours candidates in 1963. They were to be flushed out of the system with little ceremony. The year below them proved more of a problem. Among them, several potential candidates for the honours degree were considered to be outstanding—in the estimate of the old guard, of course. Goldberg seemed to have thought it necessary to indicate that he dissented from such judgments. After the results for the annual examinations were published he called a meeting of the students who had qualified to enter the final year of the course. He pointed out that their success was not necessarily an indication of their ability or an accurate gauge of how they might fare at the end of their honours year. He asked them to consider their position carefully, and advised them not to proceed unless they were prepared to risk graduating with a poorer degree than their results in the third year might have indicated.

I remember the amazement when that foolish advice became common knowledge. It was, in itself, an entirely unwise and politically damaging act. Yet Goldberg's folly had been even more egregious. Among that group of candidates was a student who had distinguished herself throughout her three years in the department. Everything she did, every essay and examination paper she wrote seemed to speak of exceptional ability, maturity and insight. People were confidently prophesying a brilliant academic career for her: she would be one we would inevitably lose to the glories of Oxford. Her results at the end of her third year confirmed all that promise. My colleagues were intent, it seemed to me, not to allow her outstanding reputation to colour their judgments. They read and re-read her work several times in order to be confident in allowing her results to be as remarkable as they felt they were. Besides including her in his general discouragement of potential honours candidates, Goldberg singled her out for additional insult by insisting that she should not receive the prize always awarded to the best student in the third year. Rumour also had it that he had sent her a discouraging letter. That student was the daughter of one of the university's most respected officers: W. M. O'Neil, Professor of Psychology for many years and at the time the Chairman of the powerful Professorial Board, one of the most powerful people in the university.

I have often tried to imagine O'Neil's consternation. He never spoke about the incident, or at least not in my hearing. It would have taken more than human forbearance, however, for him to have remained unaffected. The success and distinction his daughter later achieved abroad in another discipline might possibly have lessened the pain and the affront, but at the end of 1963 all that lay in the future. And besides, though he was not averse to involvement in the kind of power-play that resulted in Goldberg's appointment, O'Neil was an honourable man with a genuine, though at times misplaced, concern for the university's reputation. I am sure that he felt the insult very keenly. Equally, he would have been aware of the extent to which such ham-fisted tactics could damage the university's reputation. I am convinced that Goldberg's spectacular, in a way farcical fall, that parody of the fortunes of the villain-heroes of Elizabethan tragedies, began then, less than a year after his sudden rise to glory. Yet so blinded were we by his apparently inexorable progress, that even that breathtaking miscalculation seemed to many of us merely confirmation of his unlimited power. He could get away with anything, it appeared. Nevertheless, just as in those creaky plays for which he had so much contempt, Goldberg's destruction began at the outset of his blazing career. It only needed the catalyst, and an antagonist willing to bide his time. Both of those emerged when certain aspects of Wilkes's contract as the foundation Professor of Australian Literature came to be revealed.

11

When the university decided to make up the deficit in the public appeal to establish the nation's first chair in Australian Literature, it resolved to include a clause in the terms of appointment allowing the incumbent to teach and organise courses in English Literature. The reasons for that were, in all probability, merely prudential. In the early 1960s the corpus of Australian literature—or at least the body of writing deemed worthy of being regarded as literature—was restricted. Patrick White was just on the point of being discovered by the academy; Christina Stead remained all but unrecognised. There were few 'significant' poets besides A. D. Hope. In short, there was not enough literature to go around. No doubt the university was advised to harness the energies of the new professor rather than tolerate the unseemly spectacle of the incumbent of the chair twiddling thumbs while others in the English Department allegedly worked their fingers to the bone. Nevertheless, that part of the clause referring to the chair-holder's right to organise courses is puzzling. Some people were convinced that it had been insisted on by Wilkes's supporters when it became likely that he would be passed over for the Challis chair.

It never became clear how early Goldberg had found out about that curious clause. I am convinced that very few people knew about it: Wilkes certainly kept his counsel. Many of us had been troubled and even irritated by what we saw as his indifference. He seemed willing to listen to the heated lamentations around the bar of the staff club, a place studiously avoided by Goldberg and his supporters, who preferred more genteel late-afternoon sessions of sherry in his room. But even in the club Wilkes seemed aloof, perhaps unconcerned. It was all very well for him, some of us muttered, he was secure in his chair, and besides, he would take off for Macquarie soon enough and leave all those troubles behind.

Yet Wilkes gave no sign that he was contemplating a move. The result of that was further irritation: some of us had hoped that he would find an opportunity to take us with him. When it seemed likely that someone else would be appointed to the chair in the new university, we felt powerless, abandoned.

I wondered whether something was in the air when some people began to suggest that we should have lunch in a pub one day rather than at the overcrowded bar of the staff club. After experiencing the rituals of the Marlborough, the idea didn't appeal to me greatly, but I sensed that there was much more to the suggestion. So I was not altogether surprised a week or so later when Peter Edwards, one of Goldberg's victims, rang to say that we should meet in one of the seedy, poorly patronised pubs among the warren of decrepit terraces on the edge of the then distinctly unfashionable suburb of Glebe.

It was a kind of watering-hole long since replaced in Glebe by trendy pubs, smart eateries, espresso bars and vegan takeaways. In the evenings it used to be quite a lively place, crowded with students, lecturers rubbing shoulders with the locals, thin, leathery men with an uncanny resemblance to the greyhounds they kept. In the afternoon, however, the pub was deserted. One or two elderly men staring into their glasses shared the small public bar with a colony of blowflies. They lifted their gaze momentarily as the six or seven of us arrived. The publican dispensed drinks and called out to someone in the back to cut more sandwiches. Edwards invited Wilkes to comment on the state of the department. Wilkes, in turn, advised us to approach Goldberg concerning our misgivings. It was the first time he acknowledged openly that something was amiss. Subsequently, we learnt that he intended to offer an alternative programme of courses: undergraduates would have the opportunity to choose between two courses of study. He did not know whether his attempt would be successful or to how many of us he could offer employment (he confessed once he felt able to speak openly).

In later years, when those of us who were present on that warm, sleepy afternoon reminisced about the strange councils of war that began in that run-down pub, it became clear that we shared much the same recollections. We were buoyed up because at last something seemed to be happening. But a little later we were seized by panic. I remember the sensation vividly, a tight knot in the stomach following hard on the heels of heady relief—what if I turned out to be one of those who had to be left behind? The prospect of being marooned with Goldberg while some, perhaps most, of my friends and fellow victims were enjoying the fruits of salvation was hideous. I kept trying to imagine what opportunities for revenge and exquisite humiliation Goldberg would find for those of us who had been left behind. And besides, I recall thinking almost as soon as Wilkes had spoken, what if the attempt failed?

It was a measure of our desperation that we agreed to risk all. There seemed no other way of solving a hopeless situation. I think we realised straight away how easy it would be to represent the venture as a cynical exercise in power-politics, how we could be accused of compromising our professional integrity and duty. And, in truth, most of us entertained misgivings about the scheme: there seemed to be something highly questionable in the proposal to establish an entirely independent course in a subject that was already being taught exhaustively, and apparently to the satisfaction of the authorities.

Such charges were indeed raised against Wilkes and those of us who had declared our support for his proposal in many tense meetings of the department and the faculty. There are those who continue to believe that we gladly sacrificed everything for self-interest. It would be disingenuous to pretend that self-interest, or the desire to survive, had played no part in the bizarre series of events that led to an equally bizarre state of affairs for a couple of years. Every one of us who threw in our lot with Wilkes was prompted to some extent by the prospect of professional security and even perhaps advancement that his proposal seemed to promise. Equally, I am sure, a degree of calculation had influenced some of those who decided to oppose his scheme and were able, therefore, to occupy the moral high ground in the disputes that followed. For them supporting Goldberg might have seemed the safer bet—in addition, no doubt, to their conviction that to act in any other fashion would have been the greatest impropriety.

None of us who threw our lot in with Wilkes, casting our careers and reputation on treacherous waters, remained unaware of such moral and professional pitfalls. It may have been that our gloom and despair coloured our judgments, allowing us to see dubious actions in a respectable light. Nevertheless, in my case as much as with the handful of people who declared their support for Wilkes, academic and intellectual principles were uppermost in our minds when reaching our difficult and chancy decision.

In the light of later developments in literary studies throughout the English-language world and beyond, the differences between the two factions of the Sydney department seem minute. When the syllabus for Wilkes's 'B' course (as it came to be known) was published, it contained many of the names and texts on Goldberg's book lists and course requirements. In comparison with contemporary practice, both courses were highly conservative. Each addressed principles of literary value, each was grounded in traditional English literature, with little more than excursions into American writing. There were cosmetic differences, it is true, yet both courses sought to preserve and transmit a literary culture which came to be strenuously questioned after the emergence of feminist, postcolonial and postmodernist criticism. Our quarrels were, accordingly, not much more than a family squabble. For all that, the division between the two parts of the department ran along a deep cultural, academic and ideological gulf. We were diametrically opposed on fundamental questions concerning the nature and purpose of the academic study of literature. Moreover, those of us who fell in behind Wilkes believed that ours was the saner, more civilised way of teaching literature to Australian undergraduates.

The fundamental and most troubling point of dispute lay in questions of academic propriety. Though Goldberg and his supporters would not have accepted the way I and most of those who opposed him regarded his innovations, they would have agreed that they saw a literary education as a powerful moral or ethical instrument in a debased world. They were intent on employing literary culture in the service of personal, social and even perhaps political amelioration. They attempted to persuade their students that exposure to great literature would somehow refine not merely their taste or aesthetic sensibilities but their moral capacities as well. Consequently they were vigilant against what they saw as the corrosive influence of poor, second-rate or expedient writing. Great flights of the literary imagination had, in their view, the capacity to protect the world from barbarism. The allure of the less-than-great was such, however, that it would inevitably distract the attention of inexperienced or impressionable people, making them prey to a particularly insidious and dangerous aesthetic seduction.

For those reasons, syllabuses and undergraduates were both far more rigorously controlled than had been the case in my student days only a few years earlier. Under Goldberg's dispensation nothing could be left to chance, no aspect of the department's daily life could be allowed to proceed without the most stringent supervision, because temptation lurked everywhere. The atmosphere became censorious in a damaging and, to my mind at least, profoundly uncivilised way. The effect on the student population was predictable. Most of them seized (as is the wont of undergraduates) the simpler shibboleths of an easy-to-digest orthodoxy, just as their children were enthusiastically to rehash caricature versions of the complexities of deconstruction, postmodernism or feminist critiques of literature and society and, indeed, as I had done a decade earlier in my career as mimic and parodist. To say that a degree of brainwashing was implicit in Goldberg's practices would not be such an exaggeration as it might seem. Certainly, the less perceptive or more calculating students indulged in parodies of literary discriminations that had made the long journey from Downing College to the University of Sydney. Evidence of that cropped up in every class, in many essays, assignments and examination papers, but most laughably perhaps in that student literary association Goldberg and Tomlinsons fostered and encouraged—the Hitlerjugend of English studies according to Gustav Cross, who could always be trusted to find the appropriate *bon mot*.

Attending meetings of that group was more or less compulsory for the younger members of the staff, at least until the first signs of the crack in the department's fabric began to appear, after which we were (much to our relief) discouraged from attending. I remember them as nauseatingly unctuous opportunities for people to ingratiate themselves with the powerful and the influential. At each meeting one of the senior students would present a paper. The pattern was invariable. X or Y had just been reading one of the approved texts, *Middlemarch* or *Nostromo*, *The Rainbow* or *The Portrait of a Lady*. They would twitter with enthusiasm about their wonderfully uplifting experiences, how the richness and complexity of those works and their embrace of the textures of life prompted them to celebrate life itself, how they were filled with optimism, a sense of purpose and compassion for others and other possibilities of life. Yet compassion was never the keynote of those sermons, for the engagement with the fabric of life in Eliot or Conrad, Lawrence or James could not be allowed to exist in isolation. It had to be 'placed' by comparison with one of the pseudo-masterpieces of orthodox and conventional literary history. Those students had also read Dickens or Virginia Woolf, Thackeray or Hardy, though it turned out often enough that they had read little more than a passage or two chosen for their Practical Criticism classes. Those, they claimed, made them feel mean and crabbed, cynical and sceptical. In all instances, the triumphant conclusion would be that Dickens and Woolf, Thackeray and Hardy, and indeed most writers in the academic pantheon, were 'not on the side of life'. And that was a most dire judgment.

Those rituals would have been comic had their effect been less disastrous. From time to time, indeed, they provoked perilous acts of bravado. Goldberg, and to an extent the Tomlinsons, were strait-laced moralists, even by the standards of the sixties. One junior member of the department stirred up an enormous controversy when she became pregnant. Goldberg wanted her dismissed because, he argued, an obviously pregnant unmarried woman would set a most unfortunate example for our students. Somehow he was overruled on that, but the tutor's career effectively came to an end at one of those sessions of the literary society. The student giving the paper had been reading *Middlemarch* and *Bleak House*. She went through the usual motions in a less than expert fashion. George Eliot made her appreciate her life and value her friends, she claimed, whereas Dickens brought out the nasty corners of her personality, and had even made her quarrel with her best friend. Reading Eliot made her into a better person; reading Dickens made her mean and cynical. 'And reading *Fanny Hill* made me pregnant,' the tutor called out from the back of the hall.

It was easy enough to mock the pretensions of those solemn, self-satisfied revival meetings. Yet more than mockery would have been needed to counter their unfortunate and undesirable influence on cultural and academic life. In those crowded sessions, where young people delivered pompous and often parodic discourses on literary greatness and its terrible contrary, were sown the seeds of the decline that came to grip academic life in subsequent decades. The study of literature became the object of passion and zeal. Our students were persuaded that they had been charged with a mission to rescue culture and society (a favourite coupling of emotion-laden terms) from the philistine. They were endowed with a sense of purpose and even dignity: no longer would the study of literature remain the preserve of dilettantism; the English Department, and by its example the humanities, would be wrenched from amateurs, from those content merely to follow outmoded and entirely spurious notions of scholarly objectivity. These were stirring and attractive appeals. Anything that gave a sense of purpose to and imposed responsibility on a generally vague and by popular consent 'useless' pursuit, such as the study of English literature, would seem a welcome and indeed necessary reform. And such precisely were the terms of the campaign Goldberg and his supporters conducted with considerable panache in their attempt to counter Wilkes's apparently reactionary plan to drag the department back to the habits of an irresponsible past, untroubled by questions of relevance or purpose.

Many were indeed persuaded by Goldberg's arguments, as became obvious when the matter of Wilkes's proposals came to be discussed by various committees of the university. In the public arena too, those proposals were often perceived as an attempt by a discredited former regime to regain power and to oppose necessary and timely reform. Yet the very grounds on which Goldberg could appeal to some of his students at least and to considerable sectors of academic and public opinion were also the reasons why his practices and principles were so contrary to academic ideals. The danger could best be summed up by the arrogance of his convictions. He knew what constituted great literature; he understood the true purpose of literary study; he knew where the narrow limits of acceptability and propriety lay. The department was in grave danger of falling prey to dogmatism, to an arrogance that excluded other possibilities and priorities with extreme rigidity. It allowed no room for divergence of opinion, even though lip-service was occasionally paid to that ancient academic ideal. On the contrary, it demanded absolute conformism. What is more, the price of refusing to conform, as some able and dedicated students found to their dismay, was to be discarded. The system was unrelenting: once you blotted your copybook there was no prospect of salvation.

Because of that doctrinaire rigidity, intrinsically involved, moreover, with Goldberg's lust for power, the former, lackadaisical practices of the department came to seem attractive, even to some of those who had been its sharpest critics. People began to suspect that those messy, at times apparently unstructured intellectual and academic practices might have incorporated more responsible modes of operation. The general reluctance to mould taste or to harness the academic study of literature to areas of cultural, social or even political activism could be seen as a means of preserving both diversity and the legitimacy of individual interests, tastes and convictions. Several times in those difficult years, I caught myself remembering how Milgate had encouraged my interest in such a minor figure as the fascinating Richard Brome. That would have been unthinkable with Goldberg. Brome, or Shirley for that matter, enjoyed no legitimacy—nor did a gallery of other once much more celebrated and illustrious figures. In the Sydney department of the early sixties it would have been impossible to express an interest in Spenser or Sidney, in Congreve or Burney, in Tennyson or Swinburne. An inevitable concomitant of the noble ideals informing the new order was a narrowing of the range of acceptability, a censoriousness, indeed, that attached impropriety to interests beyond rigidly defined limits.

No institution can long tolerate such rigidity, least of all universities where the habits of individualism are—or were—firmly entrenched. Inevitably, even the faithful chafed at the bit during that history of spectacular falls from grace and public excommunications. Eventually Goldberg's support would have slipped away even if Wilkes had not brought matters to a head with his extraordinary proposal. No doubt the process would have extended over a much longer period, and would have been more ambiguous in its evolution. Wilkes's considerable political skills speeded the process; and he had, besides, reserves of goodwill to call on within the university. Yet the speed with which Goldberg's edifice tumbled could only have come about because of the perception that his practices were contrary to the best interests of the university and its students. There was a genuine and keenly felt need to ensure that English studies in the university would not remain trapped within a narrowly doctrinaire orthodoxy. No doubt many found the means of achieving that distasteful. Most recognised the absurdity implicit in the university's offering two rival courses in the one subject. Many, doubtless, found the way of redressing the balance questionable. And yet, after a series of surprisingly swift moves and counter-moves, Wilkes's proposals received the imprimatur of authorities which could have brought the process to a halt at any one of a number of stages. Perhaps Wilkes's skills as an academic poker player were instrumental in his winning the day, as those who saw nothing but political machination in those events insisted. Even if that had been so, however, he held some very powerful cultural and academic cards in his hand.

12

The main game was played out in meetings from which we ordinary mortals had been excluded. In all likelihood, it had begun even before the innocent suggestion that it would be pleasant to have lunch one day in the pub on the other side of Parramatta Road. Eventually, the proposal to mount a set of alternative courses in English had to be discussed in more open forums. Some of these were, no doubt, merely ceremonial, apparently democratic and collegial ways of reaching a foregone conclusion. To those of us who became participants, however, the process seemed a matter of life and death, where one's future, as much as one's reputation and integrity, was at stake.

They began with many, seemingly endless meetings of Goldberg's section of the department. The tactic he adopted was obvious and inevitable. In the early stages he assumed that we were a harmonious and unified group. The tone was quiet and measured. As sensible and responsible people, we would all, of course, swiftly dismiss such an unnecessary and divisive proposal. He glanced around the room, his look suggesting that there could be no dissent: the matter could be settled immediately without need to waste further precious time on such frivolity. It was a clever move. None of us had enough courage at that early stage to stand up to be counted. Yet all of us recognised, I think, the danger of silence, as Maggie and Jock and a few others murmured 'Yes, yes, absurd', or some such dismissive comment. Even I realised in my relative inexperience of such disputes that our silence would inevitably be interpreted as complicity and used for all its political worth.

Someone suggested that the academic principles and implications of the proposal should be discussed. I seem to recall that it was Jock Tomlinson, who could usually be counted on to misread a situation, so that he might have imagined that a fuller discussion would serve even more to discredit the scheme. If that scrap of memory is to be trusted, then the suggestion turned out to be a dire miscalculation, for it opened up the possibility for that protracted and tense poker game which Wilkes eventually won hands down. It also gave some of us an opportunity to join in without seeming to declare ourselves at that early stage. Platitudes and pieties flew around the room for an hour or so: talk of the possible virtues of diversity, the desirability of experiment and innovation in a changing world. Someone made the inspired proposal that we should listen to what Wilkes had to say for himself. So it went on, in meeting after meeting, which have merged into one anxious and despairing memory. We spent hours in Goldberg's darkened room as he sat behind his desk, the rest of us fanned out in a semicircle around his throne. I remember the sense of heightened vigilance we all experienced, something I had never encountered before, the fear that one ill-considered word, or agreeing to a seemingly innocuous proposition would spell disaster. It was an education in tactical sparring I could gladly have forgone. Suggestions and insinuations snaked around the room, all of them designed to make us reveal ourselves, to bring into the open our potential treachery and disloyalty.

That game continued after Wilkes joined the meetings. He displayed a masterly impassivity. My most abiding memory of him during those enervating sessions is his stillness. He sat, as befitted his station, in one of the two armchairs—Maggie always occupied the other. He listened politely enough, intent apparently on Goldberg's sermons about the nature of English studies and the demands of collegiality. But there was something almost provocative in the way he spent so much time polishing his glasses, inspecting the lenses for the smallest speck of dust. There was nothing overtly arrogant or flamboyant about the ritual, yet it indicated more eloquently than any statement could have done the extent of Wilkes's contempt for what he seemed to regard as so much hot air.

Hot air it indeed was mostly. Goldberg might have thought that he had justice and propriety on his side, but he went about asserting his claims in his usual devious fashion. He was intent on tricking us, or at least cornering us into impossible situations. We took countless, indecisive votes on all kinds of propositions, most of them peripheral to the central issues, yet all designed somehow to force us to identify ourselves as the enemy. And that, of course, was precisely what none of us could afford to do. The least hint of anything that could be interpreted as conspiracy would have spelt ruin for all seeking deliverance. We learnt, in short, to be as devious as Goldberg hoped to be. Throughout we pretended that we were discussing the abstract, academic and administrative implications of Wilkes's scheme as if it could have no possible impact on our lives. This was, of course, two-faced: we had fallen victims to expediency, seeing no other possibility for achieving a morally and professionally desirable aim. And our antagonists, too, were adopting similar tactics for a diametrically opposed end.

A date had been set for the Faculty of Arts to consider and either to adopt or reject Wilkes's scheme. Ominously, it was 11 November, Armistice Day. As it drew near Goldberg decided to play his trump card. At the next meeting, he announced late one night at the end of a particularly gruelling session, he would ask every member of his staff two questions: whether we would be prepared to teach courses organised by him, or whether we would prefer to join Professor Wilkes in his proposed courses. He advised us to consider our position very carefully.

He put the question about Wilkes's courses first. Eight or nine of us raised our hands. Then he asked who would be prepared to teach his courses. Every hand in the room went up. That clearly was not meant to happen, and Jock Tomlinson was heard to mutter something to that effect. We would take the vote again, Goldberg announced without giving any reason why a second show of hands was necessary. The result was the same. After that he had nowhere to turn, though he did try to finesse his way around that unsatisfactory result in various elaborate though ultimately futile ways. Finally, he had to give up trying. We had refused to grant him the one thing he needed: indisputable evidence of our rebellion and conspiracy. On that occasion, at least, we had outsmarted him.

The meeting of the Faculty of Arts promised high drama. The long benches of the Professorial Board Room were crowded half an hour or more before the scheduled start. Everyone who could make it came to what the malicious called blood sports: on that occasion there was no need to whip up a quorum for droning meetings of usually unutterable tedium. Proceedings began with a statement by the Dean, outlining the reason for calling the extraordinary meeting of the faculty. Wilkes then spoke to his proposal, followed by other influential speakers. Some were in support of Wilkes, citing the by then familiar arguments in favour of diversity, pluralism, choice. Goldberg's supporters were able to raise the discussion to a higher emotional and ethical pitch. They moved firmly to the moral high ground: the proposals were ill-conceived, detrimental to the integrity and reputation of the university, cynical, opportunist and treacherous. David Armstrong, the Professor of Philosophy who was to find himself a few years later in a situation indistinguishable from Goldberg's, was particularly passionate.

Then it was Goldberg's turn to speak, or would have been had not the Dean reminded us that it was 11 am and time, therefore, to observe a minute's silence. Of the many disturbing and bizarre events of those heady months, that silence is what I remember most vividly—the absurdity of our standing in that over-decorated room, our heads bowed reverentially. That solemn ceremony was the most vivid confirmation for me that what I had strayed into was not the world of altruism and high-mindedness I had dreamt about at a time when being able to attend such a meeting represented the height of my ambition. It was, on the contrary, a brutal world filled with those hungry for power and those who tried to save themselves, no matter how questionable their means.

When the minute's silence ended, Goldberg stood up to speak. His voice was unusually quiet, even hesitant. He had, indeed, spent the previous few days in hospital. Whether he would attend the meeting remained in doubt almost until it was about to start, so adding to the atmosphere of tension. Those expecting fireworks were to be disappointed. Whether it was the product of calculation or genuine distress, Goldberg gave every impression of one sorely disappointed, grieving because his trust and goodwill had been compromised. His seemed to be the still, sad voice of reason and humanity in an infernal world. He spoke about his hopes for the department and for the university. He had believed that with respect for each other we might have been able to forge something fine and lasting, a testament to the irreplaceable value of English studies in a great university. Now those hopes were to be compromised. How could we impress an indifferent, at times hostile world that we upheld true values rather than self-seeking anarchy?

He appeared frail and vulnerable as he stood there, beyond anger, sorrowing, betrayed. It was in its way a magnificent performance, the Overreacher's last, desperate bid to keep disaster at bay. But, of course, it was mere ceremony. He knew, I am sure, that the numbers were against him. When the vote was taken the faculty accepted Wilkes's proposals with a narrow but still decisive majority.

It was all over, even though a few much less significant hurdles remained. Slowly the administrative wheels ground on. The faculty's recommendation passed through the relevant boards and committees. Those of us who had indicated a willingness to join Wilkes's staff received in due course our amended contracts. Those who stayed with Goldberg treated us with the contempt of people who know that they have right on their side. Tony French, practically the only member of the old department to throw in his lot with Goldberg, found himself in a particularly difficult situation, obliged as he was to turn his back on former friends and colleagues. All kinds of adjustments and compromises had to be made in that surreal atmosphere. We disputed the occupancy of lecture rooms and use of the common room. The students looked on with a mixture of alarm and cynical bemusement, knowing that they would soon have to choose between the two factions, the two courses, the two radically opposed ways of going about the business of English studies.

That unnatural situation continued for a few months. Gradually, Goldberg's world disintegrated. He returned to Melbourne in 1966, broken and defeated. The Tomlinsons followed him soon after. Tony French patched up his differences with Derick Marsh and accepted a position at La Trobe. Wilbur Sanders found a place in Cambridge.

Then all that were left were a few hapless remnants who had no means of escape. Eventually that strange chapter of academic history passed into legend.

13

For a while the two rival courses continued, Montagues and Capulets snarling at each other, fists raised, wooden swords rattling. But the menace had gone out of it. As Goldberg and his supporters drifted away, their splendid vision faded and the department returned to many of its former practices. Of course, our syllabuses were not replicas of the past. Book lists had become much shorter, more practical and better geared to our students' ability to deal with difficult, often recondite material. Yet the spirit of my undergraduate years returned in large measure. Once again the courses we taught were distinguished by a generous eclecticism. Even more strenuously than before, the department seemed intent on avoiding the doctrinaire and the dogmatic. Many doors, tightly bolted for some years, were opened again. We taught Spenser and Shakespeare's lesser contemporaries as well as the poets of the late eighteenth century. Fielding returned to the syllabuses, much to my private dismay, as did Scott and Virginia Woolf and E. M. Forster and many other important writers who had been all but banished by the reformers' zeal. Everything was done, for a while at least, not to constrain our teaching within the straitjackets of convictions and certainties. To some, of course, we seemed merely to be returning to the irresponsible dilettantism of the past.

And, as always, there were spoils for the victors. Wilkes was invited to the Challis chair when it fell vacant after Goldberg's return to Melbourne in 1966. For me, for the first time in my career apart from that brief interlude in 1963, there was a chance to carry out what I regarded as real teaching, no longer sentenced to confinement in the night-watch of the first-year lectures, or floating around as an extra in the Tomlinsons' seminars. And most significant of all perhaps, it was not long before I achieved my heart's desire: a room in the main building. I felt privileged to occupy that study, which I saw as a substantial emblem of everything that university life represented for me, or had done so in the past.

By the time I gained possession of that room, some of the glamour had gone out of my dreams of university life. I had endured the tedium of trying to coax something out of Shirley's dull plays. I had also learnt that reality may never be as alluring as hopes and daydreams. Above all, I had experienced, at the very beginning of my professional life, fundamental nastiness, vanity and the display of ruthless ambition. I had learnt that those common characteristics of communal life—to which all institutions are prone—are particularly vicious in universities, or at least in the universities of the time, because fewer risks were involved than elsewhere. Most of us engaged in the squabble that consumed so much of the department's daily life had tenure. We knew that we could only lose our jobs in the most exceptional circumstances. Goldberg was certainly able to make our lives miserable, and would have been able to provoke even greater misery for us had he succeeded. But we knew that even the god-professors of the day had their power circumscribed in one all-important respect: we could not be dismissed easily, our income was at least secure. That knowledge, retrospect tells me, emboldened people, made them more prepared to stand up for what they believed, and also, sadly, to employ often underhand means to fulfil their ambitions. In later years, when university departments came to be filled by people on short-term appointments, even one-year contracts, academics became pusillanimous, fearful that putting one foot wrong might cost them their jobs.

By the time I moved my books into that low, narrow room with a quaint gas-jet in elaborately tooled brass protruding from the wall, I had experienced a degree of disillusionment. Or perhaps I had merely grown up a little. Nevertheless my most potent memory of that period is a sense of liberation, of being allowed to do what I felt I was good at, in an atmosphere of relative harmony. They were golden years.

Perhaps I shut my eyes to the signs of danger around me. Marooned for much of that time in my cosy room at the top of a steep flight of stairs, it proved possible, it now seems to me, to ignore the pressures that were to destroy that life. I believe, nevertheless, that for a decade or so, individually and communally, we were undoing much of the harm that Goldberg's presence had caused. We were, in a fundamentally important sense, achieving what I thought university life in Australia could and should achieve.

For me that came through the discovery that I enjoyed teaching, that there was considerable intellectual and even aesthetic pleasure to be had from it. Of course, part of it was mere vanity and showmanship. Those were still the years of large lectures in overcrowded, draughty halls with poor soundproofing and amplification. Initially, it is true, I was terrified by the prospect of standing at a lectern and attempting to gain the attention of several hundred chattering young people. My knees would shake, my throat would close up as I breathed the conventional words 'Ladies and gentlemen, today I will . . .' into the microphone. Soon, however, in some ways sooner than I dared hope, confidence and with it a certain flamboyance arrived. I learnt how to tailor material to fit a fifty-minute lecture. I realised that you could only hope to get across three or four salient points in that time—the rest was decoration, entertainment even. It became clear that those central and essential points had to be repeated in various guises, for the sad truth dawned on me that at any particular moment a quarter, perhaps a third of the audience was not listening. In short, I developed the skills of efficient public speaking, including certain none-too-subtle techniques of crowd control: staring out the chatterers; making it obvious by a pointed silence that it was not acceptable for someone to arrive at a lecture half an hour after it began and then to clatter down the wooden steps of the lecture hall, ostentatiously looking for the most congenial place to sit.

There was the thrill of performance too. I realised that teaching is in some ways merely a branch of show business—playing to the gallery, negotiating tricky points, even cutting corners with a questionable argument, or masking one that hadn't been sufficiently thought through. Yet something valuable, even perhaps noble in intent and significance, lay beneath the exhibitionism.

Gradually and in most ways quite imperceptibly I discovered that I was indeed following the programme I had set myself when I got it into my head that I should become an academic who would profess the glories of English literature. Of course, in those days of fantasising I saw the process painted with bold brushstrokes. Reality was nothing like that. Teaching, I found, was a steady, at times enervating process: fitting the necessary material into two or three lectures, making sure that at least the most important elements of a text or an author were covered in what often seemed ridiculously little time. Given our experiences under the former dispensation, I tried to be as even-handed as possible, sketching out a variety of possible ways of looking at difficult and often self-contradictory works. As far as I could, I was determined to avoid ramming my own theories down our students' necks. I tried at least to develop arguments to support individual judgments. Above all, I attempted to shun the doctrinaire, the suggestion that I was passing down the law from my high status behind the lectern. I fancy that I succeeded, even though I realised soon enough that whatever you said, no matter how tentatively or how much circumscribed by qualifications, was always liable to assume an entirely unintended authority. I learnt how important it was to signal, often by means of obvious rhetorical devices, warnings and reservations, danger signs in a way, to those who were prone to take every word uttered from a lectern as revealed truth.

Naturally I often failed. At times I would lose the shape of an argument or neglect to raise those little warning flags high enough. Sometimes I would be horrified to find in essays and examinations that I had misled my students, making them understand the contrary of what I had intended. It was tempting to blame it on their inattention or lack of ability; but the truth had to be faced that the fault often lay with me. I fancy, though, that I succeeded more often than I failed. And as I grew more practised and confident, those moments when success could be felt, intangible but unmistakable, increased satisfactorily. There were times when I could sense that for a portion of my audience at least, a puzzling, impenetrable or even perhaps boring text had come alive. I could sometimes detect an eagerness in them to read something again, to look at it in the light of the suggestions they had picked up from my lectures—or indeed to read a book they had, until then, no intention whatever of opening. These were some of the most satisfying moments of university teaching: something dead and inert had been brought to life for some people, even if only provisionally. I grew fascinated by the possibilities offered by the routine and mundane tasks of teaching—which many academics regard as no more than unpleasant chores, distracting them from their real work, the pursuit of their research interests. Teaching well seemed to me the most practical and honourable way of justifying a life which some people beyond the university considered of no particular benefit to any but those fortunate enough to enjoy academic sinecures.

14

In the Australia of the late sixties and the seventies, it was still possible to seek validation for such a way of life by appealing to the nation's cultural identity. Because English was our primary language, and because our institutions and modes of thought were still connected with the sensibility at the core of that language—no matter how far it might have spread beyond its original confines—the project of preservation and transmission seemed entirely valid and honourable. And essential for the sake of social cohesion. Without articulating it, or even being conscious of it, I was giving life to the process of assimilation on which I had embarked twenty years or so earlier when I tried to remake myself in the image prompted by my education into intellectual and social ways of Australia in the last phases of colonialism.

There seemed to have been nothing remarkable about that transformation. By the time I had attained the privilege of haranguing row upon row of young people on English literature, I and most of my associates and acquaintances saw my doing that as entirely natural and appropriate—after all, I had spoken English longer than most of my attentive or bored listeners. The climate had not yet arisen where my 'otherness'—the fact that I spent the first ten years of my life in Europe and had endured a measure of danger and persecution during the war—should somehow have coloured or determined the nature of experiences which belonged exclusively to my English-language self. The competence of language was enough to confer on me full citizenship in the republic of culture and the intellect, in ways indistinguishable, indeed, from a birthright. The essential impersonality of our academic practices and ideals in those days ensured that. When I attempted to elucidate for our students the implications of dynastic squabbles in Shakespeare's history plays, or the nature imagery in the poetry of Keats and Wordsworth, I spoke with an accepted and acknowledged authority. Accidents of birth or genetics were irrelevant in the light of that linguistic competence and the cultural literacy it implied.

In time I came to understand that such privileged extraterritoriality was a particular phenomenon of Australian life. Before my years in the British Museum Reading Room i had given no thought to such questions. There seemed no necessity for it. What I knew about English literature and the life it reflected was no different from the experience of my friends and acquaintances. After all, only one or two of us had ever been abroad. None but the most fortunate or wealthy could afford to travel, or find the time for the month-long sea voyage to Europe. Jill Ker, I remember, interrupted her studies to undertake a compressed version of the grand tour. She came back with stories of the marvels she had seen. Others who had left for England stayed for years, often a lifetime, and did not therefore feed our consciousness with more immediate and perhaps less superficial impressions than our reading and study had provided. Even if they had done so, it would not have influenced the almost universal sense that our cultural heritage was a country of the mind, as easily—even perhaps better—acquired from books and from the textures of the language than from experience. Thelma Herring, whose lectures spoke with such familiarity about Windsor Forest and the Vale of Arden, had spent by far the greater part of her life in Sydney, having been denied the opportunity to travel by war and family circumstances. We might have been bored by her sing-song disquisitions, but none of us, not even the handful of English-born people in her classes, thought that her erudition was in the least second-hand or imitative. It had been acquired, after all, from the most authentic sources: from Pope's poem about the great forest near Windsor and from Shakespeare's lovingly idealised images of the countryside around Stratford-upon-Avon.

It was in London, in Brown's cluttered room at University College and around the beer-stained tables of the Marlborough Arms, that I first experienced a challenge to those assumptions. In my own case the challenge was double-pronged. When Brown asked at our first meeting whether I felt confident enough of my command of English to undertake a doctoral thesis, it was a wounding moment. I felt affronted. Hadn't he seen in my *curriculum vitae* that I had graduated with First Class Honours in English? Brooding about that upsetting incident revealed even more disturbing implications. Had he been making some comment about the laxer standards in faraway, colonial Sydney? Was he suggesting that what passed for literary and linguistic competence there might not come up to scratch at the centre, indeed the navel of that culture? I am certain that some such suspicion lurked in the back of his mind, though we never returned to the topic after that day.

That impersonal, seemingly self-indulgent, Sydney style, so easy to mock and malign—by none more so than Goldberg and his associates—embodied a noble ideal. It scorned the accidents of time and place. English literature, and the possibilities of life it embraced, did not require vulgar proximity. Indeed, its great glory and the unique contribution it could make to a world far removed from the physical, and therefore impermanent, site of those glories, had something of the character of a Platonic ideal. The hill above the ruins of Tintern Abbey may be despoiled by chattering tourists, but the place itself, and all the feelings, associations and thoughts it could evoke in an exceptional sensibility, lived on in Wordsworth's poem. In that sense his Tintern Abbey, just as Pope's Windsor Forest or Shakespeare's Warwickshire, proved far more substantial and meaning-filled than their unsatisfactory physical counterparts. Similarly, the essential Englishness of the great English poets, novelists and playwrights resided in the products of their imagination, not in the physical, social or even moral circumstances that fired their imaginations. So it mattered not where in the world those flights of the intellect and imagination were studied, elucidated and preserved, nor whether English were the custodian's native language or one acquired in later life. All that mattered was competence, an ability to penetrate to the core of what had been fashioned from the raw material of experience and language.

I did not suspect at the time when I began to realise that my vocation was teaching how fragile and provisional that cultural confidence had already become. I believed that beneath what seemed to some mere posturing and vanity lay values and commitments that our society would not abandon while English continued as the centre of our imaginative and social life. We sensed that if the experience of many centuries which that language had preserved and embedded in writers' imaginations were allowed to atrophy, our lives—both individual and communal—would contract into a kind of barbarism. In the late sixties and for much of the seventies that seemed, however, the most unlikely of possibilities, despite all the signs and portents we ignored. And for that reason, as I stood behind rickety lecterns day after day, I felt that I was a fully paid-up member of a world I had come to possess in its essentials. I sometimes suspected, perhaps arrogantly, that precisely because English was my second language, I was more sensitive to its riches and nuances than those whose first words were spoken in that tongue. Having become an exponent of that language in Australia may, moreover, have helped remove the distractions of the local and the particular. Perhaps, it occurred to me, we were blessed in not being able to seek out Tintern Abbey or inspect the site of the great battle of Bosworth Field.

Writing about that vanished world a quarter of a century later makes me see these strands and currents far more clearly, and with less ambiguity, than was the case at the time. Then all manner of distractions, personal, professional and social, were liable to divert attention from the fundamental cultural and academic health of already threatened ideals and practices. Yet even then, between bouts of alarm when I knew that I was about to deliver an ill-prepared lecture or grew irritated at the obtuseness of a colleague or student, I knew that things had come together for me in an intangible but very real and satisfying sense.

My own project of self-fashioning seemed to have come to an end. At least within the confines of my professional life (but in truth beyond that too) I had become fully assimilated. That did not mean that I remained indifferent to stupidity, vulgarity and dishonesty, evidence of which was not hard to seek in the smug and inward-looking Sydney of the sixties and early seventies, a world of much cant and hypocrisy. Yet I was convinced that beneath the inevitable tarnish there lay a cultural and therefore moral and even perhaps political decency which relied in large part on the bonds that tied that world to its origins. It was no longer possible, of course, to pay much heed to the patriotic claptrap that drove me out into the blinding sunshine in 1954 to catch a glimpse of the Queen. But I suspected that all those pious acts of flag-waving and Mr Menzies's sycophancy were mere distractions from the fundamental and imperishable relevance of the true significance of our English heritage—the language and all that it embodied. With that conviction, I felt fully at home within our sandstone Gothic liberty. I had no inkling that such confidence and stability could possibly be threatened or compromised in my lifetime.

15

Imperceptibly, but inexorably, the world was changing. At some ill-defined point I began to notice how young our students seemed to have become. Then it became clear that their experience had been very different from mine. In time I found that it was no longer safe to take certain things for granted, that the assumed common knowledge which must form the basis of any kind of teaching was shrinking. The realisation came to me in small, but telling ways. I recall conducting a tutorial on a short story by Patrick White. It was, as I remember, a dull, bored group who always had to be coaxed and prodded. We came to a passage containing the phrase 'up at the junction'. No-one knew what that meant, for presumably none of them lived in those few parts of Sydney where the shopping centre is still known as the junction.

I grew impatient, irritated. Then a spark stirred in one dull brain. Like Bondi Junction?—a small triumph. Which junction did White have in mind? someone asked. Why it could be anywhere, I remember saying, there were junctions wherever the tracks crossed. Incomprehension: I realised, with something close to embarrassment, that none of those young people had ever seen a Sydney tram, that for them the system of lines and junctions was as vague and quaint as my notions of hansom cabs and horse-drawn omnibuses. We were looking at each other across the gap of the generations. We no longer shared the same world.

I also realised as the years passed that the erosion of time had been accelerated by other factors. In one respect that realisation had rueful implications for me. Year after year, as I scanned the names of students in tutorial and seminar lists, I became conscious of the presence of other cuckoos-in-the-nest. The old, familiar Anglo-Celtic names were jostling with those from many parts of Europe and Asia.

I remembered my own undergraduate days when people such as myself were lightly scattered among the descendants of the British Isles. Now we were so numerous that it was no longer possible to maintain any fiction of homogeneity. The line of direct descent—if it had ever existed—had clearly been cut. Whatever we were, we were obviously not biological legatees of a proud tradition that had spread its seeds over the oceans to survive in an inhospitable soil. And yet, I couldn't but acknowledge that the new breed of undergraduates, with names recalling the towns and villages of Greece, Sicily, Croatia, and of Lebanon, Ceylon, India, China, Malayasia and Thailand, did not seem to bring their own traditions and awareness with them—at least when they sat in my classes, they were as bored, puzzled and often resentful as their Anglo-Celtic contemporaries.

I wondered occasionally whether they too had had to learn to discard the cultural baggage they or their parents had brought with them. Had they found themselves in the same quandary as I had close to half a century earlier? Was the world from which they came—even if not directly—as menacing and dangerous as Europe had been for me, despite its peculiar and ultimately irresistible appeal? Were they, in other words, as fundamentally deracinated as I had been when we arrived in Australia in 1947 with memories of brutality and inhumanity so fresh and vivid that the greatest imperative was to disown and to forget?

I could find no satisfactory answer to those conundrums, which became a minor though fascinating preoccupation as the seventies turned into the eighties. It was obvious that, whatever the explanation, the grand endeavour of refashioning myself on which I had embarked when I decided to spend my life teaching English literature no longer seemed as legitimate as it had at the time. There was, I had to concede, ultimately little difference between those students whose families had lived in Australia for many generations and newcomers like myself, or their children. The Joneses and the Andersons, the O'Reillys and the Carpenters seemed to live in the same ahistorical fug as those other young people whose names and physical appearance spoke of places far removed from the British Isles. Eventually it became evident that it was not race, nationality or culture that determined the flavour of those decades but the particular conditions of Australian life. Of course, there could be little doubt that the presence of people such as myself in a formerly uniform society had helped to speed the changes which were reflected in the increasing difficulties I faced in the day-to-day tasks of teaching. Yet it was equally evident that the bouts of frustration and anger I experienced as the years went by were provoked by far more deeply rooted, and to my mind disastrous changes.

In the early years of my academic life—when for six months prior to leaving for England I shared that draughty room off the Vice-Chancellor's Quadrangle, or when roasting in the oven of the box intended to serve as a scientific laboratory—it was not at all unusual to see students coming to class with old, well-thumbed copies of the classics. They would bring collected volumes of Shakespeare bound in fading and cracked morocco leather, inscribed in faint copperplate with the name of a mother, father, aunt or grandmother, or squat editions of *David Copperfield* or *Pride and Prejudice* bound in commonsense, serviceable boards. They would bring the family Milton or Wordsworth and sometimes, though very rarely, more exotic treasures.

You realised that those heirlooms may have remained unread for generations, in all probability many of them had been hunted out from the back of a dusty cupboard where they had been banished by people too busy or too indifferent to read them. And yet they were, in a rudimentary and perhaps unsatisfactory sense, emblems of continuity, of a recognition, no matter how vague, that those unread words represented something meaningful and significant, no matter how much their meaning or significance might have atrophied. There was some continuity still, a sense of connection to a culture beyond the iron railings of the university.

Then those habits began to change. Partly as a consequence of the greater availability of inexpensive paperbacks, perhaps, students fell into the habit of bringing with them fresh copies of Shakespeare and Milton, Austen and Dickens—except that with increasing and infuriating frequency they would arrive with nothing other than a notepad, ready to receive wisdom about the timeless masterpieces of English literature which they had little intention of reading. I found that I was becoming a nag. What is the use of coming to seminars if they had no idea what we were supposed to be discussing, I would ask with, I was sure, increasing stridency. I remember noticing more and more their puzzled, often vacant looks as I complained and raged. I wondered what was going through their minds, just as I wondered why they had gone to the trouble of turning up. And so at length I had to admit that the world had changed, that the habits, rituals and practices we tried to maintain week after week, month after month had become hopelessly outmoded in the new (and to my mind unsatisfactory) world that had grown around us.

It struck me that we should have been following the example of our colleagues in the alarmingly shrinking modern language departments.

In other words, we should have been teaching English literature as an alien and unfamiliar culture. The evidence for that was all around us, in our students and in the experience they brought with them from their schooldays. What had held true for me and for most of my contemporaries was clearly no longer the case. We may have read very few of the great English literary figures, the canonical writers as they were termed by a strident ideology emerging in the course of the eighties, but we knew a great deal about them. I remembered the English classes in my last year at school. I had chosen to take the additional honours course in the Leaving Certificate scheme. It consisted entirely of weekly classes held in the school library with the English master dictating brief notes about the chief works of the great writers. It wasn't much of an education, but at least it provided information, kept the memory of unknown masterpieces alive, like those fragmentary verses which are all that remains of once famous epics, tragedies and odes.

Our students had obviously been denied even such tiny glimpses, yet we pretended that the old connections were still in place, that the educational modes of our schooldays hadn't been swept away. We should have known better. We should have realised that Australian schoolchildren in the seventies and then the eighties were no longer subjected to that sentimental education which sought to preserve knowledge and even perhaps love of a distant place in the late-colonial culture of my adolescence. Most of them knew little about British history, about the rituals of an alien society. We should not have been surprised that so much of what we required them to study appeared to them incomprehensible and daunting. The educational practices of the new Australia discouraged not merely what was coming to be regarded as the improper Anglocentrism of the past, but even curiosity about what their everyday language encoded. And it was that language, moreover, that misled us, that allowed us to persist with practices that were no longer valid or capable of being justified. We did not admit that we were dealing with young people who, from our perspective, were fundamentally illiterate. They could read and write—at least up to a point, though we noticed that their command of traditional grammar and spelling was often no more than rudimentary. Yet their illiteracy manifested itself at a deeper level. The language had lost those resonances which I, as a puzzled and often perplexed newcomer, had to acquire so painfully in my first years in Australia.

No doubt that competence had been replaced by other resonances, other skills. For, of course, I became aware soon enough that many of our undergraduates had access to worlds which remained closed to me, largely because I did not think it worthwhile opening the doors leading to them. In some ways we attempted to deal with such changes. Throughout those years our syllabuses grew markedly shorter as we recognised that our students were experiencing greater and greater difficulties in reading what we regarded as the standard works of English. All of us found that we had to take more time and make far greater effort to explain and elucidate what we regarded as the obvious. Expressions, figures of speech, allusions and references which we thought were entirely commonplace had become, we found, puzzling and opaque. Some traditional associations of the language—Maytime with spring, for instance—were no longer common property: they had to be explicated, laboriously and pedantically. And we realised all too often that our students weren't particularly interested in whatever we attempted to reveal to them.

Our predicament was by no means isolated to the cloud-cuckoo-land of a conventional university. These changes had far more extensive and in many ways disturbing consequences for social, cultural and even perhaps political life. The old certainties, celebrated by the portraits of the royal family hanging in schools and banking chambers, the habit of naming towns, suburbs and streets after nostalgic memories of the British Isles, had vanished. The new Australia was no longer anchored in such reassuring waters. Some insisted that we were sailing towards worlds of great promise and achievements; others suspected that we were merely drifting without purpose. It was in such circumstances that we in our sandstone stronghold, and elsewhere too, threw away a rare chance to take stock of our aims and aspirations.

In the late seventies or the early eighties, when the fabric of academic life had not yet frayed entirely, when it could have been restored with careful mending, we should have thought strenuously about how to retain the capacity of an apparently irrelevant culture to support an emerging and confused society with little faith in the models of the past. Yet by and large we turned our backs on that opportunity. We persisted in our fantasy that outmoded practices and habits of thought could survive in an ambiguous world, one vulnerable, moreover, to forces—at both extremes of the political spectrum—only too ready to exploit ambiguities and paradoxes. It would have been possible, perhaps, to embark on a project of reconciling the old and the new, of attempting to evolve structures and institutions capable of retaining the best and most relevant aspects of a linguistic heritage.

Some academic disciplines no doubt attempted that feat and may have achieved a measure of success. English studies seemed to display a regrettable resistance. We became fragmented, quarrelsome and purposeless. The reasons for that were manifold; yet from the perspective of the university which was increasingly reviled as the most retrograde and tradition-bound in the nation, it came to seem that much of the reason emerged from the quarter from which inspiration and a sense of direction should have emerged: the growing importance of Australian literature as an academic discipline.

16

In 1968 Leonie Kramer was appointed as the second incumbent of the chair of Australian Literature. She introduced to the department, even perhaps to the faculty, an unfamiliar style—one which some of her new colleagues found difficult to reconcile with their image of the academic life. Even during her years at the University of New South Wales, Kramer had been a public figure in ways almost unknown at the time. Her elevation to what remained a unique status, the only Professor of Australian Literature in the nation, brought her into greater prominence, allowing her to influence institutions and policies far beyond the confines of the university.

It would be futile to pretend that the new image of the academic she revealed was not the cause of some resentment. Her two professorial colleagues, Wilkes and Leslie Rogers (who had succeed George Russell to the McCaughey Chair of Early English Literature and Language), were cast in an older mould—even though both were younger. Each seemed content not to move too far beyond academic confines. Wilkes, it is true, continued throughout his career to play an important role in the setting of syllabuses for English in the senior years of high school. Ironically, too, he was to exert considerable influence over the study and encouragement of Australian writers through his editorship of *Southerly*, which he retained for a quarter of a century. Some suspected that Kramer was riled by that anomaly: perhaps she had expected the editorship to pass to her once she assumed the chair. But whatever her feelings, she revealed no sign of disappointment. Indeed, she seemed fully occupied by her academic duties and her additional roles in the corporate world, and even on the fringes of the political. Some people went as far as to suggest that she could not have found time to take on the additional burden of editing the journal. After all, they pointed out, a taxi with its meter ticking was often waiting outside the entrance. All in all, she was our first experience of that now familiar phenomenon: the academic as an influential public figure.

It was obvious from the beginning that Kramer intended to mould the study of Australian literature into a particular and distinct form. The maliciously inclined had suggested that during his three-year occupancy of the chair Wilkes had done little to give the discipline any particular direction because he had been merely marking time, waiting for his opportunity to shove Goldberg from the Challis chair. It seemed to me more likely that Wilkes, too, had been constrained in the atmosphere of spite and instability that pervaded the department. But certainly it was left to Kramer to evolve a means of placing the study of Australian literature on an institutional footing.

From very early on, and up to her retirement in 1989, she became the focus of certain political controversies which had made their appearance in the university as a consequence of the unrest over the Vietnam War. After Goldberg's departure, the English Department was spared another round of acrimoniously public squabbles of the kind that surrounded the fracas over Political Economy or Women's Studies, the spectacular row that saw Philosophy split into two rival departments—much as English had been. The irony of that was not lost on us as we watched the philosophers tearing themselves apart in the way we had done only a few years earlier. The political rumblings in the English Department during the seventies seemed to crowd around Kramer's conservative attitudes. Some thought that she was attempting to restrict the study of Australian literature within improperly narrow confines. She was accused of being deaf to the new, often unsettling voices that were beginning to be heard in Australian writing: Frank Moorhouse, Michael Wilding, Peter Carey among them. Her dislike of Patrick White's novels was claimed by some to reflect her highly conservative political views, especially after White emerged late in life as the figurehead of various left-wing aspirations, among them the increasingly public gay movement. There were those, indeed, that insisted that she had accepted the chair only because none other was available.

One of Kramer's early innovations certainly fuelled that suspicion. Even before she successfully established Australian Literature as a separate entity within the department—on the model of the section charged with teaching language studies and Anglo-Saxon and Middle English writing—she introduced certain famous and influential literary works into her syllabuses. Students of Australian Literature were expected to read the likes of Dostoyevsky, Melville, Tolstoy and Thomas Mann. That innovation was greeted with considerable mockery. Of course, certain cynics whispered, there wasn't enough Australian literature to go around, and much of what there was remained pretty second-rate. So you'd expect her, wouldn't you, to puff it up a bit?

I felt troubled, too. At the time it was still possible—though only by a whisker, so to speak—to remain confident in the centrality of English literature in the Australian cultural climate. The boredom and incomprehension of our students when we spoke about English life as if it were our familiar environment hadn't yet penetrated our institutional consciousness. So it seemed quite natural to regard the presence of Dostoyevsky on Australian Literature syllabuses as something of a joke, and for us to look down our noses at those who had chosen to abandon the rigours of English literary studies for the soft option of Australian Literature. The experience of two decades or more since Kramer took those unusual steps has persuaded me that, whatever her motives, the introduction of those august figures into the more pedestrian ranks of Australian writers represented a potentially valuable means of solving the cultural dilemma that few of us were prepared to face at the time. Of course, it was easy enough to accuse her of snobbery and even perhaps of a wish to denigrate the achievements of Australian writers. Few writers, it was pointed out, could stand comparison with Dostoyevsky. Yet those slightly odd practices helped, retrospect tells me, to preserve two vitally important academic and cultural priorities—both of which were compromised once the study of Australian literature became a near-autonomous pursuit.

Kramer's syllabuses sought to ensure that the study of Australian literature did not retreat into a ghetto. The British, American and European writers whose works were placed against Australian fiction and verse were there to indicate that Australian writing emerged from a rich and fully formed context, that it was not *sui generis*, and could not be understood in isolation from the cultural climate from which it evolved. In that her views seem to me entirely accurate, and in some ways prophetic. Perhaps the most harmful consequence of the growth of Australian literary studies in academic institutions all over the country was the encouragement of an essentially philistine isolationism. By the nineties a generation of academic 'experts' in Australian literature had emerged who were far less literate than the writers whose work they wished to subject to critical—and increasingly sociological—scrutiny. Kramer's insistence that practitioners of what came to be known as 'Ozlit' must keep in mind the matrix in which that literature was nurtured was timely and essential.

She may have erred in one respect. Perhaps it was not entirely wise to place complex and demanding masterpieces besides frequently halting attempts to evolve a national literature. It might have been preferable to indicate intricate cultural connections by reference to lesser works, which would not have made the local product often seem quite so feeble or derivative. And yet there, too, I have come to regard her instincts as accurate. They were one way of guarding against smugness and complacency. Isolated from broader contexts, exponents of Australian literature may easily be misled into an undue modesty of expectations, where the merely competent may well seem exceptional, where the commonplace is capable of being celebrated as outstanding.

The model Kramer evolved during the early years of her occupancy of the chair of Australian Literature contained the potential not merely to place the study of Australian writing on a respectable intellectual and academic footing, but also to preserve an essential heritage, which was fast decaying through ignorance and neglect. It was during those years that the first strident voices were raised about the irrelevance of 'Eurocentric' cultural and literary ideals. They were, of course, no more than feeble imitations of North American habits and priorities, which were then emerging in the ever-deepening rifts of social and cultural life in the United States. Yet they were persuasive for all that, appealing to the most fundamental of human characteristics: indolence. Why waste time on Shakespeare and Milton, or Dostoyevsky and Thomas Mann if it came to that, when these dead white males were irrelevant to the experience of post-colonial Australia?

Many found that siren-song irresistible. They listened to it and allowed themselves to be seduced into a disastrous cultural amnesia. They forgot that the local and the contemporary had emerged out of and existed in an intricate relationship with the past. They also ignored the possibility that the 'past' was not a homogeneous, uniform and generally inert monolith, but itself a complex and ambiguous network of strands of influences. The impoverishment of cultural and intellectual life that emerged from such circumstances was by no means exclusively focussed on the primacy of Australian writing, though that was certainly one important element.

Kramer's methods should have led to possibilities of integration and preservation in a rapidly changing world. Instead, they came to be isolated within a comfortable and reassuring cocoon. It was natural, of course, that someone of Kramer's temperament and personality would wish to command greater influence than the chair of Australian Literature, as she inherited it, exerted. During Wilkes's tenure he had no staff, no establishment beyond a secretary. Complicated negotiations with Goldberg were needed for anyone besides him to take part in the tiny segments of the courses in English set aside for Australian writing. The position held the allure and glamour of a professorship, but only in isolation. That made it largely ineffectual in the structures of negotiation, in the constant quest for funds which marked even those relatively affluent days. The solution was for Australian Literature to assume a largely independent status with staff specifically assigned to teach courses under the professor's direction, and for a portion of the funds allocated to the Department of English to be diverted to it. A possible model already existed in the division of the discipline between the two well-established chairs. Kramer argued successfully that the existing pattern should be altered to cater for changed circumstances by incorporating a third autonomous element within what was already a fairly loose federation of interests.

The results were unfortunate. Because of the fundamentally contentious nature of the academic temperament, the independence of Australian Literature led to inevitable disputes. It raised the atmosphere of suspicion which, as I had learnt by then, is an unavoidable feature of university life—revealing perhaps the origins of the calling in a world of whispering, intrigue-obsessed clerics. We looked for opportunities to belittle each other. These were no more than the normal and relatively trivial disputes of institutional life. The real harm that flowed out of Kramer's bid for independence was of far more embracing significance. It hived off the study of Australian literature from the most important of the several contexts from which it had emerged. Indeed, since the courses she organised consisted (as one would have expected at the time) almost exclusively of works by writers with a solid Anglo-Celtic heritage, the study of English literature and language was, or should have been, an indispensable adjunct to them. And so it was for a while, but in time, as more and more students committed themselves to what many of us continued to regard as a soft option, courses in Australian Literature became increasingly less dependent on English studies. To be fair, Kramer and her colleagues attempted to ensure—as their counterparts in other institutions did not always attempt—that their undergraduates and research students had some competence beyond the relatively narrow confines of 'Ozlit'. For all that, the structural independence had profound cultural, even perhaps spiritual effects. Not only did it isolate the study of Australian literature from its sustaining context, but (more damagingly from my point of view) it blocked off many of the possibilities that might have existed of revealing the pertinence of traditional writing and literary forms to the young people of Australia in the late twentieth century. Had the study of Australian literature remained an integral part of English studies—as other literatures in English remained—both the inward-looking insularity of contemporary Australian studies and some of the inanity and excesses that overtook the teaching of English literature from the mid-eighties onwards might have been avoided.

As it was, we did little to explore possibilities of forging culturally relevant modes of bridging the constantly increasing gulf between the traditional shape of English studies and the capacity of our students to understand or profit from them. We were teaching the literature of a foreign culture, as I came to realise, without acknowledging it, principally because of our foolish conviction that our students spoke the same language as the great figures of English literature.

17

By that time I had long abandoned any dream of making a mark in the great international world of scholarship. There is, I suppose, a stage in most people's lives when they have to come to terms with their own insignificance. For some, more ambitious than I happened to be, the recognition comes hard. Looking back on those years I am sometimes surprised by how easily it came to me. Of course, I experienced moments of anger and envy, but by then I had come fully to recognise that for all its vanity, teaching in a university was merely a job, a profession, perhaps more honourable than some, but nevertheless principally a way of earning a living while doing something useful—even though I knew only too well that many in an increasingly crass and materialistic world questioned the usefulness of fooling around with boring old books.

That recognition did not seem incompatible, however, with expecting the institution in which I had spent my working life to acknowledge the contribution I had made. Acknowledgment did come, by way of promotion to an associate professorship in 1972. And there it stopped, as I suspected at the time it would. I was disinclined to look for a chair in another university, as some of my colleagues were doing—John Burrows went to Newcastle, Adrian Colman to Tasmania. My life was too firmly wedged in Sydney to consider moving elsewhere. I knew also that it was no use entertaining fantasies about succeeding Wilkes to the Challis chair. He was only nine years older than me; by the time he retired, I realised, I would be considered far too old, and perhaps also the wrong sex. All in all, I was content with my lot.

As ambition waned, I discovered that I could get considerable satisfaction from much more modest publications than I had dreamt about in those years when I still wanted to conquer the world—by way, perhaps, of the august Clarendon imprint of the Oxford University Press. And it was through that trickle of publications that I came to make what I would regard as a contribution of some consequence to the world of scholarship, one intimately bound up, moreover, with the fact that I had spent by far the greater part of my life in this country.

The opportunity for that came in the late seventies, some ten years after the University of Sydney decided to establish its own academic publishing house, which was disgracefully dismantled in the late eighties. In conjunction with the press, Wilkes launched a project of locally edited texts of Shakespeare's plays: the first batch of *The Challis Shakespeare*, as the series came to be called, included my edition of *Macbeth*. To all intents and purposes *The Challis Shakespeare* was a modest, practical undertaking of a kind not designed to cover its participants in academic glory. It grew out of a need to provide undergraduates and students in the senior years of secondary school with cheap but reliable editions of Shakespeare containing annotations designed to cater for their particular requirements. British and even American editions seemed to take for granted many things which you could no longer assume to be common knowledge among young Australians. Conversely, some of them were weighed down with information of no particular relevance for our students. They were often filled, moreover, with self-satisfied displays of useless erudition, something everyone connected with the *Challis* project was determined to avoid.

My involvement in the venture offered, for me at least, the rare and significant opportunity of allowing the experience of the lifetime I had spent in Australia to flow back into the world from which my generation sought to draw sustenance. As I worked on the four volumes I edited—*Macbeth, Antony and Cleopatra, Troilus and Cressida* and *The Winter's Tale*—I was expecting initially to do no more than to use some of the skills I had acquired decades earlier in my struggles with James Shirley. At first I feared that I might have forgotten some of those highly specialised techniques, but I discovered that the arcane business of textual scholarship was rather like riding bicycles, something you never entirely forget how to do. I soon realised, however, something far more fascinating and even thrilling in a way.

Anyone addressing the task of preparing a modern edition of a Shakespeare play is faced with a seemingly impossible tangle of contradictions. The original editions themselves are filled with errors, corruptions, ambiguities and omissions. Because of the chaotic nature of even the more respectable of the original texts, there has been a tradition of several centuries' standing of 'correcting' Shakespeare, of trying to tidy up texts that were written for recitation and came to be transmitted in various haphazard ways. In the early, heroic days of editorial work, from the middle of the eighteenth century to the early decades of the nineteenth, much of the task fell into the hands of scholars trained in Latin and Greek—they were frequently underemployed clergymen—who did their best to guess the probable meaning behind what seemed to them nonsensical utterances. Their ingenuity occasionally produced spectacularly successful results. But their ignorance of all but the highest forms of literary English also misled them—laughably at times as we discovered while working on the *Challis* texts.

I was alerted to that in the early stages of preparing my edition of *Macbeth*. In several places where eighteenth- and nineteenth-century editors declared the sole original text to be incomprehensible, and altered it accordingly, I was surprised to find that I had no trouble making sense—indeed better sense than the usually accepted emendations—of the original. I realised that this had to do with the substantial layer of sixteenth- and early-seventeenth-century colloquialisms in Shakespeare's language, something of which those honourable men in the great colleges of Oxford and Cambridge or in their comfortable country parsonages were ignorant. But so were several more recent British scholars of Shakespeare's language. The reason for that soon became clear. Important aspects of Shakespeare's diction, especially those derived from the argot of the London underworld of his day, had passed out of currency in England, but survived the sea-change of carriage to the antipodes two centuries or so after his time, when men and women who still had access to that language were conveyed to the colony of New South Wales to safeguard honest British folk from felons and malefactors.

One of the most famous and also most altered lines of *Macbeth* made me tumble to that possibility. As he is tormented by the terrible tussle between his ambition and his conscience, Macbeth comes to the not very startling realisation that only fear of the consequences makes him hold his hand, hesitate over murdering his kinsman and sovereign in order to achieve the power he lusts after. Were it not for that, he would risk all, even judgment in the afterlife—or as Shakespeare puts it: 'upon this bank and shoal of time we'd jump the life to come'. Or so it reads, at least, in all editions since the mid-eighteenth century.

The expression is one of the most puzzling in the play. There may be some residual sense in the concept of leaping over the bank and shoal of time, that is the present life, though the implication is not entirely clear. Scholars have long acknowledged this, and pointed out moreover that in Shakespeare's time the verb 'to jump' could also mean to hazard or to wager. That nevertheless does not do much to clarify why the present life might be a 'bank and shoal of time'. The oldest, and therefore what is for our purposes the original, text of the play, contains however a rather different phrase. There Macbeth says that he would be prepared to hazard the afterlife on the 'bank and school of time'.

The thrill of recognition has stayed with me since the moment when I hit on the obvious. I buried myself in the library with dictionaries, word-books, concordances, whatever I could lay my hands on that contained hints about slang in the late sixteenth century. And there was evidence enough. Shakespeare's contemporaries knew the word 'school' as a place where one played games of chance, and by extension as a word suggesting games of chance, just as they knew the word 'bank' in the same way that contemporary devotees of games of chance know it. Eighteenth-century gentlemen-scholars were obviously ignorant of such sleazy aspects of life, even though they recognised that Shakespeare's austere tragedy—about a pair of adventurers who hazard everything and lose all—contained many images of and allusions to gambling. By printing 'the bank and school of time', my edition of *Macbeth* was the first since the eighteenth century to restore a tiny fragment of what, I was convinced, had been Shakespeare's original intention.

It might be hard for those outside the artificial world of the academy to appreciate the satisfaction of that discovery. Yet that small point, together with half a dozen or so other restorations of the original expressions in the four plays I worked on for the *Challis* series, represents, I think, the only true contributions to knowledge it was my good fortune to make. It may not have been much, I admit. Yet as scientific researchers will also confirm, the advancement of knowledge occurs in small, unremarkable steps. Few of us are granted the privilege of making the spectacular discovery, the great breakthrough— deciphering Linear B or discovering the double helix. I, like almost everyone else setting out on the academic path, dreamt at one time of achieving something as grand as that in my own field. Even after I had learnt better, I sometimes imagined that I might come upon the exceptional find while sifting through the yellowing sheets of paper in the Public Record Office or turning the pages of old books in the

North Library. I did not know what that might have been—perhaps an undiscovered play by Shirley which turned out to be the equal of *Hamlet* or *King Lear*, enough to put his name in the first rank on the strength of that single play. I realised, of course, that such was unlikely to be my lot. You had to be content with the small-scale, the less than earth-shaking, which would nevertheless be sufficient to inscribe your name—if only in tiny letters—in the record of scholarly achievements.

For such reasons I was pleased at having helped to rub the tarnish of time off one or two corners of Shakespeare's plays. It does not matter greatly, of course, whether Macbeth wagers all on the 'school' or 'shoal' of time. Yet it did matter in another way, for my contribution was another step—perhaps a fairly important one—in the task of restoration, of better understanding, of allowing us to get one small pace closer to the words spoken on the stage of a London theatre in the first decade of the seventeenth century. And besides, the kind of work that led to that discovery appealed to me greatly. It was a wonderfully astringent contrast to the self-important arrogance of so-called academic criticism. It was governed by certain more-or-less objective and verifiable conditions. It was incumbent on me to try to establish my case, if not to prove it. Criticism, as it was practised in the inspirational fug of the Goldberg years or in the new jargon-ridden and polysyllabic mode coming into fashion at the time, seemed far more self-indulgent and ultimately pointless.

Those Shakespearian *trouvées* prompted me to try my hand once more at publishing something in what most of my colleagues still regarded as the great centres of learning. For the first time in a quarter of a century I sent off a short note—about 'the bank and school of time'—to *The Review of English Studies*. The reply took months to arrive, by surface mail. They were sorry but they weren't convinced. I was annoyed and spent a day or two muttering about stuck-up, self-satisfied Poms. But it didn't last long, for by then I had come to know that nothing mattered very much, apart from a few deeply personal things. I could live without appearing between the covers of *The Review of English Studies* or any august journal. Perhaps one day, probably long after my death, someone might realise that the lifetime I had spent in Australia had provoked one or two minuscule discoveries which the proud scholars at the navel of the English-speaking world would have to acknowledge. And if not, then at least I wouldn't be around to get annoyed by their intransigence. I went on with my editorial work. One or two further discoveries of the kind came to me, though none as satisfying or significant, at least from my point of view, as resolving that puzzle in *Macbeth*. Whether the great world beyond the seas recognised it or not, I felt I was reversing the flow of knowledge, research and discovery. At least privately and individually I was something more than a passive recipient of wisdom that came coursing down from the great seats of learning. I knew something they could not easily have come to know, and that in its way was satisfaction enough.

18

By the early nineties the Department of English was not the happiest of places. Most of my colleagues felt neglected, hard done by; everyone had a grievance. We fought and bickered. As always, our disputes seemed to be about matters of high principle but, just beneath the surface, they revealed the usual mixture of ambition and frustration, the exercise of power for the sake of power, intrigue, nastiness, backbiting and malice. The causes for our discontent were many, and indeed the sad, demoralised state of the department was by no means unique: most institutions were suffering from the rapid, often poorly considered changes that had swept over tertiary education by that time. The glittering world promised us by a succession of governments turned out to be a dull, leaden experience of ever-increasing interference by bureaucrats both from within and outside. It was the beginnings of the corporate universities—vulgar, mercenary institutions that seemed entirely to have forgotten the reason for their existence, self-perpetuating organisations bloated with the sense of their own importance.

No facet of academic life was immune from the inroads made on it by officious meddling, especially after severe restrictions on funding followed a period of rapid and in some ways unwarranted expansion at a cost the community was clearly unwilling to sustain. There were obvious differences, nevertheless, in the fortunes of the various sections of universities. In general, the professional faculties, with their greater political influence and ability to attract donations and bequests, were insulated to some considerable extent from ravages other disciplines had to endure. Among the latter, the humanities fared worst, at least in the University of Sydney.

The reasons for that were complex. A large part was due to the rigid way in which university places were allocated by the central authority. The more glamorous faculties, those capable of promising their graduates the likelihood of high-earning careers, were able to call the tune. By severely limiting the number of places available each year, they contrived to control competition among members of their professions and also to confine entry to school-leavers with the highest achievements. The effect of such narrow-minded selectivity had detrimental effects on some professions, medicine in particular. Its consequences for the generalist faculties were equally unfortunate. Arts and Science became second, third or fourth level preferences for many aspiring students. These faculties—particularly Arts—were filled with young people without any particular aptitude for or interest in the disciplines in which they had enrolled. Many were there only because they had not performed well enough at school to gain entry to Medicine or Dentistry.

In that less than happy climate, English was particularly vulnerable on two counts. On the surface English studies were prospering; enrolments in the department remained high, much to the chagrin of several branches of the humanities that saw the English Department as a three-headed monster gobbling up an ever-increasing proportion of the miserable funding allotted to the generalist faculties. Yet the quality and dedication of our students declined, or so it seemed to many, each year. English became something of a soft option, undemanding, willing to tolerate levels of accomplishment even lower than other parts of the faculty, and therefore discouraging many potentially valuable and eager students. Our troubles were exacerbated by the considerable proportion of our students who came to us from the Faculty of Education, where entrance requirements were even lower than those for Arts. Though no one was prepared to admit it publicly, it was obvious that we were reaching a state where a worrying number of our students was clearly not equipped for university study, even at the then current generally undemanding levels of expectation. So our syllabuses became simpler and simpler as we found that our students, as a body, found it difficult to read certain standard literary works—Dickens's longer novels, for instance—which a generation before had been widely studied at school. Moreover, because the Canberra bureaucracy came to exert increasing control over the operation and practices of universities, it proved almost impossible to remove from the system most of those undergraduates who were incapable of meeting generally lax and indulgent demands. As long as they managed to fulfil relatively minimal requirements for completing written work and attending examinations, their success was more or less guaranteed. Only when they emerged as graduates and attempted to find employment in the great, cruel world beyond the university did their inadequacies come to be revealed. Some may have been experts at recondite literary jargon, but basic literary and literacy skills proved sadly lacking in many of them.

It is fashionable in conservative academic and intellectual circles nowadays to ascribe the blame for the sorry state of literary studies in universities and elsewhere to certain contemporary fads: structuralism, poststructuralism, deconstruction, postmodernism—these terms are practically interchangeable in the public arena. Undoubtedly these modish academic preoccupations encourage jargon-plagued, pretentious nonsense. The obscurantist critical language much favoured by some literary theorists, together with certain easily imitable stylistic devices, provide a convenient template which anyone who has learnt its basic techniques can apply at will. And the writings of many academics also betray word-spinning, obscurantism and even gobbledegook on occasions. The situation is to be deplored and lamented, but it is not entirely surprising. Undergraduates, and many postgraduate students too, are by their very nature imitative, easily led by example. It could not be otherwise, for no matter how superficially democratic or non-interventionist educational philosophies or practices might be, the primary function of a university teacher remains nevertheless the filling of empty vessels. The dreadful, often comic, attempts at theoretical sophistication I encountered among students in my last years in the Sydney department were not of a vastly different order from their parents' attempts to emulate the palpitating style encouraged by Goldberg. Nor, I suppose, was it fundamentally different from my generation's essays in the high scholarly style that was then fashionable among literary academics. The unfortunate consequences of contemporary critical preoccupations among students are a result, rather, of the haphazard manner of many literary academics' acquiring (over the course of the last two decades) the superficial characteristics of complex and highly specialised skills, which demand considerable linguistic and epistemological competence.

The quandary reaches back to the deep-seated dilettantism of the British model of academic literary criticism. The cult of the amateur, of the person of taste and sensibility, remained dominant even with Leavis and his followers and imitators. Though Goldberg and his colleagues laid claim to greater intellectual rigour than the Sydney department had (in their opinion) professed, they too failed to depart from what was essentially no more than connoisseurship. Matthew Arnold's *Culture and Anarchy*, the foundation myth on which much of Leavis's theories were based, did not reach far beyond the inspirational in its over-simplified division of nineteenth-century British society into Philistines and Barbarians. With Leavis and his followers, as much as with Arnold, acts of faith rather than consistency of argument were needed to give validity to large-scale and essentially unprovable literary, cultural, moral and even perhaps political convictions.

In that respect, the intellectual climate of the Goldberg years in Sydney was little different from the despised atmosphere of the system of which I turned out to be the last product. As I look back on those years when Herring, Wilkes, Oliver and Milgate conducted us on those detailed tours of English literary history, I am struck by a particular and worrying anomaly—an anomaly which I, too, revealed (hindsight tells me) throughout my professional life. They gave us an excellent grounding in historical and literary scholarship. I came to enjoy its fruits in London, in a very similar academic and intellectual climate. Yet both the Sydney department of the time and the climate of University College (or more accurately perhaps of the seminars in the Marlborough Arms) were shy of the world of ideas. You could have felt at times that to engage in any but the mildest of philosophical, political or cultural speculation was a tad vulgar.

That was very much the flavour of the Sydney department as I remembered it. My teachers were honourable and conscientious enough to make some gestures towards literary discriminations, also introducing us to the rudiments of conventional critical and literary theory. Yet their hearts did not seem to be in it. They gave the impression that it would have been somewhat improper for them to stray too far into questions of aesthetics: their duty seemed more directly concerned with passing on to their students a body of knowledge which would allow—or so they hoped perhaps—each individual to reach responsible and well-informed judgments. Nevertheless, to take more than a few elementary steps towards shaping taste would have seemed improper, an invasion of individual integrity and something with which an institution concerned with knowledge must not meddle.

When I returned to the department in 1963, I was vaguely aware of a slightly altered climate. Two colleagues in particular, Tulip and Simmonds, recent arrivals from the intellectually more strenuous world of American scholarship, seemed intent on much more coherent epistemological and even perhaps philosophical procedures. I remember that some of the older members of the department found them a trifle too radical—too intellectualised as they revealingly put it. I also found their strenuousness a little puzzling, for nothing in my undergraduate or postgraduate experience prepared me for accepting the proposition that scholarly care and rigour were not enough.

In such ways, the climate that formed my own professional aspirations was restricted and probably ill-designed to serve the needs of changing circumstances. Yet the education I had received, for all its nostalgia and sentimentality, at least possessed the virtue of modesty. The Sydney department produced very good literary scholars and historians. In that way it kept alive a culture and its traditions, which were in danger of atrophying in an environment where the outward and substantial signs of that tradition were disappearing. Perhaps they failed to acknowledge—even in my undergraduate days, in a much more homogeneous and less sceptical climate than the present—that those traditions would inevitably suffer a sea-change when transported across great distances. Nevertheless, even that apparent failing may have been justified. Lurking behind the department's unspoken assumptions was, I think, the concept of a social and cultural dynamic: in a changing world it was necessary to retain as far as possible the integrity of a vital, perhaps even central part of our cultural heritage. That could ensure that developing social and cultural institutions might aspire towards greater integrity. Such, at least, seemed to be the unacknowledged hope: to go beyond it, towards directing or shaping culture, might have seemed improper in the intellectual climate of the time. For that reason Goldberg's deliberate attempts to mould taste and sensibility appeared arrogant and dangerous.

Even those troubled years came nevertheless to appear almost benign in the light of what was to come. In the last decade of my academic life I witnessed what seemed to me the growth of an arrogance as great as that of Goldberg and his associates among literary academics often insufficiently trained in the complex and highly specialised skills of contemporary linguistic and philosophical theories they sought to disseminate. The results were in many cases parodies—just as derivative as the Australian Leavisites' fighting the social and cultural battles of a distant society or indeed the undercurrent of nostalgia in my own education both at school and university.

The heady mixture of philosophical, cultural, anthropological and linguistic theories that arose in France around the time of the near-revolution of 1968 was never predominantly literary in bias. Of the several (and often quite sharply antagonistic) culture-heroes that emerged, only Roland Barthes, the most approachable and therefore most influential, concerned himself extensively with the nature of imaginative texts and writing. The remainder, Derrida, Foucault and Lacan among them, certainly employed literary texts in their often highly technical arguments, yet their interests and their significance lay beyond the normal competency of the academic study of literature.

That the various phenomena flowing more or less directly out of French thought of the late sixties came to dominate the literary academy in later decades is due almost entirely to the domestication, so to speak, of these theorists by American academics, many of whom were also involved in the fierce battles that came to be known as the culture wars of American universities and produced in consequence a strange hybrid composed from essentially incompatible elements.

Australian universities never experienced the fury of the disputes that wracked many North American institutions. The reason for that was not hard to find. To our shame, in my time there were very few Aboriginal students at the University of Sydney. In all my years in the Department of English I encountered only a handful, and in those instances they were mostly children of well-to-do, educated people who had made their way in the world at large. Nor were migrants or the children of migrants particularly vocal activists. Most seemed to me to be acting in the way I had acted almost half a century earlier: their inclination was to become as far as possible indistinguishable from their Anglo-Celtic contemporaries. In such circumstances, women formed the main body of the 'marginalised', those suffering the ill-effects of discrimination and prejudice. Their case was not as open and shut as they liked to claim; the disadvantages they suffered were far less severe than the conditions American blacks, for instance, had to endure at colleges and universities, or Australian Aborigines encounter every day of their lives.

This is a difficult area, where reason is easily swept aside by passion. Undoubtedly in the fifties and even for much of the sixties there were few women of power in universities—though I could never entirely forget Maggie Tomlinson. By the eighties, however, that situation had changed. Several women, Leonie Kramer among them, occupied chairs. Women were also represented on the upper levels of the academic hierarchy—they numbered among their ranks associate professors and readers, besides many senior lecturers. Yet the eighties saw a remarkable rise of temperature in complaints about discrimination. Women members of staff pointed to their lack of opportunities for advancement, promotion, access to research funding besides complaints about the lack of child-care facilities. Women students followed suit. They were often loud in their protest that the syllabuses privileged 'patriarchal' writers and points of view. The fashion arose of looking at courses of study to ensure that women were properly represented— even in such periods as the sixteenth and seventeenth centuries, when women writers were in short supply and (unhappily) of only limited value and interest, despite many attempts to present them as highly gifted though largely ignored voices. Such complaints and the disputes to which they led were often couched in language as febrile and immoderate as that of the controversies that wracked North American life. And in Australia, too, they were often articulated in terms of the arcane and opaque discourse appropriated from the much more cerebral practices of French linguistics, philosophy and social theory.

In the Sydney department, as throughout universities in every part of the country, feminism provided the centre of the various attempts to redraw the cultural map. Unlike their North American counterparts, Australian feminists did not find uneasy allies and occasional antagonists among the black or coloured population. In this country, radicalism in academic and intellectual circles remained more or less the sole property of middle-class men and women of predominantly European ancestry. Ostensibly, the plight and viewpoints of migrants and ethnic minorities occupied increasingly larger parts of the syllabus. Yet in terms of institutional politics the question of ethnicity almost never arose. Far more vocal, at least in the humanities, were exponents or proponents of the study of gay writing, though even that did not reach the level of abstraction or vituperativeness characteristic of North American 'queer' literary criticism. Oxford Street more or less ignored the universities, having far more interesting concerns to address on its own terrain.

There was, accordingly, a suspicion of the half-baked, even perhaps of the provisional in the heated disputes that kept us busy through long staff meetings. Much passion was generated, certainly, but it often seemed to lack conviction, or else it disguised mere play for power, maintaining the rage in the hope of richer prizes. It was not a question of sincerity: the articulate and at times passionate advocates of the cause of women, or of gays, believed that the world in which they lived was seriously unbalanced, biased in favour of (mostly ageing) 'straight' men. It was, rather, a matter of tone, of suggestions of injustice and the intolerable exercise of power by the privileged few, which did not seem to be borne out by the realities of academic life in the eighties and nineties, or by day-to-day practice. It reminded me a little of the political passions of students during the years of the Vietnam War. They might have occupied the offices of the administration on a Monday, but by Friday, especially if the weather was fine, they would pack up and leave—no doubt to spend the weekend at the beach.

Ideology was not, indeed, the most detrimental legacy to English studies of the unrest of the eighties and the nineties. It might have been so in other, more theoretical and rigorous disciplines, or even in other English departments, where theory bit much deeper than in the largely conservative, perhaps even fuddy-duddy Sydney department—that, certainly, was Stephen Knight's view when he took up a chair at the University of Melbourne. In Sydney, however, the infatuation with the heady world of deconstruction and postmodernism was more playful, almost decorative. Several people retooled quickly, and with some efficiency—at least efficiently enough to mask their inability to read French, for instance, or their no more than nodding acquaintance with the arcana of the holy texts of their new religion. Their command of the new orthodoxy was superficial, but it was effective, and impressed students sufficiently to prompt some of them into arid word-spinning, into language games without much pertinence or substance. But none of that mattered too much; we were living, after all, in the age of surfaces.

The greater harm of political (or at least pseudo-political) passions brought to English studies lay in another quarter. There, again, the Sydney department was more cautious and conservative than most others. During a pompous review of our standards by a visiting panel, which took place in the year before I left the university, a solemnly earnest professor of English—from Adelaide as I recall—ticked us off for being, in her view, insufficiently innovative. Someone asked her what the value of innovation for its own sake might have been. I remember her looking at her questioner in disbelief. And yet we did, up to a point, join in the mindless pursuit of novelty. Some innovations were timely and well-judged, many others seemed merely to answer the dictates of fashion; they were cosmetic more than substantial. Our syllabuses became unstable, they gave the impression not so much that they had been thought through but invented on the spur of the moment. That, in turn, made our practices (together with every other institution's in the country) suspect to those who controlled the purse-strings, and therefore our well-being. We seemed to have abandoned our duties and responsibilities. While some of the accusations hurled at English studies during the late eighties and early nineties were no more than the usual philistinism endemic to society at large as well as to certain sectors of the academy, many hit their mark. We seemed to have become irresponsible and therefore vulnerable to damaging criticism.

By the late eighties the assault on the 'canon' by influential North American literary academics had trickled down to the south. It was deemed improper for an institution such as ours to make more than quite minimal demands on the way our students constructed their courses of study. The enemy was the old way, the so-called monolithic syllabuses of the conventional English department that required students to progress, without deviation, through a succession of writers and books allegedly privileged by those classes which controlled the dissemination of texts and writers' reputations. Such control, in terms of the simple Marxism underlying these notions, was an impropriety. Indeed, any notion of literary value or of the strength and validity of traditions was deemed to be chimerical, a product of the same control and oppression that marginalised the less privileged groups of society. For a university to continue in its authoritarian way of locking students into inflexible courses of study was contrary, therefore, to the highest ideal of academic life.

The consequence of our adopting such dreams was laughable and destructive. There was a great deal of heated rhetoric about the improper, authoritarian bias of syllabuses that paid insufficient heed to students' individual aspirations and preferences. Why should everyone have to study Shakespeare, or any other 'great' literary figure, for that matter? The superiority of Shakespeare was merely culturally conditioned; his plays had no more right to be studied than other, less conventional texts. As a result our syllabuses became unmanageable jumbles among which hapless students, given almost unconstrained freedom of choice, wandered like lost souls. We had abrogated our responsibility because of our dire confusions about the difference between taste and individual preference on the one hand, and on the other the purpose and justification of the academic study of literature. We were, in effect, admitting that we had nothing to teach our students.

English studies became little more than discussion groups or self-improvement courses. We could only exploit that which our students already knew or happened to be curious about. If they thought that it might be interesting to study Milton, for instance, well and good. If they had never heard of *Paradise Lost*, or if what little they knew about it did not appeal to them, that was well and good too; they could get a degree without bothering about it. Such procedures are well suited to interest groups, bodies of enthusiasts intent on pursuing their likes and curiosity. To confuse their interests with the nature of academic study seemed irresponsible.

Even in those years when the department retained a measure of control over syllabuses, prescribing approximately fifty percent of a student's work, leaving the rest to choice, many of us were already aware of the pressures that led to a largely consumer-oriented bias in the department's practices. Why do we have to read *The Faerie Queene*, honours students would ask more and more frequently. It was *so* boring, *so* irrelevant to their lives. The truth was, of course, that they were only required to study a fraction of the six books of his grand project that Edmund Spenser managed to finish. The answers we gave were clearly not convincing: boring or irrelevant though it might be to some twentieth-century sensibilities, *The Faerie Queene* was greatly admired by Spenser's contemporaries, and continued to exert a substantial influence over English literature for the best part of three hundred years. It was impossible to understand the literature and culture of the English Renaissance, I used to argue, and what came after it, without some familiarity with one of the most influential books ever published. The argument did not wash: the concept of historical understanding was almost irrecoverably lost.

The intellectual and academic implications of our more or less opting out of teaching in the strictest sense of the word, being content to act as no more than moderators of discussion sessions, had grave implications for the future of English studies. Most worrying of all was the possible loss of skills. What if Spenser were rehabilitated one day? What if, far from representing the worst aspects of Elizabethan misogyny and paternalism, a shake of the ideological kaleidoscope were to reveal his work in a new and irresistibly attractive light? How would the academy cope then? Would Spenser have to undergo something like the painful restitution of Dickens after Leavis decided that his novels were, after all, admissible into the 'great tradition'? There were other concerns too. The department's practices, because of our noisy disavowal of authoritarianism, seemed to me highly authoritarian, and arrogantly so in our refusal of our duty towards our students, who came to us as the years passed with an ever-decreasing reservoir of literary competence. We did little to educate the new 'barbarians'; mostly we were content to indulge their prejudices, or prejudices they had acquired second-hand on their stumbling road to university.

We were harming ourselves, too, in the eyes of many other parts of the university. I fell into a shabby but, or so I thought, effective rhetorical trick when students used to complain about how unfair it was to have to read Spenser or Milton or any writer that happened not to please them. Would they argue, I asked (remembering my dismal days in the Faculty of Medicine), that medical students should be able to avoid studying the central nervous system because it bored them? There was usually a long silence, followed by a comment that literary studies were different, that there were no essentials—the standard response of the time. Yet that question was precisely what other academics, even some within the humanities, were asking about us. It was during the late eighties that I began to hear the English Department being referred to as the sheltered workshop. People were no longer taking us seriously; our loss of esteem reached its nadir as more rigorous disciplines began arguing that we had abandoned even the most rudimentary of scholarly standards. And those who held the purse-strings had obviously listened.

19

In the increasingly stringent funding cuts universities sustained after the economy went sour in the eighties, the Sydney English Department was singled out for especially savage treatment. A large part of this seemed to be due to rivalries and enmities in the administration of the Faculty of Arts. English had long been regarded as the most bloated resource-gobbler in the faculty. Several influential administrators, moreover, were suspected of being particularly hostile towards certain members of the department. We suffered, some of us thought, because of antipathies that had almost nothing to do with professional or educational matters. Despite all that, it should have become obvious by the late eighties that the new mode of English Studies which became fashionable during that decade was insupportable in a climate of severe financial restraint.

The central platform of the anti-authoritarian, democratic department which had evolved by that time was the almost total lack of compulsion. Gone were the traditional 'core' courses which were taught, in part at least, in large lectures of several hundred students at a time. Instead options multiplied, incidentally necessitating a bizarre system of course numbers (with complicated decimals) and a galaxy of exclusions and prerequisites that occupied many pages in the student handbook, so adding to undergraduates' sense of confusion. Many of these options were the traditional staples of literary study; others were bizarre fantasies reflecting individual academics' obsessions more than any pedagogic necessity. It was a self-indulgent and appallingly expensive system to operate.

There had been some virtue in shifting the department's emphasis to small-group teaching—at times with classes of half a dozen or so. That was, after all, the favoured method of Oxford and Cambridge, great institutions we still admired in an oblique way, no matter how much the ideological rhetoric of the time urged us to regard them as elitist exploiters of unwarranted privilege. Yet whatever the benefits of such a system, the drain on resources it provoked was unsustainable. What is more, the proliferation of little 'thematic' options came to seem—with much justice—less and less respectable to those who controlled the allocation of funding. Each of us appeared to be acting as though we were running our own separate universities. Large-scale differences in workloads emerged. Those who taught a course with several hundred students for one semester ended up with several hundred pieces of written work to read. Others, whose recherché courses did not attract more than ten or fifteen undergraduates, had a much easier time. Resentments inevitably arose, adding to an already quarrelsome atmosphere.

It was in that context that the drive to encourage some of us into early retirement began. The funding cuts to the department were severe, excessive even, and radical steps were needed in order to stay within the inflexible boundaries of annual budgets. Inevitably, given the ideological climate, senior middle-aged male members of the department, myself among them, were exposed to an unsubtle campaign of discouragement. At first I ignored the appeals that I should retire, throwing them contemptuously where I felt they belonged, in the wastepaper basket. I was determined to hang on, out of cussedness perhaps, but also because leaving behind a lifetime's vocation—no matter how uncongenial it may have become—was an appalling prospect.

Hindsight suggests, however, that those petty gestures of defiance were largely futile. My disillusionment with university life had grown imperceptibly throughout the eighties. Admittedly, it was not—or at least not until a year or so before I resolved to make the break in 1994—a matter of overpowering anxiety. In most ways I was content and fulfilled. I continued to enjoy teaching and tried to ignore the sad fact that I had fewer and fewer postgraduate students, some of whom were intent on writing theses about such matters as the nuclear threat—not, to my mind, preoccupations immediately relevant to the academic study of literature. The greatest satisfaction came from elsewhere: from my marriage, from our sons and the friends we had made in a lifetime spent in the one city.

Over the years Nina and I faced the usual hurdles and crises. The illness and death of my parents within three years of each other was followed not long after by Nina's mother's protracted illness and death—her father had died some years before we were married. There were the expected alarms with our sons: childhood sickness, accidents, broken limbs. There was, too, the chronic shortage of money; that together with our preoccupation with our children and ailing parents made travel impossible for many years. And in any event, the world of the leisurely sabbatical was fast disappearing under the suspicious scrutiny of bureaucrats who multiplied alarmingly in the years after Whitlam persuaded universities to grant Canberra exclusive control over funding. Nevertheless, I knew that life had dealt kindly with me, and I was (and remain) grateful for the peace and security I had discovered in Australia.

Such satisfaction cushioned me for many years from realisations that could not, however, be ignored by the latter half of the eighties. Not to put too fine a point on it, I had to acknowledge by then that my academic career had turned out to be no more than mediocre when measured by the institutional yardstick of honours, distinctions, status and the like. Many factors accounted for that, I realised, not the least perhaps the disastrous beginning of my professional life during the Goldberg years. Distress, alarm and the ever-pressing political imperatives of that dreadful time robbed me of any inclination to pursue a scholarly reputation. I should have been searching for opportunities of making my name known. I should have tried to consolidate the few contacts I had made in my time in the British Museum. In other words, I should have been busily networking, as the saying goes nowadays, in a competitive field which was, even then, fast becoming overcrowded.

I did none of that. I wasted my energies in the slippery game of survival, in trying to learn fancy footwork to protect me in those meetings and cabals in Goldberg's room or in a broken-down pub in Glebe. In retrospect I realise that I had wasted what could have been the most productive years of my life according to the normal expectations of academic advancement. When the department returned to equilibrium after Goldberg left and his allies followed him, I imagined for a while that it might be possible to do something about establishing a name for myself beyond the confines of our sandstone university. I suspected, however, that it might already have been too late. I had turned thirty; by that age someone like Schoenbaum had begun to be respected in the scholarly world at large.

The truth of that was brought home by two half-hearted attempts I made in 1980 and 1981—around the time when I was engaged in editing Shakespeare—to give a push to my stalled scholarly career. On two occasions, I spent a week or ten days in Stratford-upon-Avon among the brightest stars of the Shakespearean firmament at conferences which were supposed to celebrate the Bard, the Swan of Avon, but were fundamentally nothing other than opportunities to establish and confirm the pecking-order of that illustrious universe.

I listened to aggressive Americans scoring points off each other as if they were prize-fighters in a ring. I sat through an endless slide-lecture by a humourless, self-impressed German on images of Fortune in Renaissance drama—a wearying succession of indistinct photographs of woodcuts and engravings projected onto a wobbly screen. I sat politely while an elderly Japanese scholar, blissfully ignorant of the passions he was stirring up, provoked a noisy walk-out by a group of Israelis as he read a paper on the anti-Semitism of Shakespeare and his contemporaries, waxing eloquent about the usurious practices of Jewish merchants and moneylenders and the villainies of the notorious Dr Lopez. I witnessed spectacular fallings-out and also the forging of new alliances.

I, too, had been invited to present a paper. It turned out to be just that: an opportunity to place my essay in the conference archives but certainly not to deliver it in front of an audience. That honour was reserved for the more famous or at least the better known.

I saw Schoenbaum there. By then he had reached the height of his career. Now ambitious young Shakespearians were courting him as I used to see him, two decades earlier, paying respect to the grandees of the North Library. When we gathered for conference photographs on a mellow summer afternoon, with bumble-bees, heavy with nectar, lazily circling the assembly, I noticed that Schoenbaum's position was very close to the centre of the carefully arranged semicircle standing around the elderly Muriel Bradbrook, placed, like a latter-day monarch, among her adoring courtiers. I ordered a copy of the photograph and was able eventually to find myself among the hundreds of faces, at the edge, half-obscured by the long shadows cast by the afternoon sun.

20

As the years passed, I looked at that photograph from time to time. It became an emblem, a symbol-charged image, like those illustrations of Lady Fortune the German scholar found so irresistibly fascinating, of my position in a world I had once dreamt of conquering—fame, renown, the respect of celebrated scholars, influential works published in the discreet blue binding of the Clarendon Press. None of that, I realised at length, would happen. I would never be anything other than a teacher in an Australian university.

In those years I also found myself thinking more and more about people whose lives had taken very different directions from mine. Had I made the right choices? I began asking myself, not very seriously nor very often, but sufficiently for it to become a minor preoccupation.

I recalled, for instance, a fleeting encounter with Robert Hughes one day in London in 1969. It was a foul, windy day of rain and sleet. I noticed a figure in a strange yellow hooded cape walking towards me. It stopped. I was about to walk past when I recognised the voice inside that swathe of oilcloth. We dashed into a café in a side street. I can no longer remember clearly what we talked about as we sat for fifteen or twenty minutes drinking watery coffee from thick, heavily crazed cups. Hughes mentioned that he was working for the BBC, but it was only temporary. He spoke about his plans and ambitions, of the books he would write one day and even perhaps the pictures he would paint, for he hadn't entirely given up his early desire to be a painter.

Years before, in Sydney, when he used to treat his friends to seemingly endless monologues about his aspirations, many of us were tempted to dismiss him as another loudmouth. Sitting in that café, at a counter covered in what seemed like century-old stains, I was just as disinclined to believe him. I was still convinced that people of our kind weren't cut out for such glories. I am ashamed now to think of my smugness. There I was, the 'successful' Sydney academic listening to what I regarded as so much hot air. My notion of how one of us might conquer the world was narrowly confined. You could do it, perhaps, by worming your way into the centres of academic life: one or two Australians had, I knew, achieved precisely that. Any other way—in the arts, by writing or by becoming a cultural figure, a public intellectual in a manner of speaking—seemed presumption: we didn't have that kind of stuff in us, despite Joan Sutherland or Barry Humphries.

The most remarkable thing about Hughes, of course, was not that he achieved much of what he used to speak about, eyes shining with ambition, in the *Honi Soit* office in Sydney or in that grubby London café, but that he did not transform himself in the way people I had known who succeeded in the academy had transformed themselves into parodies of Ivy-League professors or Oxbridge dons. The Hughes I read nowadays in his pungent, rhetorical flourishes has the same turns of phrase as the young man who was once a good friend. The thick-set, middle-aged image on the television screen bears only fleeting similarity to that slim, athletic twenty-year-old. But the voice and above all the ideas spilling over each other remain the same; the same extravagance, the same rush of words—disciplined by practice and experience, it is true, yet the same enthusiasm which, long ago, seemed merely misplaced ambition.

I have often wondered whether it would have been possible for Hughes to have acquired not merely international fame but also his intellectual boldness had he stayed in Sydney. Mostly I am inclined to think that it would have been impossible. Over the years, that has made me wonder whether my life would have been much different had I too set out on an adventure which, in the final count, I was too cowardly to attempt. In my bleaker or perhaps more candid moments I have no choice but to admit that my temperament, talent, personality and perhaps also the peculiar circumstances of the early years of my life would have debarred me from such achievements, no matter how bold or reckless I might have been.

It took some years for me to unravel at least a part of the puzzle posed by the careers of such people as Hughes. Looking back, I now realise that the most telling clue was provided by another of those accidental meetings, though again its significance took a long time to sink in. It also happened in 1969, when I was again spending time in the British Museum in the course of the only full sabbatical year I was able to take. One day I ran into Germaine Greer, who was in London putting the finishing touches to a 'potboiler', as she called it—*The Female Eunuch* and the first step in her extraordinary public career.

I remember thinking at the time that she looked a little depressed. Some of the fire of her Sydney days had gone out of her eyes. The weather was damp and miserable; she was dressed in an odd assortment of clothes obviously intended to keep out the weather—without, as I now realise, any attempt to look fashionable or to resemble what passed for middle-class, even academic sophistication. I thought she looked scruffy, without realising that she was ahead not merely of fashion but of all that clothes and appearance implied. We chatted for a few minutes. She spoke about how irritated she was by university life—that was, I think, during her years at the University of Warwick. Which was why, she added, she had decided to get away from academic work for a while and write a different kind of book. And anyway, she needed to make some money.

I bristled, of course. Whatever private and unacknowledged misgivings I might have had even at the time about universities and my own career, I was still enamoured with the cloistered ideal. Fancy abandoning academic work for a potboiler, I remember thinking. So I was ready to write Greer off: a waste of great potential. I did not understand her realisation that if she were to fulfil that potential or give rein to her intellectual ambitions, she would have to look beyond the constraints of conventional academic writing. Of course, she offered little help or encouragement by putting her ambitions in such an off-hand manner. Even then she must have known that *The Female*

Eunuch would turn out to be anything but a potboiler, no matter how notorious it might become, or how much it would pitch her into controversies. Clearly, she was setting out for uncharted territory. Perhaps she was troubled by doubts and anxieties—would she succeed? What price would she have to pay for straying from the consolations of an ordered, even predictable world?

These are all guesses. We chatted for five or ten minutes, and then went on our way. For many years I gave little thought to those few minutes. But when Germaine emerged as one of the best-known figures in the English-language world (and beyond), respected and even worshipped as much as she is reviled and demonised, I began thinking back on that brief encounter on the steps of the British Museum. I kept telling myself that I should have paid more attention to the undercurrents of what she was saying, just as I should have realised that Hughes's chatter had not been as idle or self-indulgent as I had thought.

Both of them had to break away or at least distance themselves from strictly academic life or from expectations of steady careers. Hughes, as I remember, was not a particularly conscientious or successful undergraduate. He liked cutting lectures, wasting time (as I did) hanging around the *Honi Soit* office. Judging by a few remarks she dropped, his mother seemed to fear that Bob mightn't be able to pull himself together and forge as steady and successful a life as his elder brothers.

I would like to think that Hughes had been endowed with prophetic powers; that he realised, in the 1960s, or perhaps earlier, that the age of the universities and even of steady professions was passing, that the kind of respect the humanities were supposed to command would not stand up against the pressures of a radically altered world. Obviously, Greer came to that recognition too, though she held out in a sense, and has never entirely abandoned academic life or the tone and cast of mind that go with it. And it was something I also came to realise, or stumble into, though much too late—and in a climate with far fewer opportunities to break out, to seek some way of escaping the increasing irrelevance of universities. I came to suspect that geography might have had a great deal to do with that. By the time I made the jump—only a few years short of normal retirement age, it is true—I fancied that in Britain and America I might have been ready to sever the ties earlier (despite my caution, even diffidence) because in those more populous and intricate societies much greater and more honourable opportunities and incentives might have been available.

Our friend Jill Ker Conway's career threw that situation into sharp relief as I watched her over the years gradually detach herself from academic life, without however abandoning associations. In *True North*, she discusses the reasons that drove her, relatively early in her academic career, to be diverted from teaching and research, the traditional arena of the profession as I and many others of my generation understood it. As she discovered how much women were at a disadvantage at the University of Toronto in the 1960s—sometimes in trivial and merely annoying ways, often with much more dire consequences—she realised that she must engage in university administration in order to bring about change and amelioration for women, both students and staff. That led to a waning of her purely academic activities, and to the major decision she took in 1974 when she agreed to become the President of Smith College, one of the best respected academic institutions in the United States. That appointment effectively led her away from most people's understanding of true academic life into bureaucracy and administration, and from there into the financial and corporate world except for seminars she takes each year at the prestigious Massachusetts Institute of Technology and her continuing involvement in academic publishing. Nevertheless, her life nowadays is taken up with pursuits which most university people—in Australia at least—would regard as contrary to academic ideals.

I have often wondered what people like Germaine Greer would think of that kind of feminist activism. For Greer, obviously, it was better to take a different road into the initially perilous arena of the public literary and intellectual life. Would she regard Ker Conway's later career within established, largely male-dominated institutional structures as irresponsible? Certainly some of Ker Conway's noisier and less thoughtful former compatriots see the steps she has taken into the corporate world precisely as betrayal.

In the Australian context there may be some justification for that suspicion. I sometimes think Jill is a trifle too harsh about a country where she has not lived since the early 1960s. I do not think that contemporary Australia (for all its sad, shabby shortcomings) is so constrained by the manacles of the past as she argues—or at least I used not to think so, until certain alarming phenomena on both sides of the political and social divide gave cause for reconsideration. Yet it is undoubtedly true that there are major differences in ethical standards between American and Australian society, certainly where academic and intellectual life are concerned. Too many of the local academics I have known who became powerful administrators have strayed into betraying even minimal standards of scholarly and intellectual integrity.

As the years passed, I watched those people, one by one, identifying themselves with grey bureaucrats profoundly inimical to the intellectual and scholarly life. I saw how contemptuous they had grown of their so-called colleagues, how they encouraged an atmosphere of suspicion in the faculties and departments from which they had emerged. I watched them turn themselves into self-promoters, ruthless in their quest for power. Observing the rituals of the new breed of academic administrators, I found it impossible to avoid heretical thoughts. Those high-powered academics turned administrators and bureaucrats, loud in their arrogance, seemed to speak with a pronounced Australian cultural accent. Is there something fundamental to our society, two centuries and more after its shameful beginnings, I asked myself, that keeps us trapped within the mentality of gaolers and their prisoners? It was with such possibly jaundiced and cynical eyes that I compared Jill's transformation from historian to academic and corporate high-flier with the posturings of those at the University of Sydney who had scaled the heights of the corporate university.

In 1994 I spent a few days with the Conways—John her husband died not many months later—in their Boston apartment and in a house deep in the Massachusetts countryside. Had the iron also entered into her soul, I wondered. Jill busied herself with a hectic life: appearances in several cities both in the United States and Canada to promote *True North*, meetings of some of the boards she serves on, a weekend session to choose the head of a New England college. Fortunately, she remarked, she was not teaching that semester at the Massachusetts Institute of Technology where she takes a seminar on the history of ideas, so her schedule was not as hectic as it might have been.

A few days provide, of course, insufficient grounds for generalisations. And yet, having recently left the academic life behind, with memories of the Sydney movers and shakers still fresh in my mind, I was struck—as I had been struck in the past—by what I can only call, imprecisely I know, Jill's connectedness. The direction which her life and career had taken did not seem to entail conflict between the intellectual and practical, the academic and the corporate. I suspected that she had retained her integrity in ways that her Australian counterparts had not always contrived to achieve. I suspected therefore that in certain parts of North America at least, university people were not as isolated from or hostile to the outside world as many Australians were in my experience.

It was a dispiriting recognition, compounded by the fact that I was still mourning a way of life which I had left behind only a few weeks earlier. That recognition made me realise moreover the particular disadvantage of the kind of life I had led for the previous forty years. It had encouraged a divorce from broader intellectual seams of a kind that Hughes and Greer had tapped into—beyond institutions, it is true—and Jill was also following, even though, to all intents and purposes, her career had taken her far from narrow concepts of academic life.

By the time I had begun to entertain such depressing thoughts in the last years of my academic career, I had mostly reconciled myself to the constrictions of my own professional life. I was certain that even if my talents and accomplishments had been exceptional, they could not have achieved free play in Australia. That was, to my mind, an incontestable fact: the kinds of opportunities Hughes and Greer were able to exploit in the public, intellectual and cultural spheres were not available in a society which, in that respect, remained underdeveloped. Nor did academic life, whether at its scholarly core or on the administrative and bureaucratic fringes, offer conditions of the kind that allowed Jill to move easily between the scholarly and the public, the institutional and the corporate. Contemporary Australia is a far more sophisticated society than the sleepy, inward-looking country my parents and I came to after the Second World War, or for that matter the society Jill left behind in 1960. But no amount of selfsatisfaction with our cultural achievements is able to mask the fact that our intellectual life cannot rival the richness of the older cultures of the Northern Hemisphere.

There were times when I used to be troubled and even angered by that. Occasionally I would catch myself indulging in the wildest fantasies—not merely about that vague offer of some kind of employment Brown had dangled before me in 1962, but by even more outrageous daydreams. What would have happened if war had not broken out in the early years of my childhood? What kind of life would I have been able to lead had not the complex cosmopolitan culture of Budapest been destroyed by the madness and fury that grew steadily in the years after 1918? Would it have been any more satisfying than the life I had made for myself in our make-believe stronghold above Parramatta Road—or would it, on the contrary, have been stifled by Central European bourgeois propriety? I knew, of course, that those questions were futile. Besides, there were much more important consolations: as I went about my daily academic tasks, I was beginning to understand more and more clearly that another, probably far more satisfying way of life, was waiting for me elsewhere, beyond the increasingly irrelevant academic world.

21

I began to realise by the early nineties that it had become possible to play some role in the public cultural sphere. For several years I had been engaged in book reviewing and cultural journalism—rediscovering the interest in contemporary writing that had arisen, many years earlier, at the same time as I discovered the heady world of Renaissance drama. My entry into that world was accidental too. Margaret Jones, the literary editor of the *Sydney Morning Herald*, commissioned me to review a book about Shakespeare. She liked the piece I wrote and so, a few months later, asked whether I would take on another assignment: Christina Stead's unfinished novel *I Could Die Laughing* which had just been published in a version prepared by Ron Geering. With that my second and perhaps much more fulfilling career got under way.

By that time I had been writing essays on Australian books for some twenty years, chiefly for *Southerly*, the journal Wilkes edited until 1987. For many years I had remained mostly deaf to Australian writers. The reason for that probably extended back as far as my teens, my early years at school in the Sydney suburbs, when the few snippets we were required to read—'Bell Birds' and 'Clancy of the Overflow', 'The Loaded Dog' and *Man-Shy*—did not speak to me at all eloquently. Nor were my later explorations of Australian writing much more alluring. Occasionally I received prizes at school, mostly as it happened for Scripture. These were almost invariably books by Ion L. Idriess. They seemed as uninteresting as anything else I had come across; they were all abandoned after a few pages. I much preferred reading what I regarded as the height of sophistication: Aldous Huxley and Evelyn Waugh. There, I felt, was my proper milieu.

Later, there was that copy of *The Tree of Man* a friend gave me when I turned twenty-one. Don Finley's dustjacket design did nothing to make me rush to read the novel. It depicted a man with an axe standing among a clump of trees. The low hills on the horizon looked just like the Blue Mountains. The same old stuff, I thought, especially after my conscience forced me at least to dip into what had been a well-intentioned gift. After that I avoided Australian books until the last month or two of my life among the monuments of English civilisation in the Reading Room of the British Museum.

In London in the autumn of 1962, as I was waiting for Brown to finish reading *A Study of the Life and Works of James Shirley*, when I was at a loose end, edgy and apprehensive, I borrowed a friend's copy of *Riders in the Chariot* which had been published not long before, with some mild and condescending critical praise in the Sunday papers. I thought I might as well give Patrick White another try, though I remember that I didn't hold out much hope of finding this book any more satisfying than the little of *The Tree of Man* I had managed to read.

To say that encountering *Riders in the Chariot* in that grey city swathed in smoke and mist was a revelation is a cliché, yet nevertheless true. Primarily, I recognised that I was in the presence of an exceptional imagination. Yet the appeal of that disturbing and unwieldy novel proved far more personal. There in London, as I was about to commit myself to returning to Australia, a world both familiar and alien, I was surprised to find that my own doubts and hesitations were mirrored by White's unsettling novel—not merely in the figure of Himmelfarb, the uneasy European haunted by images of a life not entirely unlike mine in the early years of my childhood, but (I suspected) in the writer himself. I knew nothing about the circumstances of White's life, but I glimpsed behind the complex, four-fold tale of misfits and outsiders in *Riders in the Chariot* a sensibility as ambivalent about Australian life as I had been, and also feared that I might become once more. White spoke to me in a way none of the few Australian books I had read (or half read) had ever spoken. From that time on, as far as opportunity allowed, I read everything of his I could lay my hands on.

Another facet of *Riders in the Chariot*, and *The Tree of Man* when I went back to it, and also of *Voss*, *The Aunt's Story* and subsequently of the later novels prompted me eventually to try my hand at writing something about an area of literature I used to consider remote from my interests and training. The more I read and re-read White's novels, the more I was surprised to discover that the world they explored was not entirely remote from what had by then become my academic speciality, the literature of the English Renaissance.

One particular strand of White's imagination suggested extraordinary resonances with the work I regarded as my fundamental academic interest. *The Solid Mandala*, as well as a superbly perceptive and erudite discussion Thelma Herring published only a few months after it was released in 1966, alerted me to something remarkable. Here was Patrick White exploring the most arcane corners of Neoplatonic, Gnostic and cabbalistic lore in ways not very different from those of the poets and dramatists of the seventeenth century who were beginning to interest me: Herbert, Vaughan, Traherne and Crashaw, Ben Jonson's strangely learned masques to entertain the court of the scholarly James

I, and even the last plays of Shakespeare. I discovered what seemed to me a thrilling conjunction, allowing the two sides of my life—of the person who had known no other world as well as Australia yet led an imaginative life directed towards England and Europe—to come together in satisfying and meaningful ways.

I thought that I could harness some of the skills I had acquired in the study of the English, indeed the European Renaissance to an essay on a contemporary Australian novel. In 1967 I wrote an essay on *The Tree of Man*, attempting to establish a link between the novel and sections of C. G. Jung's *Philosophy and Alchemy*. Tentatively, and with some misgivings about straying so far from my 'field', I offered it to Wilkes, who published it in an issue of *Southerly* later that year. My formal engagement with Australian writing came about, therefore, largely as a consequence of Wilkes's continuing editorship of *Southerly*. We had forged a close professional and personal association by the time I set out to offer him that essay on *The Tree of Man*. If I had made a fool of myself, I felt, the damage could be contained: no-one would have found out that I had written a jejune, unpublishable piece in an area far beyond my formal competence.

Even then I was able to recognise a distinct pattern behind those pieces. Each of them was in a sense an attempt at self-therapy. The writers who came to interest me in later years—Elizabeth Jolley, David Foster, Henry Handel Richardson, Christina Stead besides White himself—all teased away at the ambiguous and paradoxical questions that many Australians continue to ask about their European heritage and inclinations. All seemed immersed in European art, culture and thought. The artists, thinkers, writers and composers they evoked in direct or cunningly disguised ways had also been the household gods of my own wholly secular and fundamentally Central European family. I felt an affinity with them and their books which prompted me, arrogantly perhaps, to bring my own preoccupations to bear on their novels and stories.

I discovered great satisfaction in those essays and discussions—certainly much more pleasure than from the two books of Shakespeare criticism I wrote, largely because I felt an obligation to fulfil conventional academic expectations. And yet I did not regard those essays on Australian writers as central to my professional or even perhaps intellectual life. They were more of a hobby or relaxation, enjoyable tasks where I did not feel entirely constrained by academic proprieties. Writing about White and Jolley, Foster and other recent writers was my playtime, where I could fashion a critical prose notably different from the magisterial tone I attempted to adopt in my 'real' vocation.

That provided, as I now realise, invaluable training for my life as a book reviewer and literary journalist.

Initially, book reviewing seemed to me a rather paltry endeavour compared with the rigours of academic scholarship. But as I gained more confidence in what is, in its own way, a highly specialised skill, and as I grew to enjoy it more and more, I also realised that the academic world I had known had vanished forever. A thousand words for the Saturday papers might not have had the glamour and self-importance of a magnum opus which I never managed to write, but it did provide a forum, an outlet and, in an honourable way I hoped, an informative tool of a kind as well.

As time went on, the work became increasingly satisfying. I had stumbled into something the image-conscious administrators of the contemporary university were urging us to do: to 'sell' our skills to the community at large, and so enhance the university's standing. I did not expect plaudits, and was not surprised when John Ward, the former Vice-Chancellor, said to me one day that he did not think academics should make a habit of writing for the papers. I got the very strong impression that he regarded the kind of work I was doing as vulgar. I did not imagine, however, that my modest forays into the public literary sphere would be an indirect cause for leaving the university.

Despite those intimations of a life beyond the academy, I found it impossible to abandon ingrained habits and prejudices. I was determined to stay in the profession as long as possible, especially after the New South Wales Government passed legislation abolishing compulsory retirement at sixty-five. Even though all the signals were discouraging, I decided to apply for a personal chair after these positions were inaugurated by the university, much to the distress of junior teaching staff who—quite correctly—regarded their establishment as an unwarranted drain on finances. They saw only too clearly that the privileged would be prospering at the expense of their own promotion to the former career grade of senior lecturer.

The committee appointed to look into my application listened to me politely, and then informed me that I had been spending too much of my time on peripheral activities. They had enjoyed, they told me, my account of a migrant childhood in a book I had published not long before, *Inside Outside*, and several of them mentioned that they had profited from its discussion of cultural and social predicaments of the kind I had experienced. But it wasn't what you'd call academic work, was it? I ought to do a bit more academic publishing, they advised, and try again in a few years.

I didn't have the inclination or the energy to remind them that the official claptrap of recent years, urging us to prepare for the bright new millennium, had recommended precisely what I had been doing in that book and in writing for the press. And besides, I asked myself, how much time did I have left? I should have realised then that I had come to the end of the road. It took, nevertheless, a combination of largely trivial circumstances—though with a nasty undercurrent—to prompt me into leaving the university.

How I was eased out requires some prudence and tact to relate: whereof one cannot speak, thereof one must be silent. From all appearances I left the university of my own volition. At first I resisted the blandishments of those offers that came every few months from the administration, with cash and tax incentives, to persuade older people to clear out. My life needed a structure, I felt. I wanted to avoid at all costs becoming some kind of Ancient Mariner, hanging around after retirement when I no longer had any function. I realised that if I were to leave the university I would never darken the doors of the place again. Perhaps that was a harsh and arrogant decision, but it seemed, and still seems, the correct instinct. Yet all it did was to confirm my determination not to listen to seductive offers and incentives for early retirement.

All the same, I found myself becoming reckless and cantankerous. Much against my inclinations, I was catapulted into several public disputes with my colleagues just as we were contemplating yet another radical overhaul of our syllabuses, taking one more step (it seemed to me) towards irresponsible indulgence of ignorance, failing in our duty to direct our students towards cultural possibilities remote from their experience. Being ticked off in the correspondence columns of the press was not pleasant. I often wondered why I bothered to raise my voice in the first place. But I went on, out of a desire to annoy, perhaps, as much as out of a sense of duty. I was irked by the silence of some colleagues who offered support and encouragement in private but held their peace in public. In my blacker moments I was tempted to accuse them of being no more than fair-weather friends, opportunists and time servers. Then, of course, the realisation came that they would have to remain trapped in that world for many years.

I suspect that it was around that time that some people began to recognise that it would need only one little push to make me leave. It came when I accepted an invitation to appear at the 1993 Melbourne Writers' Festival. I reorganised my teaching for a few days, arranged for a colleague to take some classes that could not be rescheduled, all with the knowledge and blessings of Wilkes, the professor I was answerable to according to the terms of my contract.

When I returned to Sydney I found a tart and discourteous note waiting for me from Margaret Clunies Ross, the Head of Department, reprimanding me for having been AWOL. That was enough to tip the balance. I was fed up with pettiness and nitpicking. I filled in a sheaf of documents about voluntary early retirement, spent the next six months drowning in a bureaucratic sea, and so, at the end of the first semester of 1994, brought my academic life to a premature end.

I gave my last class, delivered my last lecture, signed the last of a seemingly endless succession of documents and gradually cleared out my study. I decided to get rid of everything except my books. Out went the lectures I had written; out went notes I had taken for seminars and tutorials; out went the papers I had given at conferences. I almost threw out *A Study of the Life and Works of James Shirley* but something—sentimentality no doubt—stopped me at the last minute. It might as well gather dust in the back of another cupboard for a few years longer, I thought.

Then it was done. My room—no longer in Blacket's superb building but in a much more pedestrian structure which the department had been occupying for some years—looked desolate and depressing. I did one last quick scan, of the kind you do when leaving a hotel room to make sure that you haven't forgotten to pack something. Then I shut the door behind me and dropped off the keys at the front office. I was free. As I walked past the main building—the university standard was fluttering above the clock tower—it struck me, not for the first time, and certainly not without a sense of elation, that it was 14 July, Bastille Day.